ISABELLE
The Life of Isabelle Eberhardt

ISABELLE

The Life of Isabelle Eberhardt

BY

ANNETTE KOBAK

Chatto & Windus

LONDON

First published in 1988 by Chatto & Windus Ltd
30 Bedford Square, London WC1B 3RP

A CIP catalogue record for this book is available
from the British Library

Copyright © Annette Kobak 1988

ISBN 0 7011 2773 2

Photoset in Linotron Sabon by
Rowland Phototypesetting Ltd
Bury St Edmunds, Suffolk
Printed in Great Britain by
Redwood Burn Ltd
Trowbridge, Wiltshire

TO GUY AND AMY
WITH LOVE

Contents

ONE · NORTH

1. The Anarchist   3
2. An Inconvenient Birth   11
3. The Villa Neuve   15
4. Poison I   19
5. The Old Turk   25
6. Brotherly Love   30
7. Masquerades   38
8. Correspondences   44
9. The Move   48
10. Dar El Islam   50
11. The Nail   58
12. Islam   61
13. The Hypochondriac   66
14. Rachid   69
15. Poison II   73

TWO · ADRIFT

1. Rebirth   81
2. Oasis I   87
3. Tax and Sex   96
4. Paris: Fin de siècle   101
5. January 1900   106
6. Adrift   109
7. The de Morès Connection   114
8. Room to Let   121

THREE · SOUTH

1. Oasis II   127
2. Idyll   132
3. Dangerous Liaisons   142
4. Winter   148
5. Assassination   152
6. Convalescence   156
7. Slimène   161
8. Exile   165
9. Trial   172
10. Marseilles   177
11. Marriage   183
12. Politics and the High Plateaux   188
13. Mischief   193
14. War   207
15. Peace   220
16. An Equivocal Death   231
17. Post Mortem   239
18. Postscript   246
Bibliography   249
Index   253

Illustrations

(Between pages 82–83)

1. Isabelle Eberhardt as a sailor, 1895
2. Sheikh Abou Naddara
3. Isabelle as an Arab, 1895
4. The marquis de Morès
5. Isabelle as a Tunisian, 1895
6. Biskra
7. Sheikhs El Hachemi and El Taïeb
8. El Oued
9. Isabelle as an Arab girl
10. A Moorish café
11. Isabelle on horseback
12. The staff of the *commune mixte* at Ténès
13. Algerian *tirailleurs*
14. Algerian soldiers under French command
15. Brigadier-General Lyautey, 1903
16. Lyautey as an Arab
17. Lyautey and staff at Aïn Sefra, 1904
18. Isabelle in 1904
19. Isabelle in Aïn Sefra hospital
20. Isabelle's body being carried from the rubble in Aïn Sefra
21. Portrait of Isabelle by Pruna

Map of France, Switzerland and parts of North Africa, 1900

The pen drawings are by Isabelle Eberhardt, and are taken from her diaries, *Mes Journaliers*

Acknowledgements

As with any biography, a narrative of my own shadowed that of Isabelle as I wrote this book. Mine included a series of lucky finds and serendipitous introductions to people who have become valued friends: none more so than Elizabeth Claridge, who first suggested the idea of writing about Isabelle Eberhardt to me, and to whom my first and most heartfelt thanks are due. With her unparalleled knowledge of the area and her generosity, she has been the moving spirit behind much of the recouping of women travellers' lives in recent years.

My thanks are also due to Cecily Mackworth in Paris for her considerate assistance: any subsequent biographer must always be indebted to her pioneering *The Destiny of Isabelle Eberhardt*; to M. Becherif of the Algerian Embassy for pointing me in the right direction (particularly to the Isabelle Eberhardt archive in Aix-en-Provence); to Simone Rezzoug of Algiers University for generously sharing her expertise with me (and particularly for alerting me to an uncatalogued military file on Isabelle); to Abdulhamid Zoubir of Algiers University for his interest and help; to MM. Jean-François Maurel and Jean-Etienne Genequand, Head Archivists at the Archives d'Outre-Mer at Aix and the Archives d'Etat in Geneva respectively, for their efficiency and sleuthing; to the obliging staff of the Société Historique de l'Armée de Terre in Paris; to Oleg Kuzmenko of Kiev University for an illuminating correspondence; to Alissa and Galia Feigin for their excellent translations from Russian for me; to Tim Fox in Paris for his hospitality and encouragement; to Jane and Jim Whittell in Algiers, Fay and the late Michael Curtin in Geneva, and Marjorie Malina in Paris, for their hospitality.

I should also like to thank Michael Church, Susan Hagan, Kate Kavanagh and Lisa Jardine for their comments on the manuscript at various stages, and Rana Kabbani for some final, much-valued insights.

Upon my word, upon my word, we Russians are a drunken lot. Intoxication of some sort we must have: to get ourselves wild with sorrow or maudlin with resignation; to lie inert like a log or set fire to the house. What is a sober man to do, I should like to know? To cut oneself off entirely from one's kind is impossible. To live in the desert one must be a saint.

JOSEPH CONRAD
Under Western Eyes

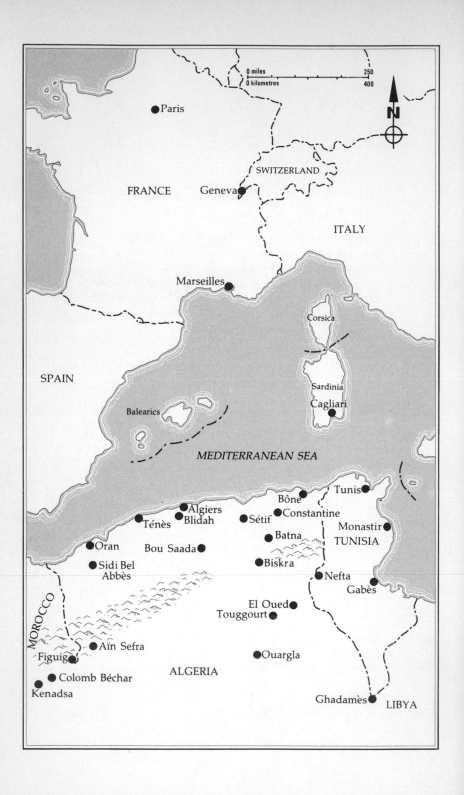

ONE

NORTH

Nejdanov was not born under a lucky star, and did not find life an easy matter.

TURGENEV,
Virgin Soil

❧ I ❧

THE ANARCHIST

Le nihilisme, petit prologue.
NIETZSCHE

The morality of the future will not dictate to people. It will absolutely refuse to shape the individual according to some abstract idea, just as it will refuse to shackle him through religion, laws or government. It will give the individual full and complete liberty. It will become a simple acknowledgement of the facts, a science.

What this science will say to men is this: if you do not feel strength within you, if your energy is just sufficient to keep up a greyish, monotonous kind of a life, with no powerful experiences, no great pleasures, but also with no great suffering, well then, keep to the simple principles of egalitarian ethics. When all is said and done, you will find in egalitarian relationships the greatest amount of happiness possible, given your mediocre energies.

But if you feel the force of youth inside you, if you want to live, if you want to enjoy the whole range of life in all its overflowing fullness, if you want to feel the greatest joy that a human being can know – then be strong, be great, be energetic in everything that you do.

It is up to you to choose.

PETER KROPOTKIN, *The Anarchist Morality*

On 2 December 1872 a small, dark-eyed Russian woman arrived on the newly built Geneva railway station with her four young children and their tutor. She was probably a pretty woman, in view of her history, although her passport only logs prosaically a jutting chin, a wide mouth and a domed forehead. Prey to a 'nervous condition', she was linked to the minor Russian aristocracy at one remove both by birth and by marriage. Her companion, the tutor, was athletically built, black-bearded, inclined to fulminate, and an anarchist. Since Mme de Moerder's elderly husband, whom she had left behind in Russia over a year and half before, was a general and a close adviser to Tsar Alexander II, it was an odd thing for her to be travelling with an anarchist, vowed to the destruction of the autocracy and all that went with it.

On the face of it, what had brought them to Geneva was her health: she to seek milder climes, he to accompany her, and to teach the older children. But underneath the pretext, nearer the truth, was another motive: the tutor's heady, apocalyptic idealism, secretly shared by Mme de Moerder, which had led them, like so many other Russians – even other aristocrats, like Kropotkin – to flee the Tsar's regime. They were also lovers; but a more specific guilt which they shared ensured that they would never admit the fact, in spite of spending the rest of their lives – a quarter of a century – together. From the moment they left Russia, the couple had drawn a veil of evasiveness around them, to protect their secrets from interested parties, and to keep their own high-minded conception of themselves untarnished by un-comfortable home truths.

The train had brought them from Montreux, skirting the northern shore of the crescent-shaped lake of Geneva, lac Léman. Clearings intermittently revealed the glistening breadth of the lake, circled by the Jura and the Savoy mountains, which had been a magnet for individuals with turbulent lives, and turbulent thoughts, ever since Calvin's time. The mountains gave protection, the lake a vista of freedom, the geography quick access to frontiers, and, since 1815, the politics neutrality. More, something about that vast, landlocked stretch of water, Europe's biggest lake, had kindled some of Western man's most radical and unquiet thoughts, particularly about the nature of freedom and constraint: here Saint-Simon, the founder of French socialism, composed his *Lettres d'un habitant de Genève*, Voltaire wrote *Candide*, Rousseau spent his childhood, and Mary Shelley conceived her own noble savage in *Frankenstein*. In lakeside châteaux the exiled Mme de Stäel wrote her novels of the 'misunderstood woman', and Byron, in self-imposed exile from scandal, wrote of the paradoxes of freedom and imprisonment in his poem *The Prisoner of Chillon*. More recently the Russian revolutionaries Herzen, Kropotkin and the 'one-man storm-troop' Bakunin had plotted, in their different ways, the overthrow of bourgeois society from the lake's calm shores. And only seven months before Mme de Moerder's arrival, in the spring of 1871, a new wave of revolutionaries – socialists, anarch-ists, one or two Marxists – had begun to flow in, fleeing the aftermath of the bloody Paris Commune. And in due course Lenin, born the year before the Commune, would live and work in a quiet Geneva library, often in an exalted state, plotting to 'put Europe to the flames'. Revolution itself, so often fomented here, would never take place here. Around it all the clock-watching, clock-making, money-making tradition of the Swiss ticked on, punctiliously uninvolved.

Mme de Moerder had been born Nathalie Charlotte Dorothée Eberhardt (the Charlotte a quick genuflection towards the ruling Tsar Nicolas II's wife) on 23 September 1838 in Moscow, into a branch of the kind of old, aristocratic Prussian family which had provided the Tsars' courts with some of its highest-ranking officials ever since the days of Catherine the Great. At some early stage in her life Nathalie's father had died, or had parted company with her mother, and her mother had remarried, very much within the same social circle, to a Baron Nicolas Korff, who was one of three generations of Korff barons in Russia, descended from an old Baltic family. Both a Korff and an Eberhardt were included in the new Tsar Alexander II's court in the late 1850s, as part of the new, young team which he hoped would take Russia into the modern world, and it was no doubt through these court connections that Nathalie had met her future husband, the General, a senior adviser to the Tsar.

Senator-General Pavel Carlovitch de Moerder came from similar stock: he had been born in 1795 into the Russian branch of a German aristocratic family close to the Tsar. The family tradition continued with Pavel and his older brother Carl. Carl became an Imperial aide-de-camp and tutor to the young Alexander, and all of Carl's five children in due course served the Tsar in some capacity, from general to maid of honour. Pavel himself became both a general and a senator, a rare dual honour. His first wife, Nadezhda Alekseevna, died in 1857, leaving him two daughters, Olga and Elisaveta, and it was some time after her death that he had married Nathalie. They then had three children in swift succession, Nicolas in 1864, Nathalie in 1866, and Vladimir in 1868.

During the 1860s, whilst Mme de Moerder was having her babies, Russia was in the throes of some of the most radical changes in its history, characterized by urgent demands for personal and political emancipation. From her position of privilege Mme de Moerder watched the country become increasingly riven, and the court increasingly punitive. Tsar Alexander had been the first of the Romanovs to acknowledge the imperative need for reform in his monolithic country, which appeared embarrassingly backward in comparison with a Western Europe where Marx had already published his *Communist Manifesto* (seven years before Alexander had come to power), and where Darwin's, Spencer's and J. S. Mill's ideas were revolutionizing the sciences and social and philosophical thought. Russia's system of serfdom was looking particularly indefensible, and defeat under inept leadership and amidst much suffering in the Crimean War had further damaged Russia's self-esteem as well as its finances. But Alexander's attempts at reform, including the tardy and half-hearted freeing of the serfs in 1861, merely gave leeway to the discontent to express and organize itself more effectively than it had been able to under centuries of despotic autocracy. A new and peculiarly Russian class came into being: the intelligentsia, which, with no tradition of gradual change behind it, began to devise extreme solutions to the country's problems, and agitate for total revolution.

One of the Tsar's attempted reforms backfired on him specifically: out of the science faculties of the universities, which he had particularly fostered, hoping to make them the seedbed for the men and women who would help forge a new Russia, came, like Frankenstein's monster, extremists bent on his destruction. At first they were known as the negative tendency, but in 1861 Turgenev gave currency to a simpler term in his book *Fathers and Sons*: the nihilists. Defined in the book as people who did not take any principle for granted 'however much that principle may be revered', the nihilists' particular sport was to reverse the traditional order of things for the sake of it, which included the men growing their hair long and the woman cropping theirs. The family and conventional morality were particularly scorned, to the point where, as Dostoevsky – a great nihilist-baiter – complained, the nihilists would commit adultery as a matter of solemn duty, almost on principle (if they had not deplored the very concept of principles, which they saw as bondage to despised tradition). In *Fathers and Sons* the hero's elderly uncle is saddened: 'without principles taken as you say on trust one cannot move an inch or draw a single breath . . . We shall see how you manage to exist in a void, in an airless vacuum.' Coincidentally, in the same year Count Bismarck, leaving Russia after three years at the Prussian Embassy, applied the word 'void' to the climate in the country as a whole: he had his ring engraved with the words 'La Russie, c'est le néant'.

The nihilists had no coherent world view; what united them was the rejection of existing reality. They soon merged into the revolutionary anarchists' movement, which had been developing alongside it, rooted in ideas of individual liberty going back to the Stoics. At one wing of the Russian anarchists of the 1860s was Tolstoy, an implicit anarchist, with his long hair and peasant clothes, who attacked the Church, the state, the law and property rights, and who had freed the serfs on his own estate in advance of the Tsar's Emancipation Act. At the other wing was the hot-headed revolutionary Mikhail Bakunin, in exile in Europe since 1848, who preached that 'the passion for destruction is a creative passion', and wanted to fuel the fire of 'divine discontent' wherever he saw its spark. Unlike the profoundly moralistic Tolstoyan 'anarchism', his anarchism made scant plans for the future beyond bringing down every kind of social order that existed, in a flamboyant 'après nous le déluge', a wilful, moral apocalypse. The only new society he envisaged was one where no man or woman 'will in any way have to search for any sanction for their actions other than what they find in their own conscience and reason, determine them by anything other than their own will, and be responsible for them only to themselves'.

All of these ideas were manifestly alarming to the autocracy, but it was not until a revolutionary made the first attempt on the Tsar's life in 1866 that Alexander suddenly halted his reforms and began the long, vindictive process of counter-revolution which came to be known as the White Terror. From this point onwards, anyone remotely subversive (which meant most of the intelligentsia) was remorselessly hounded – even, through the long arm of the Third Section, those who fled to more clement European shores.

*

Witnessing the changes, Mme de Moerder perhaps felt the stirrings of some latent idealism, and perhaps felt increasingly dissatisfied at being so squarely wedded to the old order. In her own mind, she had an adventurous, independent side, so far entirely subsumed in breeding future fodder for the Tsar's court, and since she was singularly devoid of maternal feelings, she felt more put-upon with each successive birth. Yet her character was too undeveloped, and her vanity still too dependent on the status of her position, for her to take an open stand. Instead, she retired more and more to their country estate in Pawlowsk outside Moscow, where she exercised her urge for independence in riding horses, whilst the General's duties kept him close to the court in St Petersburg.

When Alexander Nikolaevitch Trophimowsky was appointed as tutor in the household, some time around 1870, the new ideas of the last decade suddenly came close to home, and her discontent could be focused through one man, and validated by his intellectual grasp of the wider discontent of the masses. She could suddenly be part of the spirit of the times, not on the sidelines.

At five foot nine inches, Trophimowsky was not a tall man, although he was still eight inches taller than she was; at forty-four, he was not a young man, but he was still thirty-three years younger than her husband. Of Armenian extraction, he was born on 15 August 1826, and had married his wife Akilin Polgorow in June 1854 in his native Kherson, on the Black Sea near Odessa. They had three sons. Trophimowsky had what was described later by perhaps his only well-disposed Geneva neighbours as 'a venerable face, a real Tolstoy face', with a high forehead, strong nose, bushy beard (beloved of both priests and nihilists at the time) and blue eyes. His ironic, sometimes abrasive manner was the disappointed face of his romanticism, which found it hard to bear life as it was, and sought solace in well-intentioned but grandiose hopes for humanity as a whole. He was an erudite man, well versed in the classics, and fluent in French, German, Italian, Arabic and Hebrew as well as Russian. He talked to Mme de Moerder about the great philosophies of the past, and of the new ideas coming out of Europe. Life did not have to be a sedate progression from cradle to grave, fulfilling duties to country and family. You could choose. She could choose. In the new Utopia women were equal to men, had an equal destiny and an equal responsibility for their lives. As for marriage, it was, as George Sand had said, 'the most barbarous institution known to man'. And these seemed to be no idle words: Trophimowsky himself had acted out his beliefs, leaving behind his wife and family in Kherson. Her position began to look daily more false, her commitment to a pillar of the establishment more of a cowardly, materialistic compromise.

Yet Trophimowsky had a darker side, and was not all that he seemed. Ten years later in Geneva a police report on him unearthed the information that before arriving at the de Moerders' household he had 'previously led quite a stormy life, having been an Orthodox priest, a solicitor, a superintendent of livestock etc, and seems to have left a very bad impression in his country'. Did the General know of this unpromising curriculum vitae? Did the General know that he was an anarchist? The answer is probably that Trophimowsky gave him an edited version of his past, stressing his wide-ranging knowledge and perhaps his connections, for he is rumoured to have known Tolstoy and even (presumably as a young man) Gogol. (He was certainly to share with Gogol an almost farcical paranoia.) His other strong suit, in the General's eyes, was that he was a keen botanist and naturalist, for the General had himself published a slim tome of his own thirty years before, called 'The instinct of animals, or letters from two friends about natural history and some of nature's phenomena'. The General might even have felt that Trophimowsky's previous position as an Orthodox priest was recommendation enough, since the Church was so cravenly attached to the state. In fact, Trophimowsky had left it precisely for that reason, rejecting it, as most of the intelligentsia had done by then, as the people's opiate. (He had probably only joined it for ideological reasons, as part of a wave of fashionable Slavophilism which saw salvation in returning to old Russian values, rather than in straining artificially – as the whole city of St Petersburg did – towards the West.)

As for Trophimowsky's own motives in taking on a post within such a Tsarist household, the circumstantial evidence shows him to have been playing a highly duplicitous game. Within Russia we do not know what his anarchist connections were: they were of their essence secret and undocumented. But rumour had it that he would have had to leave the country anyway in 1871 to avoid being sent to Siberia, or worse, for his anarchist beliefs. However, after his arrival in Switzerland there is evidence linking him directly with the arch-anarchist Bakunin, as from April 1872 his name appears on a list of twenty-five Bakuninists meeting in Zürich, and as one of those funding Bakunin's printing-office. Crucially, by this time the ageing Bakunin was abjectly in thrall to the extremist anarchist Sergei Nechayev, whose highly influential *Revolutionary Catechism* (written and circulated in 1869, but only published in Russian in July 1871, it was to inspire Lenin more than any other piece of writing, including Marx's) stated his creed plainly: 'Our task is terrible, total, universal and merciless destruction.' He also gave advice on the 'duties of the revolutionary towards himself', which included any kind of subterfuge: 'the revolutionary may and frequently must live within society while pretending to be completely different from what he really is, for he must penetrate everywhere, into the higher and middle classes, into the houses of commerce, the churches and the palaces of the aristocracy, into the worlds of the bureaucracy, literature and the military, and also into the Third Section and the Winter Palace of the Tsar.' Could Trophimowsky, close to Bakunin, have come into a seat of the aristocracy, bureaucracy and military like a Trojan horse, in a politically calculating way, 'pretending to be completely different from what he really [was]'? Judged by its long-term effects, his arrival certainly decimated the whole of the de Moerder family. But whatever his initial intentions, dogma evidently gave way at some stage to passion, just as it had with Turgenev's Bazarov in *Fathers and Sons*. In high bourgeois fashion, the tutor fell in love with his employer's wife.

It was in March 1871 that Mme de Moerder, pleading illness, left Russia with her children for milder climes. Trophimowsky may have been detailed to accompany her, or may have joined her along the way. At first they went to Istanbul, then on to Naples, and then to Montreux, where, on 11 December, an ambiguous nine months after she had left, Mme de Moerder gave birth to her fourth child. He was named Augustin Pavlovitch de Moerder, as if he were the regular son of the General; and the General continued to fund the growing family's travels, as if this were indeed the case. On the face of it, he had been roundly hoodwinked.

AN INCONVENIENT
BIRTH

When they arrived in Geneva, Trophimowsky and Mme de Moerder took two sets of rooms, both a stone's throw from the station, but in opposite directions. The first was an elegant third-floor apartment at 8 rue Mont Blanc, on the broad street which runs down from the station to the lake. The front rooms looked down to the lac Léman, and the back of the flat overlooked a leafy, Parisian-style square. The other address was less prepossessing: a lodging-house known as the Maison Fendt, in the rue des Grottes, a narrow street rising steeply behind the station, amongst a maze of small, run-down houses, shops and cafés. They applied for a *permis de séjour*, clearly intending to stay. Each gave both addresses, leaving room, characteristically, for ambiguity about who lived where.

Four months after their arrival an event occurred which might have released them from their double life: on 23 April 1873, General de Moerder, now aged seventy-eight, died suddenly of an apoplectic fit. It was a very convenient death for them. The General's fortune was left to Mme de Moerder and the children, with the proviso that the bulk of the capital would remain in trust in Russia, awaiting the return of his heirs to their native country. The young Nathalie claimed later that Trophimowsky broke the news to her 'brutally', saying simply 'Your father is dead'. To be fair to Trophimowsky, he, like Turgenev's nihilist Bazarov in *Fathers and Sons*, despised all sentimentality, particularly that connected with the family, and his brusqueness was probably determined. It was, however, symptomatic of the new order of things that it should be Trophimowsky, and not their mother, who broke the news.

In spite of the main obstacle to their liaison being now out of the way, the couple still did not admit to being lovers, either within the family or without, although the rue Mont Blanc address now faded out and they seem to have all been living in the rue des Grottes. Of course, Trophimowsky was still married, and his wife would not divorce him, shrewdly refusing to give up the one thing left of her shell of a marriage, the family's inheritance rights. Yet, although concern for conventions was unlikely to have influenced an anarchist such as Trophimowsky, he still continued to be cast as the tutor, whilst in practice gradually assuming all the reigns of domestic power. He became the children's legal guardian, was registered as head of the family on any census, and took over the day-to-day running of the household, which Mme de Moerder had not been brought up to do, and had no strength for. One of the reasons they lied over their relationship was probably financial, to do with Mme de Moerder's legacy, almost their only source of income. Another was no doubt the de Moerder children's dislike of Trophimowsky. But there was also another reason, which would take some fifteen years to emerge.

Until the General's death, the de Moerder children had probably not been too affected by the ménage, which had a veneer of propriety. Knowing they were their father's children, they no doubt assumed underneath it all that they would in due course return to the gracious life they remembered. But now, with the General's death, and with their mother an ineffectual, and frequently ill, presence, they were suddenly at the mercy of someone they profoundly distrusted. A bitter resentment took root in them towards the man who seemed to be the cause of the drastic change in their lives. The two eldest, Nicolas (who was now nine) and Nathalie (now seven), remembered their father best, and as they grew up they began to piece together the sequence of events behind the evasiveness of their mother and the tutor. The picture that emerged became etched vividly on their children's minds in almost fairy-tale terms: the ogre-tutor had abducted their mother from the castle and made off with her, with them and with their father's money, and now they were exiled from their rightful kingdom. As in all good fairy tales, they would kill the ogre, and regain their paradise lost.

*

Nothing is known of the family in the three years following the General's death: they were an anonymous part of the large community of Russian exiles in Geneva, and might have stayed that way. But something is known of their particular community, which was marked by a high degree of secrecy and conspiracy.

Nechayev had been arrested by the Russian secret police in a Zürich café in August 1872, and was now imprisoned in the Peter and Paul Fortress in St Petersburg. Before his arrest, he had already left his mark on the city, where he had specialized in setting up fake conspiracies, escalating the prevailing atmosphere of paranoia. Many of the exiles, including Bakunin himself, positively revelled in the paraphernalia of conspiracy – the aliases, the secrets, the false passports, the edgy thrill of possible betrayal. Even the police had set up their own, fake anarchist newpaper – called, ironically enough, *Pravda*, the truth – to catch revolutionaries. The old romantic revolutionary writer Herzen, who could lay claim to having started the momentum towards revolution earlier in the century, had found the atmosphere claustrophobic: 'Geneva is impossible, or at any rate almost impossible, owing to these busybodies and intriguers.' Conrad observed the climate at a later stage in *Under Western Eyes* and understood from the inside what it felt like to be involved in what to Westerners seems an atmosphere of 'morbid theatricality':

the shadow of autocracy had already fallen upon the boulevard des Philosophes, in the free, independent and democratic city of Geneva, where there is a quarter called 'la petite Russie'. Wherever two Russians come together, the shadow of autocracy is with them, tingeing their thoughts, their views, their most intimate feelings, their private life, their public utterances – haunting the secret of their silences.

In 1876, Bakunin died, a spent force, and by then the groups of anarchists were warring as much against themselves as against the autocracy. He ensured it should carry on that way by signing a document before his death recognizing the imprisoned Nechayev as the movement's leader for the future.

*

What stopped Mme de Moerder and Trophimowsky sinking back into the anonymity of most of the other exiles was an unexpected event in the year of Bakunin's death: Mme de Moerder became pregnant again, aged thirty-eight, with no acknowledged father for the child.

The prospect of the birth sent a ruffle of what was more likely to have been embarrassment than anticipation through the household.

As the time drew near, Trophimowsky left for Moscow – perhaps to try to negotiate on Mme de Moerder's behalf the release of some of her capital – while Nathalie was sent off to a convent in Evian, and Nicolas was farmed out elsewhere. (There is no mention of Vladimir, which was very much the story of his life.)

At six in the morning of 17 February 1877, a baby girl was born to Mme de Moerder in the Villa Fendt. She was registered 'Isabelle Wilhelmine Marie Eberhardt, illegitimate daughter [more agreeably in French *fille naturelle*] of Nathalie Charlotte Dorothée Eberhardt' – '*du nom de mon père*', as Mme de Moerder put it later in her will. The surname gave Isabelle only half an identity, with only the maternal line acknowledged. With characteristic contrariness, and since she would always retain certain vanities about her Imperial connections, Mme de Moerder gave her daughter middle names derived from the original name of the current Tsaritsa, 'Wilhelmine Marie'. (This is a very obvious connection, although it has never been mentioned; instead, Isabelle's names have inspired the colourful and spectacularly improbable theory that her father was the eighteen-year-old homosexual Arthur Rimbaud.)

Nicolas and Nathalie arrived back at the Maison Fendt to find that a 'sickly' baby had arrived, unannounced, in the household. Now fourteen and eleven, they found the new baby shaming: another, and blatant, irregularity in the household. It probably confirmed, if confirmation were needed, their suspicions about Trophimowsky. This last maternity failed to conjure up maternal feelings in Mme de Moerder, and Nathalie later claimed that she had to act as nursemaid, as well as being the only one to attend to ordinary domestic proprieties in the house. Trophimowsky, when he returned, spoilt the new baby, she claimed resentfully.

THE VILLA NEUVE

Trophimowsky was already fifty-one when Isabelle was born. After her birth, and in the wake of Bakunin's death the previous year, he began to lose heart for the apocalyptic ideals of his earlier years. The bickering revolutionary factions no longer seemed worthy of his hopes for a better humanity, and he decided, like Candide, to cultivate his own garden.

When Isabelle was two and a half, the family moved out of central Geneva and into the country near Meyrin, some five kilometres to the west of the city, on the road to Lyons. On 15 October 1879, Trophimowsky bought a property known as the Villa Tropicale, in the area called Les Avenchets. Registering his profession as 'tutor', he paid 9,239 francs 80 centimes for the property, which was purchased in his name, but with Mme de Moerder's money – apparently capital had been successfully negotiated from her estate. Astutely, more the ex-solicitor than the anarchist, he had a clause written into the contract protecting himself from any claims on the property by his wife. The fact that he owned it rather than Mme de Moerder probably lessened the possibility of claims from the General's family in Russia; it also strengthened his domestic position.

The Villa, which Trophimowsky renamed the Villa Neuve, was huge and rambling. It was set in four and a half acres of overgrown grounds, hidden behind a screen of pines. There were lilac groves in the grounds, and a large, stagnant, weed-filled pond (which, a generation later, the local people nicknamed the Caspian Sea, after its shape and its Russian owners). The Villa's particular attraction for Trophimowsky lay in its large greenhouses, which had given the property its original, incongruous name. The young Nathalie later told neighbours that Trophimowsky lavished her mother's money on extravagant equipment for the hothouses in order to cultivate the rare orchids and cacti which became his speciality. His exotic blooms soon gave him a certain reputation amongst local botanists; but the greenhouses, a playground for Trophimowsky's obsessive perfectionism, flourished at the expense of the garden, the house, and the children. In the gardens, he would sporadically try out the latest horticultural fads, but they all flopped expensively for lack of care and attention. He would have liked the Villa to be a self-sufficient commune on Fourierist lines, or a Tolstoyan estate, with the children all tilling the soil for the good of their souls, but the necessary goodwill and cooperation were in short supply. The de Moerder children saw Trophimowsky's ideals as yet another demeaning exploitation by the usurping ex-domestic. To them there was nothing high-minded in doing the gardening.

The inside of the Villa was stark and spartan, with only one or two pieces of furniture in each large room. Trophimowsky had stretched his anarchist principles to acquiring property (it was one of his mentors, Proudhon, who had said 'Property is theft'), but not to making it comfortable, which smacked of the bourgeois; and Mme de Moerder was too wan to create a home. There was always a temporary feel to the house, large as it was: a sense of camping. It was in this atmosphere that Isabelle spent her early years, never told who her father was, slightly resented by her oldest step-brother and -sister, spoilt by the 'tutor', and much of the time left to her own devices. Neighbours gave a rather fanciful picture: the young Isabelle used to 'dance about like a little wild animal along the garden paths. Untamed and unfettered, she did whatever took her fancy from morning to night. Her fantasies knew no bounds.' The one thing other neighbours remembered about the girl they used to glimpse occasionally as they passed by the garden was that she always seemed to be carrying things which were too heavy for her. Trophimowsky kept her hair cropped, dressed her like a boy, and brought her up like a boy, in keeping with Bakunin's dictum that 'every child of either sex should be prepared as much for a life of the mind as for a life of work, so that all may grow up equally into complete men.' Mistrusting what he saw as the lies of civilization, he refused to let the children go to school, but taught them himself, in an intermittent way. Augustin and Isabelle were responsive pupils, and with instinctive children's flair devised a nickname for him: 'Vava', which appropriately aped, and yet avoided, 'Papa'. Nicolas and Nathalie, however, were as resistant to his theories and passions as they were to him, and Nathalie refused point-blank to wear her hair cropped. He had more success with Vladimir, too young to remember his father, and a nervous, sickly child, whom Trophimowsky managed to cajole into poring as obsessively over the cacti as he did.

Above all, for fear of contaminating his charges with the small-minded mentality of the surrounding community, but also out of a growing paranoia, he kept the children confined in the house and grounds, which exacerbated the tensions within the household.

Isabelle's later easy and proficient horsemanship suggests that she learnt to ride now, when she was young, and perhaps even had a horse of her own (although there is no record of either). There were certainly other animals, dogs, geese and ducks, all with 'such very distinctive faces', according to a letter a visitor wrote later to Isabelle, adding 'I think animals are very influenced by their surroundings, and yours reflect the intelligence around them.' As she grew to puberty, Isabelle sketched and painted and daydreamed. There was a lot of time for her to dream, and particularly, like so many, very different, Victorian girls, to dream of what was beyond the garden gate. She wrote later in her diaries: 'I was already a nomad as a young girl, when I used to daydream as I gazed at the enticing white road leading off, under a more brilliant sun, it seemed to me, into the delicious unknown.' She remembered the 'first awakenings of my intelligence, when I used to admire the melancholy sunsets behind the high, gloomy silhouette of the Jura, and try to fathom the huge mystery of my future'. She recalled her 'great obsession with what lay beyond, which used to make me daydream so much in those days. I used to spend long hours at night leaning on the windowsill in my bedroom, watching the vast sky, the jagged, often snowy outline of the Jura mountains, and the huge, blurred black sweep of trees, with the old poplar of the nearby farm towering over it.' Isabelle's quietism was born in these reveries, as she watched the world and did not feel a part of it; and alongside it, seemingly, but not really, in contradiction to it, its counterpoint was born: a compulsive quest for something beyond – beyond the garden, beyond the mountains, and beyond what seemed to be there.

Meanwhile Trophimowsky and Mme de Moerder began to succumb to the worst side of the exile's mentality: nothing would ever seem quite so real to them again as the turbulent upheaval they had left behind. They fell prey to a backward-looking inertia and introspection, unwilling to make contact with their new surroundings, but living at an increasingly fantastic distance from the reality they had left behind. The only visitors who came to the Villa were exiles like themselves – mainly Russians, sometimes Turks, who would brood around the samovar with them, ever alert to the distant thunder of events in the mother country. Isabelle looked back almost wistfully on the timbre of these occasions later in a short story ('Doctorat'): 'Ah! the happiness of these fanatics who pass their existence in a dream of the absolute!' In 1881, when Isabelle was four, the Winter Palace was dynamited and Alexander II was finally assassinated, as he was riding through the snowbound streets of St Petersburg. (A picture postcard of the attack was found in Isabelle's papers after her death.) The signal for the attack had been given by a tiny, flaxen-haired young woman, born into a situation of privilege similar to Mme de Moerder's. In 1882, Nechayev, who at one point had written a letter to the Tsar in his own blood, died in the Peter and Paul Fortress. In 1887, when Isabelle was ten, Lenin's brother was executed for trying to assassinate the new Tsar. These heady, dangerous, far-away events were still closer to home for Trophimowsky and Mme de Moerder than any local reality.

⚜ 4 ⚜

POISON I

The constraints at the Villa provoked in all the children an urge to escape, which took different forms with each child. The first to leave was Nicolas. In 1885, when he was twenty-one (and Isabelle eight), he enrolled briefly for external courses in botany at Geneva University, and then left home, joining the French Foreign Legion, in a grand gesture of escape. He relinquished name and identity to become No. 8817 in the 2nd Company of the 1st Regiment of the Legion in Sidi Bel Abbès in Algeria. He soon deserted, leaving his French ship in Singapore as it was about to set off for Tongking (now Vietnam), and making his way back to Russia – which may have been his intention in the first place, since he had been secretly in correspondence with some of the de Moerder family there for several years. He was now welcomed back as the General's son and heir, and was given a government post in the Ministry of Foreign Affairs under Tsar Alexander III. The new Tsar was even more autocratic than his predecessor, more effective at quelling any opposition, and with a far more dominant police force.

In his brief time at the university, Nicolas had met a young student, Alexandre (sometimes Jules) Perez-Moreyra, to whom he confided his story of the ogre at the Villa. Perez was indignant and sympathetic, and now became the first port of call for any of the de Moerder children who wanted to abscond. After Nicolas had left, Vladimir repaired once or twice to Perez's house, in the Eaux-Vives district of Geneva, in half-hearted and abortive attempts to follow in his brother's footsteps. Trophimowsky, who unaccountably but disturbingly doted on Vladimir, probably coaxed him back. In September 1886, the fifteen-year-old Augustin, spurred on by his older brothers' examples, also left home for Perez-Moreyra's, but he was hauled back to the fold by Trophimowsky, this time with the help of the police.

From her relatively protected position as the youngest, and as the only child who was not nominally a de Moerder, the young Isabelle watched these attempts to escape, and sensed the increasingly fraught atmosphere. Soon came the most dramatic escape of all, which dominated life at the Villa for over a year.

*

Nathalie, too – who, according to a later police report, had 'a certain disposition for sex' – was also introduced to Perez-Moreyra sometime in 1886, and the two fell in love. She was as anxious as Nicolas had been to leave the Villa, and in the summer of 1887, Perez asked Mme de Moerder's permission to marry Nathalie. Under the direction of Trophimowsky, who held an understandable grudge against Perez for having harboured his three other wards, Mme de Moerder refused, and during the night of 23 November 1887, when she was just twenty-one, Nathalie left clandestinely to join Perez. The cleaning woman at the Villa, Mme Mallet, claimed that Mme de Moerder had known of the impending escape, and condoned it, but the records otherwise show Mme de Moerder toeing Trophimowsky's line in whatever he said – a characteristically ambiguous piece of behaviour.

Nathalie poured out her heart to Perez about the injustices of Trophimowsky's regime. He was already disposed, through her brothers, to be appalled by it, and what he now heard incited his bellicose temperament to a pitch of fury. Trophimowsky, she claimed, was the father not only of Isabelle but also of Augustin, but would not admit it. He had looked down on her, she said, begrudged her food and had – a particular horror to her since Zola's works were considered 'obscene' at the time by most of the general public – *made her read Zola*. But she also levelled two startling new charges: firstly that Trophimowsky had engineered the death by poisoning of her father in Russia; and secondly that, in the words of the subsequent police report, 'she was daily prey to the disreputable and obscene propositions of M. Trophimowsky, who wanted to force her to become his mistress, going so far as to attempt to take her clothes off in her bedroom.' On Christmas Day 1887 Perez swore to Vladimir, with graphic mathematics, that he would 'come one day and ram eleven Wetterly bullets into the villain'. The couple went ahead and got married on 7 April 1888, having obtained official permission to do so without Mme de Moerder's consent, since Nathalie was now twenty-one. Perez then began bombarding the household with accusing postcards. On 20 April he wrote to Mme de Moerder: 'M. Trophimowsky entered the Senator-General's household as a servant . . . and the villain took advantage of it to steal from him and to make off with you; he's living off money stolen from his master, but shielded by your presence.' Another card on 15 May, addressed to Nicolas – although he knew him to have been in Russia for three years – said: 'I've just learnt that the attack of apoplexy was invented to cover up the whole affair; now I know what happened, I know how the General died; but although the papers have disappeared, and the man hired by this scum to do his business for him has been sent to Siberia, I'm going to disinter this whole affair and get an arrest.' To Mme de Moerder he wrote: 'Now it's an unremitting fight to the last between the coward and me, and whatever it costs me, even if I have to leave the country, I'll see this through to the bitter end. Tell him to keep what he's taken, and bury it with him in his coffin when his time comes – his *imminent* time.'

Trophimowsky now wrote to the police in alarm, detailing the threats and asking for their protection. As it happens, they had already been approached the previous December by a local philatelist to whom Augustin owed money, who had asked for a confidential investigation of the family's affairs. Did Mme de Moerder exist? What rights did the so-called tutor have over the children? Were they political refugees, given the mysterious airs that everyone in the household affected? Had the guardian already had brushes with the police, as he'd been told? The police were therefore disposed to take a sceptical view of Trophimowsky's complaints, and to wait for both sides of the matter to present themselves before acting. Their impassive attitude exacerbated Trophimowsky's growing panic, which, on 26 May, suddenly seemed amply justified.

Called to the Civil Tribunal to present his case, Trophimowsky sat down on a bench and in doing so pricked his leg on a needle which was 'stuck to the bench with a piece of leather and tar', as he told the police. When he got home, he found that an anonymous telegram had been sent to Mme de Moerder at about the same moment that he was jabbed, saying 'DEAD ON ARRIVAL, NO HOPE OF RECOVERY'. In his elegant, shaky handwriting, Trophimowsky wrote a long, repetitive letter to the police, obsessively going over the build-up of threats, trying to get them to take the issue as he did, as a matter of life or death:

Conclusion: this individual had decided to finish me off ('*I'll see this through to the bitter end*') and conceived this plan as a way of doing it. It seemed to him foolproof, and offered him a decisive and swift result ('when his time comes – his *imminent* time'). In view of the moral state governing the black soul of this individual, the needle in the Civil Tribunal must be seen as the instrument of his plan. Since the telegram announces my death as an accomplished fact, it is a proof - psychologically comprehensible – that the *doctored* needle led the criminal to believe that his action would be devastating. I therefore contend that on 26 May Perez attempted to poison me with a poisoned needle.

But before the processes of the law could address themselves to Trophimowsky's claims, Perez came closer to home. Just after five on the afternoon of 5 June, he arrived in person at the gates of the Villa in the company of seven 'friends' to pay what he termed a 'courtesy' visit to Mme de Moerder. He and one of the others broke away from the rest and approached the house. Trophimowsky came out and barred their way, shouting at them to get off his property, but Perez pushed past him, shouting back that he wanted to see his mother-in-law. Normally, there would have been no one but the family at the Villa, but as luck would have it, both the cleaning woman and a workman, Antoine Clochet, were there. Mme Mallet, 'seeing Mme de Moerder's extreme terror', ran off to get the help of a neighbour, M. Stämpfli. Trophimowsky got Vladimir and Augustin to run to get the police, and then he and Clochet together managed to hold the fort. According to Trophimowsky, Perez was gesticulating wildly and shouting, but Perez claimed he was merely passing the time of day, enquiring innocently about the health of his mother-in-law. M. Stämpfli and the police arrived, the police took statements from all concerned, and everyone dispersed.

Mme de Moerder, whose 'nervous condition' was driven to a crisis by this siege, retired to stay at the house of her doctor, M. Vuillet. She herself, by her own account 'ill and very weak for a number of years', now wrote to the police, in a tone of high moral indignation. She deplored the 'whole diabolical influence [Perez] exerts over the morals of my children', but even more the fact that his accusations had been deliberately written on postcards, so that postmen and post office employees could read and comment on them, and repeat them throughout the neighbourhood. 'I would never allow myself to pursue Perez in the courts, in spite of the exceptional gravity of his vile calumnies, because he is indifferent to public scandal, whereas I am in no way accustomed to it. He is a danger not only to me and to my children, but to well-organized social life in general.' Her sudden concern for 'well-organized social life' was decidedly pious.

In a last salvo, Perez now threatened to have the General's body exhumed as evidence, and Trophimowsky (perhaps rattled?) wrote asking the police to 'put the slanderer in a position to show proof of his terrible accusations and his sources for them'. But Perez was in no position to find the kind of legal proof that would be necessary to pursue the matter in the courts, and, for the moment, he had to leave it at that. He and Nathalie now severed all relations with the Villa.

On 21 August, the seventeen-year-old Augustin made a second bid to abscond, leaving behind a note saying 'I'm leaving home because I've lost all right to the affection of my mother.' Trophimowsky asked the police for their help in finding him, and wrote that 'this note proves this miserable boy's state of moral perversity'. The scant supply of maternal affection no doubt accounted for much in all these troubles. Mme Mallet gave her opinion to the police that, whilst the children were well fed, 'Mme de Moerder does not love her children, who in consequence have no affection for her, which is understandable in the conditions in which they've been brought up.'

Perez told the details of the ménage to the all-too-ready ears of a neighbour, Françoise Guillermet, who, years later, when she was editor of the *Gazette de Lausanne*, wrote a scandalized article about Isabelle's childhood in a Paris journal called *Les Marges*. Trophimowsky, she claimed, had told Nathalie before she left, 'If you leave this house, even if you come begging at the door like a dog, I shan't so much as throw you a bone.' She never met Trophimowsky or Isabelle, but she was not someone to let this prevent her giving her categorical views: 'He was a vile man, if ever there was one, this Russian ex-priest, but he was also a magnetic personality. You could understand if you saw him how he had bewitched the miserable creature who sacrificed husband, children and position to him.' Mlle Guillermet seemed a little seduced herself by the idea of this magnetic tyrant.

*

The eleven-and-a-half-year-old Isabelle was now left more or less alone in the house with Trophimowsky. Nicolas and Nathalie had left, her mother was recovering at the doctor's house, Augustin was temporarily (as it transpired) absent, and the twenty-year-old Vladimir, whom Isabelle only ever referred to once in her writings and that as 'the unhappy Volodia', was an enfeebled presence. She is not mentioned in any of the accounts, nor did she ever refer to these events, but she was undoubtedly there, watching and listening. If she had not been aware before from her own experience of Trophimowsky's nocturnal advances to Nathalie, she probably was now. It was as she was coming up to puberty that she now found herself for much of the time the only female in the house, together with the man whom Nathalie openly asserted was her father.

❧ 5 ❧

THE OLD TURK

In the autumn of 1888 Trophimowsky retrieved Augustin from his latest escapade and returned the 'miserable boy' to the Villa. He had spotted early on that Augustin's weak character would get the better of his promising intellect, and despised him for it. He confided as much to Isabelle as she grew up, seeing her to be made of stauncher stuff, but Isabelle for the moment was blind to Augustin's faults. Indeed, she had always rather hero-worshipped this brother five years older than herself, and for her the one good result of the recent exodus of her step-siblings was that she would be thrown together more intimately with him. He had grown to a striking six foot tall, and his height, his notably large blue eyes, and his air of romantically unfulfilled promise were beginning to give him a particular appeal to women. Even his mother, otherwise rather remote emotionally, doted on him. To Isabelle, the mere fact of their physical similarity – with their high cheekbones, wide brows, fine features and slim figures – had, she felt, destined them to be soul-mates. She wrote in her diary later of 'this being who is very mysteriously like me physically and who, I'm sure without being able to say why, must have many psychological affinities with me.' (The 'mystery' she saw in her 'half-brother' being like her suggests that even at twenty she did not consciously admit he was her full brother.) The bond she felt was further sealed by their having shared the ambiguous terrors of the past few months, so difficult for anyone else to understand. Now Augustin had the added glamour of appearing the misunderstood rebel, and Isabelle warmed to the task of saving him from himself – not only for his own sake, but for hers, since she started to cast him as the trailblazer for their future together.

Trophimowsky was now sixty-two, and his beard and eyebrows were turning white, but he still kept up his anarchic tutoring at the Villa. Isabelle, whose precocity allowed her to keep up with her brother, found a particular charm in his lessons since they brought her closer to Augustin. Both children inherited a talent for languages, which flourished in the cosmopolitan atmosphere of Switzerland. They had been brought up bilingually in French and Russian (although Isabelle made slight grammatical errors in both), and soon became fluent in German. Trophimowsky also taught them Latin, Arabic, Italian and even a smattering of English (although he passed on to Isabelle his dislike of English 'hypocrisy'). Cutting great swathes through history and literature, the tutor expounded to them about the great civilizations, races and thinkers according to the lights of his own eclectic, but mellowing, philosophy. If Isabelle lacked an ordinary social context as she grew up, she gained in exchange an intense, even exalted, imaginative life through the authors she read: Plato, Heraclitus, Rousseau, Voltaire, Tolstoy, Turgenev, Zola and Paul Adam (whose deeply pessimistic, merciless attacks on the moral turpitude of the society around echoed exactly Trophimowsky's own sentiments).

She showed an early preference for writers with the quality that Tolstoy valued above any other: that of 'heart'. When she was about fifteen she wrote an essay comparing Voltaire and Rousseau, which concluded (with an apocalyptic strain, and a sense of the healing power of nature, which were both to become characteristic of her):

With all the power of his tireless genius, Voltaire defended humanity's sacred and misunderstood rights and in his long life he fought until his last breath for the definitive emancipation of the human spirit; therefore it seems to me right that his work will last as long as that same humanity does on our globe. But it was with his heart that the humble son of a Geneva clockmaker pleaded for creatures' rights, the right to happiness, the right to love; and it is through the eloquence of his soul that he opened their eyes to the beauties of nature, the sovereign consoler of our ills. And that is why Jean-Jacques deserves to be read by the inhabitants of surviving planets when ours is no more than a pale moon wandering in the night. And it's also why I would give the *Philosophical Dictionary* for eight pages of the *Confessions*.

As she grew to adolescence her love of 'heart' verged on sentimentality, as she discovered, and fell for, Pierre Loti's tormented and melancholy escapism, which seemed to accord so much with her own and which indelibly marked her own style and way of thinking. She loved his talk of solitude, abandon and exile, and strongly identified with the magnetic attraction he felt for Islam and Muslims: 'Everything that touches Islam, near or afar, casts a spell over me,' he wrote, 'and likewise, the Musselmen of every country seem to accept me, and welcome me differently to others, as if, somehow, I am one of them.' The ground had been well prepared for Isabelle by Trophimowsky: by the time she was sixteen she could read the Koran in Arabic, and write an elegant classical Arabic hand.

Loti's first book, *Aziyadé*, published in 1879 and set in Turkey, was Isabelle's favourite at this time. His exotic depiction of 'the orient' (which at the time denoted for the French the Near and Middle East, and even North Africa) – together with his own languid, sensual and heroic role in it – fired her imagination. *Aziyadé* was no doubt one of the books she recalled later to Augustin, when she wrote of 'certain books which arouse in our two almost identical souls the same feelings, the same anxieties, the *same sad calls* towards the *Unknown*, towards an *Elsewhere*'. In walks they used to take in the valley above Collonges, full of what Proust calls 'l'angoisse qui plus tard émigre dans l'amour', they brooded on the 'Elsewhere': 'We were alone in the great eternal silence: [in Arabic] facing the great mountain', and shared their 'fantasies, hopes, plans for the future'. If they longed for escape to more exotic lands, their longing was born of a very Russian cult of suffering which developed between them: 'All the sombre philosophy of our lives was formed down there on the great roads to France,' she reminded him later, 'farther, farther, always farther on.'

At some point the generalized longing towards an Elsewhere, channelled and exoticized through their reading of Loti, became more specific for them both: it became a dream of going to North Africa, to the Maghreb. Isabelle wrote to Augustin later of 'this land of the Maghreb, which, you remember, was always the sacred touchstone of Mecca [*la sainte kaaba*] for us both', and wrote in her diary of 'that extraordinary attraction, which I felt for [the land of Africa] before I'd ever seen it, long ago in the monotonous Villa'. Her own account of the origins of this attraction was given to the writer Robert Randau later.

She had, she told him, an independent nature, and considered herself free from social constraints of any kind – from all of the conventions, received ideas and prejudices which narrowed the horizons of the bourgeoisie. Free of such trammels, and yet tired, she said, of new doctrines which denied the existence of deep and simple human values, she longed to 'expand freely in the margin of the world', to detach herself from the rich, the self-satisfied, the resigned. She felt she was emancipated, particularly, Randau said, since she was young and believed that happinesss lay with simple people. 'Thus prepared to find refuge in the vast spaces of the desert', she suddenly discovered Loti, was dazzled, and longed to become part of a world which was as far removed as possible from the vices of civilization.

This account was given in retrospect, omitting any of the troubles at the Villa, but there may have been another spur to her attraction to the Maghreb, one of which she was not consciously aware, and which centred around Trophimowsky and the ambivalence over her origins.

Trophimowsky's own familiarity with the language and culture of Islam went back to his Armenian origins: his family were probably some of the thousands of Armenians who emigrated from Turkish to Russian territory in the early years of the century. Arabic was not the language of Turkish Armenia, but Islam was its principal religion, and the vast Muslim majority were well acquainted with Arabic through the Koran. Culturally the 'oriental' world and its history were closer to Trophimowsky's background than the European. Teaching Isabelle and Augustin about the cradle of civilization between the Euphrates and Tigris, he was teaching them about places which were geographically familiar to him from his recent ancestral history. He also talked to Isabelle of the Caucasian and Kalmuck steppes between Armenia and his native town of Kherson – barren, mountainous regions, home to millions of nomadic Muslim Tatars, the mixed descendants of Genghis Khan's far-off Mongol hordes, and described them so well that Isabelle's later writing is suffused with detailed nostalgia for steppes which she herself had never seen. Significantly, she felt an obscure, subconscious ancestral bond with this area around the Black Sea, which had so recently become part of Russia, and which had been so much more oriental in its history.

Trophimowsky's interest in Islam seems to have revived in the early 1890s, during Isabelle's adolescence, partly no doubt through re-reading the Koran with her, and partly because by the 1880s Islam, under its charismatic leader Jamal al-Din al-Afghani, was beginning to present itself as a radical force for the Arab peoples' liberation from the expansionism of the European colonial powers. The methods of Al-Afghani, who left Egypt for Paris in 1883, must have recalled those of Trophimowsky's revolutionary days: secret societies, peoples' solidarity, assassinations; and his agnostic's view of Islam as a civilization rather than a religion coincided with Trophimowsky's own. Whilst Trophimowsky began to sign all his letters with the Muslim greeting 'Be happy!' during the 1890s, he could often be heard banging his fist on the table at the Villa and shouting 'That bastard Jesus Christ!' - something no strict Muslim would say, since Christ was also a prophet. (It did however echo Bakunin's thundering against the 'tyrannous and murderous God of the Jews'.)

Isabelle's own knowledge of Islam was kindled by Trophimowsky, but her instant affinity with it as a touchstone of salvation and escape was something more elusive and deep-rooted. Although she must have known of Nicolas and Nathalie's assertions that Trophimowsky was her (and Augustin's) father, Trophimowsky seems never to have admitted it to her. Instead a cover story developed, which may have been of Isabelle's or her parents' devising. Like many illegitimate children (including T. E. Lawrence) given leeway for fantasy by parental evasiveness, she was oblique and inconsistent in her few references to her parentage, and her comments are coloured by her particular fantasies at the time. However, the story that she later stood by whenever she was called on to give an account of her background was embodied in a letter she wrote to the newspaper *La Petite Gironde* in 1903: 'As the daughter of a Muslim Russian father and Christian-Russian mother, I was born a Muslim and have never changed my religion. My father having died shortly after my birth in Geneva, where he lived, my mother lived on in that city with my old great-uncle, who brought me up absolutely like a boy.' It is very likely that Trophimowsky and her mother sowed the seeds of this cover story for Isabelle. If so, she needed to believe their version of events, for otherwise the pair would have been lying, which meant that all kinds of other, more terrible, accusations against them, which they had hotly denied, might have also been true.

One fact is clear: her conscious mind wanted to believe she had had a Muslim father who had died but her subconscious knew otherwise, and dramatically asserted itself at later crises in her life. Her 'extraordinary attraction' for the Maghreb may have originated in a determined effort to validate a story she knew in her heart to be less than the truth. It was only less than the truth, and not a complete lie, because, like a murderer who is impelled to revisit the scene of his crimes, Trophimowsky and Mme de Moerder invented a story which was very near the truth: Trophimowsky was indeed, by the time the story came to be suggested to Isabelle, a 'Muslim Russian'. The only difference was that he did not die after her birth, but was very much alive.

🎄 6 🎄

BROTHERLY LOVE

Isabelle urged Augustin to work hard to become a writer, to travel, to go to the Maghreb. In doing so, she was both living out vicariously her own ambitions and instinctively seeking out ways of escaping the unfathomable impasse at the Villa with self-esteem, and without the traumatic upheaval of the previous departures. Unlike her older siblings, she wanted to love her mother and Trophimowsky, and needed to keep their precarious dignity intact.

But Augustin's own weakness of character was beginning to show through. When he was nineteen, he had enrolled in an external course in chemistry at the university at Trophimowsky's insistence, in an attempt to give him a profession. Instead of working, he had fallen in with the vagrant fringes of city life, drinking, consorting with prostitutes and dabbling with opium and hashish. By the time he was twenty-one, he was becoming addicted to drugs and drink, and would turn to the odd louche deal to finance supplies, sometimes even stealing money from the Villa. Still his charm saw him through: Mme de Moerder and Isabelle, still not aware of quite how low he had sunk in his private life, covered up for him, believing that his rebellion was fundamentally a philosophic, heroic one. Dmitri, the hero of Isabelle's later novel *Trimardeur* (*Vagabond*), owes a great deal to Augustin:

Dmitri Orschanoff had the rare ability to *be able* to succeed in anything he wanted to, almost without trying. If he'd had a strong will power and some order in his ideas, this quality would have been invaluable, but in the moral and intellectual confusion in which Dmitri struggled, it was disastrous, allowing him to forgive himself his faults, always promising to make up for lost time *later* . . . At the first hint of criticism, Dmitri felt misunderstood and rebellious. He felt he was not wanted, and marched off.

It still seemed possible that all this was just a regrettable phase. In 1893 Augustin met a portrait photographer called Louis David and his wife Cécile in Geneva. They divided their time between Blidah in

Algeria, where they lived, and Geneva, where David had a studio. (They also used to travel to Paris whenever there was an interesting exhibition to photograph.) Augustin was so taken with their ebullient and well-managed way of life, so different from that of the Villa, that it kindled a flicker of purpose in him. He, too, wanted to live in Algeria. He, too, wanted to become a photographer. The couple duly invited him to come and stay with them in Blidah. Isabelle, now sixteen, encouraged him to accept and make the dreamed-of voyage to the Maghreb.

His visit was a success, and he came back to Geneva full of plans. Throughout late 1893 and early 1894 he bombarded the Davids with letters and gifts, including flypaper and a Swiss army penknife, and even sent the local Blidah police some absinthe, to keep them sweet. (The Davids, amused, felt this was going a bit too far.) But once back in his old haunts he began to fall prey to his old vices, and by early summer his drinking and drug-taking had left him so debilitated that he could barely sleep or stand upright. Although his letters to the Davids had tailed off, the couple still had no idea of his problems, and in June 1894 they wrote a genial letter saying they were coming to Geneva in July, and hoped to meet him and the rest of his family.

But now Augustin disappeared again without telling anyone, even Isabelle. He turned up in Marseilles, where he was taken under the wing of a practical girlfriend, Madeleine Bernard. When she met him he was 'as pale and distraught as a man on his deathbed, and up to his eyes in trouble', so she decided to take him off to an 'eagle's nest' in Corsica for a rest cure. She realized that it looked rather compromising to be going off with him, but wrote diplomatic letters to Trophimowsky and Isabelle explaining where he was. She assured them that their intentions were honourable: 'in spite of the daily intimacy we have, there's nothing between us that I would be ashamed to talk about.' He needed a rest, and then he would return to 'his dear family whom he adores and whom he speaks of constantly with such affection. He's always thinking of his dear mother and of you, his beloved sister.' By 22 July the cure seemed to be working: 'since he's been sleeping properly, stopped drinking and smoking and is leading a calm life he says himself that he feels quite different and can stand up without any pain, something he hasn't been able to do for some time.'

Meanwhile Madeleine's aunt, one Mlle Joliet, who ran a bookshop in Geneva, had also been placating Trophimowsky on their behalf, to such good effect that he began to order books from her. The area he was particularly interested in, he wrote, was 'the secret life of priests'.

Whilst Augustin was away, the Davids had arrived at the Villa and had met the rest of the family. They wrote to Augustin on 4 August, trying to persuade him to return: 'We don't doubt that Corsica's charms are quite enough to keep you there, but we also trust it won't be long before you return to your beloved family.' Another family acquaintance, a chemist called Schoenlaub, wrote in similar vein:

I'm writing as a friend to beg you to come back, because of your mother's extreme anxiety and ill health. I've been with your charming family on several occasions. My dear friend, you're a reasonable and erudite man, a philosopher – don't stay away from your home and family any longer. It's so sad to see the state your beloved mother is in. She's a good and kind woman, you are her most adored son, and she's by nature of a very nervous disposition. Be a man, be courageous; prove you adore your dear mother and come back at once.

By the autumn this honeyed talk had succeeded in returning Augustin to the fold, although he had by now missed the Davids, who had meanwhile returned to Algeria.

Reluctantly, Isabelle began to sense that Augustin was not up to the role of alter ego that she had cast him in, and began to take over the initiative in areas where she had hoped he would lead the way. In March 1895, now aged eighteen, she herself wrote to the Davids suggesting that she, Augustin and her mother come out to Blidah, and asking advice on how to set up there for a while. Cécile David replied that hotel life was costly and inconvenient, and suggested renting a villa near them. Once they were there, she wrote, they would find the cost of living very low, and she reassured her that, whatever anyone told her, it was safe there, and foreigners were warmly welcomed.

This promising plan was thwarted by a recurrence of the Augustin problem. In April he disappeared once more, and another hue and cry was set up to find him. Isabelle wrote to his current girlfriend, Hélène Long, in Marseilles – they knew her brother in Geneva – asking if she knew where he was. Isabelle received a breathless and illiterate reply saying 'it seems ever so sad to me that he left just like that without even writing to all of us who never done him any harm.'

Mme de Moerder's health deteriorated with the worry, and Isabelle had to put off her plans to get the family to Algeria. The Davids, on their yearly Geneva visit in the summer of 1895, found Augustin missing once again. Unable for the time being to fulfil her fantasy of going to North Africa, Isabelle did the next best thing and had herself photographed in David's studio in 'Arab' costume, looking at first glance very much the dashing desert cavalier. On closer inspection, the camouflage is clear: her face is troubled, her eyes veiled with melancholy, and her costume makeshift. Underneath her burnous she is wearing an assortment of jumbled Turkish and *spahi* oddments from David's costume cupboard, geared to the orientalist tastes of the period, and Turkish slippers which would have fallen off at the first sign of action. But the fantasy accurately anticipated the reality, and the photograph strikingly embodies a notion of how she wanted to be, well before she had set foot in Africa. She had another picture taken of her, this time as a sailor, which was another role she was drawn to, and which she sublimated for the moment through Augustin. Her choice of hat, which bears the ship's name, the *Vengeance*, was deliberate, since she saw herself (and Augustin) as destined to avenge the injustices of the de Moerder family. (When she sent the picture to a friend some months later she drew his attention meaningfully to the motto, and later still, on 18 January 1900, she wrote in her diary that she wanted to 'become someone, and in that way alone achieve the sacred aim of my life: revenge'.

It was not until September that Augustin returned home. Perhaps those at the Villa decided that a long sea voyage might keep him out of trouble and make a man of him, for on 12 October he set off again, primed to join the French navy. He bade Isabelle an affectionate farewell which she later recalled in terms which imply the suggestion of incest which hovers over their relationship – 'do you remember those kisses we exchanged on the doorstep that day?' – and, amid mutual promises of devotion, Augustin set off. With an unerring talent for bathos, he soon wrote Isabelle a plaintive letter saying he wanted to come home. Isabelle was exasperated, both at his maddening lack of resolve, and at his continual sabotaging of her plans for their joint salvation. She wrote angrily on 23 October, 'You write "Everything's finished". What do you mean, everything? Yes, the old life is finished, dead and gone, relegated to the past.' However much she wanted him back, it was imperative to her that he should now stay away and break with the past:

For Mama's sake, in the name of my love for you, I forbid you to come back. God, if he existed, alone knows what it costs me to write that sentence to you! But it's my formal duty. To come back here, to take up that odious and pointless life again – no, that would be your downfall, morally and physically. Vava wants you to come back and start a *nursery garden*!! . . . The uncertainty is making Mama ill, very ill. You can save *everything*. Save it!

She insisted he join the navy at once.

Within days of receiving the letter, Augustin joined the Foreign Legion. Isabelle first heard the news through a sailor friend of Augustin's, Vivicorsi, to whom she had been writing, under the pseudonym of Nicolas Podolinsky, apparently to keep tabs on Augustin. Then Augustin sent a note to her on 12 November confirming it:

My love, Augustin de Moerder, soldier in the 1st Regiment, Foreign Legion, 18th Company, No. 19686 in Sidi-bel-Abbès, near Oran (Algeria). There, my beloved, is the whole sad truth. And yet I think of you, and Mama, and Vava. And I tell myself again: *Hieme et aestate, et prope et procul, usque dum vivam et ultra* [In winter and summer, near and far, as long as I live and beyond]. Yours ever, Augustin.

The news threw Isabelle into despair. The Legion did not even have its subsequent Beau Geste glamour, but was known to be a last ditch for drop-outs, convicts and failures, and a sure passport to death through fighting, disease or drink. (The Legion made no bones about it: the recruiting-room in Marseilles had its 'law' inscribed on the wall – 'You are soldiers in order to die, and I am sending you to the place where you will die.') Isabelle also knew that signing on meant an engagement of five years – five years in which she would not see him, in which he could no longer be of any help in her own predicament. She wrote him a furious letter:

This is a thunderbolt for me. What have you done?!! What have you done, you wretch?! Have you really gone completely mad, have you no idea what you're doing? I'm in the depths of despair. No one knows about it yet here. *Impossible to mention this letter*. And what does all this incoherent behaviour mean? Why didn't you join the navy somehow? You really must be out of your mind! Don't you understand the ghastly result of what you've done, you miserable creature?! No, really, I don't know what to do any more. I'm finished after this evening, completely and utterly finished. Everything's over for me. All right, so be it! No, no, life isn't possible any longer! And why do *all* of you whom I've loved, loved so madly, why do you kill me like this?! Already – without this hideous news – my own life had absolutely collapsed here, because of the terrible things going on. Everything's finished, thoroughly finished for me . . . I formally *forbid* you to write anything to me before you've written to *Mama*, just to *her*. *You must do this. Damn you if you don't!* Don't finish her off completely! You're lost. And in losing yourself, you've also lost me, completely lost me. I put my last hope in you, and now that's gone. I don't know what to do or think! No, no, there's no hope for me in this damnable life of eternal darkness. And the only thing I can do to save myself from this endless misery . . . I *must* not do! But can I hold out much longer?

Augustin probably did write a conciliatory letter, because by Christmas Eve Mme de Moerder and Trophimowsky both knew of his fate, and Isabelle, although still in despair, was no longer angry. Searching for somewhere to turn in her misery, and feeling a gathering need to believe in something, she decided to go to Christmas Mass at the Catholic church with their 'old maid'. The letter she wrote Augustin before going there shows her still a non-believer, and yet worrying the idea of a God:

It's the first time, my beloved, that we shall be spending this festival apart, separated perhaps for all Time and Eternity! Who knows if we shall meet again? What misery, what desolate sadness, deep and implacable. No more hope and no more faith. No God to whom we can cry out our nameless misery, all the atrocious injustice of our suffering. The heavens stay empty and silent, nothing, no one anywhere. Solitude is *absolute*. For us two, solitude is absolute, remember that! No one, *ever*, will understand our suffering, our aspirations and disappointments. And why must we live apart, far from each other? 'My God', a mechanical phrase, a habit! God! What's happened to our dreams, our hopes, our plans for the future?

In the same letter Isabelle writes of a new romantic attachment, although comparing it still with how she feels for Augustin. She writes a poem in Arabic:

My body is in the West/ And my soul is in the Orient/ My body is in infidel country/ And my heart is in Istanbul/ And my heart is in Oran! . . . In Istanbul! you know why . . . no doubt you've managed to unravel the truth, the distressing truth, about everything that, with our impossible character, I've told you about the engagement. You must have understood and guessed. But no, that love, that desolate love, never reciprocated, is nothing in comparison with the immaterial love I have for you.

She adapts a quote from Loti:

If Eternity exists, with which of the two shall I go and live, with him, my beloved brother, or with you? Oh! with you, always with you. And if Eternity exists, these immaterial, deep and inexplicable loves must be reborn with us.

Only they give us that tremulous sense of the Unknown and a kind of vague premonition of a very mysterious *tomorrow* and a *beyond*. Love alone, the two kinds of love . . . the one which is like ours, and the other, the one which I felt for the brown-eyed Levantine. 'Is it the supreme effort of the soul towards the skies or the blind law of nature?' But always, always with you, near or far, always.

Isabelle's passing infatuation with the young Turk is not mentioned again, but unreciprocated though it was, it evidently played some part in weaning her off her emotional dependence on Augustin.

Mme de Moerder's health was given yet another blow with the news of Augustin's enlistment. On 2 January 1896 the chemist Schoenlaub wrote to Augustin again describing Mme de Moerder as 'looking into a gulf, searching for her son at the bottom of a chasm'. Trophimowsky resolved to use any means to get Augustin out of the Legion, normally a difficult manoeuvre, but Isabelle now thought differently. By early 1896 she had accepted the *fait accompli*, and advised Augustin to try to redeem the situation by committing himself fully to the decision he had made. He must not 'stagnate intellectually', but should read and write whenever possible and keep a diary, which he could send her to use later as material for a story. 'This time at least try and stand on your own two feet and be resourceful. Your future depends on you alone now.' She warned him that Trophimowsky was thinking of trying to get him out of the Legion by appealing for the help of the Russian consulate, and she begged him to pre-empt this by writing at once to the Emperor himself relinquishing his Russian nationality, and applying for French nationality. 'Then you'll be free for ever of any possible prosecutions. And you know that you planned to give up this Russian nationality anyway, which you know as well as I do is far from being a sinecure. The letter to the Emperor is a *sine qua non*, otherwise the embassy will become involved and send you to Russia for a medical examination, and then you know you'll be lost and never get out.' (No doubt she had in mind the potential influence of Nicolas, working his way up in the Ministry of Foreign Affairs.) She told Augustin to write and tell Trophimowsky plainly what he intended to do: 'Above all no phrase-making, no sentimentality.'

Meanwhile Trophimowsky had dictated a letter for Mme de Moerder to write to Augustin's commanding officer, pleading his release on grounds of poor health. The colonel grudgingly conceded, although he explained it would take at least eighteeen months to effect. However, shortly afterwards Augustin got involved in some unspecified criminal episode which so appalled the colonel that he was suddenly only too glad to let him go. To be kicked out of the Legion was rejection indeed, and by the end of February Augustin was back home in disgrace, with the illusions of those close to him finally dashed.

During the four months Augustin had been away Isabelle's own life had altered in many ways. Just before he returned, she wrote saying 'You'll find me infinitely changed. I'm not proud of it! These last months have taken away the last of my illusions. The era of dreams is finished for me. God grant that it'll be over for you, too. Your dreams have led you to the Foreign Legion, without your even managing to stay. That's quite enough, isn't it?' That obsessively close, probably not fully incestuous, bond had finally snapped.

7

MASQUERADES

'When you come back,' Isabelle had written,

remember you won't find me at all the same person you left me, you'll have to get to know someone quite different. You'll find me working austerely and making my way in the world. As soon as you've recovered a bit, you'll find your way too, I'll help you. Think soberly and seriously about your situation, about your future, about the age you've reached [he was now twenty-four] without having done anything to secure your future. Listen to the voice of reason this time, and get it into your head that you cannot live off illusions and phantoms any more. It's impossible, it's deadly. Think it over and decide to do what I've done and change your old morbid way of life with all those drugs etc.

The abrupt change in tone in her letters to Augustin in the New Year reflected not only her resolve to take charge of her own life, but also a new amorous adventure with a married man five years her senior, Charles Schwarz. Isabelle was now nineteen, and Trophimowsky allowed her to go into Geneva on her own – on the condition that she went dressed as a man, which he claimed was 'more convenient in town' – and it was there she had met Schwarz. Initially he had helped her send medicines, money and books out to Augustin; but by mid-January he had become her 'great friend'. On 30 January she wrote to Augustin in a quite different vein to recent letters (she herself was to complain of the 'really distressing instability' of her moods) telling him of a meeting with Schwarz:

My life here is quite funny. Just imagine – I go around dressed as a sailor, even in town, right under the noses of agents. The other evening I was sitting in the pharmacy and to my great confusion (I remembered my complaints to you about drinking!) I got so drunk on beer (six of them!), happily in the company of Schwarz, that I found the . . . singular courage to make a bet with him that I would never dare kiss him . . . I told him, yes, I would dare. Probably without the six beers he would have won the idiotic bet, because

I'd have realized what a nonsense it was. But no! I kissed him and I even carried on kissing him in the empty pharmacy.

For Schwarz, who was, Isabelle wrote, 'a sensualist, who likes to live fast', it was no doubt piquant to be kissing a girl dressed as a sailor. For Isabelle, it was the first hint that her attraction to disguise was not merely circumstantial, but the result of a deeper compulsion.

The flirtation with Schwarz, although brief, may even have been consummated: in February 1896 a Greek artillery officer called Christos Christidi threatened to write to Mrs Schwarz to tell her that Isabelle was her husband's mistress; and at the same time Isabelle was writing off to Paris for a booklet on 'neo-Malthusian practices', presumably contraception. However, by the spring the relationship had petered out, probably because, as Isabelle had intimated to Augustin before, 'he really does love his Julie.'

Not all men found Isabelle's sexual prevarication stimulating: Christidi himself found it very resistible. She had evidently been sending him teasing, pseudonymous letters and he wrote curtly, 'I didn't know and still don't know what kind of a person I'm dealing with, what their real name is and to what sex or nationality he or she belongs. Meanwhile I haven't the time to write to unknown people hiding behind diverse pseudonyms.'

Isabelle's own confusion over her identity, which she now began to cultivate, was more than just an adolescent phase. In part, it was obviously circumstantial. She was given at birth a surname which not only failed to give her an acknowledged social identity, but which was a cover-up, something she probably always felt was negotiable. Amongst the anarchists she grew up with, *noms de guerre* and disguises were common currency, often as a matter of survival. Her sense of fluidity over her gender was also established well before she was of an age to have any say in the matter. In addition, as she grew into a young woman, her body stayed boyishly flat-chested and slim-hipped, and she was not encouraged to draw attention with her clothes to womanly characteristics she did not possess, especially since the corsets, tight waists and long skirts of the time would have inhibited the physical freedom she was used to. If challenged later about her cross-dressing, she would always stress this practical side – 'I was brought up just like a boy', 'Men's clothes are more practical for riding'. However, this was not the whole story. Some undefined malaise was behind both the cross-dressing, and the exceptionally – and often melodramatically – high content of pain that runs through her life, her letters, and her diaries.

What that something was can only be conjectured. Certainly even the matter of her physical make-up was probably not as simple as it seems, for there may have been an anorexic component in her failure to develop physically, a reluctance to grow into a woman stemming from a possible fear of incest with Trophimowsky. But deeper still perhaps was a certain narcissistic disturbance, rooted in her relationship with him. By obeying, to the point of adopting as her own, or internalizing, Trophimowsky's insistence that she wear men's clothes, she was acting out her desire to please him on his terms. As sometimes happens with the gifted child in a family, she became to a certain extent the scapegoat of her parents' unacknowledged guilts and problems. She sensed that to gain Trophimowsky's love – a prerequisite for survival in the Villa since her mother was ineffectual – she had to validate him and his theories. But the high, hidden price she paid in the process was to lose access to her own real self, which included her femininity: as she had written to Augustin, unconsciously articulating the problem, 'why do all of you whom I've loved, loved so *madly*, why do you *kill* me like this?' (my italics); and it may have been this loss which shrouded her life in premature mourning. What is certain is that disguise for her, as for T. E. Lawrence, was not the simple, daredevil caprice it has been seen to be, nor was it only an escape. It was in part a compulsive re-enacting of a deep childhood trauma: that the man she subconsciously knew was her father would not acknowledge her real self. So whilst she turned to disguise on one level as an escape from her confusion about her identity, on another level it relentlessly earthed her back into her old grief, which could not be discharged until it could find its proper object of mourning: her own real self. Fear of incest, however potent a fear, was trumped by an even greater one, one that threatened survival more: fear of the loss of a parent's love. Meanwhile, unless she could be freed of the compulsion to re-enact the drama, cross-dressing increasingly became, in the manner of a perversion, the only way she could experience a sexual thrill. Her personality has been seen by biographers as 'enigmatic', and many would-be biographers have been put off the task by discovering that underneath a spectacularly colourful and adventurous

life lay not only an 'enigmatic' and elusive personality, but also a
paradoxically empty one. Yet this emptiness itself becomes a powerfully interesting factor once it is understood as a central loss, and not
as a failure.

*

Nineteenth-century writers frequently took on pen-names, often so as
not to shock the family they depended on for support – while men's
names were thought to give women writers a more serious hearing
than they might otherwise have had. These considerations motivated
Isabelle, too, but she also took on a man's name for writing as a way
of testing herself in the open market, of matching her mind against
others' without really laying herself open. She now took the pseudonym of Nicolas Podolinsky, which she had adopted the previous
summer to write to Augustin's friend Vivicorsi, and used it as a
pen-name for her first published piece of writing. It was a short story
called 'Infernalia', and was published in September 1895 in a new
Paris magazine, the *Nouvelle Revue Moderne*, one of many literary
magazines springing up in Paris in its artistic heyday. It was a bizarre
début: a piece of Baudelairean necromancy about a voyeur in a
mortuary, looking at the dead body of a girl and being roused to
desire. It has the ghoulish subtitle 'Sepulchral Sensuality', and is
headed by a poem by Jean Richepin, the Algerian-born rebel-turned-
Académicien, one of the favourite poets of Isabelle's youth. His poem
speaks of 'love without end, love without a name', in a romantic
exhortation to love at whatever cost, even if it is dreams and shadows,
in order to seize a spark of the divine fire.

The language of 'Infernalia' is vague and overblown, and its theme,
death's seductive power, coincides with fashionably *fin-de-siècle* deca-
dence. Yet the morbid fascination with death was part of Isabelle's
very own obsession, vividly adumbrated here before her family's fates
had made death familiar to her. She describes two shrouded bodies
lying in a mortuary room which reeks of entrails, curdled blood and
drugs. One of them is a young man with 'the very gentle profile of a
white statue, his lips scarcely pale, and with a lugubrious smile on his
livid face'. The other is a woman, 'a mystical and pure image in her
transcendent martyred beauty', the sensual curves of her now rigid
form lifting the shroud. Their human form is still there, but otherwise
they are gone, struck off the list of the living for ever, and now destined

to be cut about under the scalpel the next day for the benefit of students, other young men and women still 'avid to live, to know and to love'. Their ultimate wretchedness would be laid out under an indifferent sun, but 'what does it matter? In the great, eternal and enigmatic process of Becoming, how could the sacrifice of blood, life and flesh be regretted?' Those who would be touching this flesh tomorrow were still alive and warm-blooded; another day they would be alleviating others' sufferings, and then they too would suddenly be inert, and fall into 'the great Void, formless, timeless, nameless', and so it would go on. But beside the young woman's body was someone living, a student doing guard duty – and fighting an inner battle against dark forces which threatened to overpower him. As he looked at her, his skin bristled with desire. 'With all his will power, with all his energy, he was resisting the sinister and neurotic call . . .'

Since Isabelle later said that she had studied medicine for a while in Geneva (although there are no extant records of her having done so), the story may have been prompted by her medical class's first visit to a mortuary. Yet it also heralded Isabelle's own two prevailing dark forces: the necrophilia, considered as a graphic metaphor for the mesmeric pull of death, and a notably voyeuristic strain.

The publication of the story stimulated her to more writing. She wrote to various publishers about her work, including to one Henri Rainaldy, who was so confused about her identity that he addressed his letters to Mlle I. P. de Moerder, Madame Isabelle de Moerder, Monsieur N. Podolinsky and Mlle N. Podolinsky. Perhaps he thought they all lived at the same house, and in a sense they did.

In April and May 1896 the *Nouvelle Revue Moderne* published two more of her stories under the name of Podolinsky: 'Dholema' and 'Per fas et nefas'. A correspondence soon developed betweeen Isabelle and the magazine's editor, J. Manin (who addressed her as 'Mademoiselle'). In May 1896 she asked him for the address of a new magazine which was about to appear, called *L'Athénée*. He replied that it was an upstart magazine run by juveniles, particularly the editor, who was a friend of his. In Manin's opinion, it was 'destined to vegetate into oblivion'. In fact, his own magazine vegetated into oblivion within the year, and *L'Athénée* took over its subscribers, its debts and some of its writers. Its editor, J. Bonneval, began what proved to be a long-lasting correspondence and friendship with Isabelle. She sent him her stories from the *NRM* and he replied in

October 1896: 'I can see you are in love with the sacred flame. I can tell I'm dealing with a frank and exceptional nature, and although we normally get the opinion of our panel first, in your case your writing qualifies you immediately for inclusion.' He gave her six months' free subscription. In January 1897 he wrote to her:

Dear Mademoiselle and *confrère*, I easily forget in reading your letters whether you're a girl or a boy. If it weren't for your feminine handwriting, I'd believe the latter supposition more easily. In any case, this proves you have an unusual virility, although moderated by your feelings and your aspirations. Don't ever be completely masculine because a superior woman is superior to her masculine colleague. In you as a woman there are some exceptional qualities, but they would cease to be so attractive and so remarkable if you got too close to that other part of the human species that is egoism personified.

In January, February and May 1897 he published her translations into prose of poems by the Russian poet Siméon Nadson, who had died in 1887 at the age of twenty-five, and who, along with Richepin, was her favourite poet at the time.

❧ 8 ❧

CORRESPONDENCES

In early 1896 Augustin returned to Algeria, and Isabelle made a last attempt to get him to settle there. She wrote:

I've proved you can count on me – you should have followed *my* advice in the first place. Stay in Algeria now, take advantage of this final opportunity, and save everything. With some capital you could do anything, I promise you. Even if it was just a minute orange farm in Blidah, we'd be saved. Above all think what a joy it would be to be able to say that it was you in the end who had saved the whole lamentable tribe called Beni-Moerder!

But Augustin drifted back to Geneva again, and Isabelle finally gave up the attempt to make him the advance guard for her own journey to the Maghreb.

It was during this period (probably from 1895 to 1896), Isabelle told her writer friend Robert Randau many years later, that she acted as 'secretary' for a 'central committee of Russian terrorists' in Lausanne. Randau thought this was melodramatic talk and took it with a pinch of salt, but he was probably wrong. Isabelle had indeed grown up in an atmosphere steeped in the cross-currents of European anarchism; her later novel *Trimardeur* (*Vagabond*) and some of her short stories reveal a detailed knowledge of anarchist cells in Geneva; and her reference earlier that year in her letter to Augustin about dressing as a sailor 'even in town, under the noses of the agents' suggests her own involvement. However, by 1896 she was beginning to lose patience with the intrigues and cabales of latter-day anarchism. Like her hero Dmitri in *Vagabond*, she had initially responded avidly to the idealistic talk of individual freedom, but soon found that the movement created its own tyrannies, with its 'Dumas *père* scenes, and all its committees with a president, a vice-president and so on, all this puerile and illogical imitation of just those forms of government which we're fighting against'. The cause of freedom, she came to feel, would be better served by each individual simply taking the liberty he or she wanted, rather than being the 'harbingers of a problematic liberty a thousand years from now', as Dmitri put it – 'people who haven't the courage to shake up imbecile, judgemental society and everything that is deadening right now.' Her disillusion with revolutionary politics reinforced her dream of escape.

In autumn 1896 she began a new correspondence, under a new pseudonym, with Abou Naddara, a flamboyant Egyptian man of letters who lived in Paris and was well known as an Arabic scholar. She wrote in Arabic, in the guise of a young Slav writer who had 'embraced the Muslim religion' and taken the Muslim name Mahmoud Saadi, and wanted to settle in Algeria in order to improve his Arabic. She even enclosed a photograph of herself – the one Louis David had taken of her dressed as a sailor. Her choice of pseudonym was revealing: the year had begun with her complaint to Augustin that there was 'no God to whom we can cry out our nameless misery' and now, in October, she was choosing a name with plainly religious connotations: 'Mahmoud' (a form of Mohammed), meaning 'chosen by God', and 'Saadi', with its sense of fate or destiny.

Abou Naddara was the pseudonym of James Sanua, a playwright who had been exiled in Paris since June 1878 for starting a satirical magazine in his native Egypt openly ridiculing his country's occupation by the British. He had been a precocious scholar, able to read the Bible in Hebrew, the Koran in Arabic and the Gospels in English by the age of thirteen. He remained a polyglot, and had an expansive charm which won him friends from all walks of life. In Paris he started up his own magazine, corresponded with a catholic selection of people from famous explorers to Hugo and Dumas *fils*, and was given the nickname 'Abou Naddara Zarga', 'the man with the blue spectacles'. He also undertook to give lessons in Arabic to the increasing numbers of people interested in learning it, in a Paris obsessed by things oriental.

Isabelle took particular care with her first letter to him. He was charmed, and began his reply by writing her a poem in Arabic, inspired, he wrote, by her magnificent letter and her 'perfect knowledge of the Arabic language'. He goes on: 'Your style and your handwriting have captivated me and I've put your incomparable missive amongst my autograph letters from oriental and occidental scholars, as a very precious memento. Thank you for the honour you did me by sending your charming letter, which astounds everyone to whom I proudly show it.' Encouraged by this response, Isabelle decided to reveal her real identity and sex to him in her next letter. He replied on 16 November:

Dear Mademoiselle, I'd like to express in Arabic the pleasure that I felt in receiving your *sublime* writings and my admiration for your calligraphy and your drawings. You asked me to reply in Arabic, and I do so below, to express my joy at knowing that it's a young lady I'm dealing with, a young lady of genius and blessed with great virtues and superior qualities, and to express my regret that I'm old and cannot lay my heart at the feet of someone as accomplished as you are.

He made an elegant promise to write her an ode in sixty-one languages on the day of her marriage. Isabelle was delighted with his courtesy and charm, and resolved to go to Paris to study personally with him when she could.

Abou Naddara soon introduced her to another correspondent who was to play a formative role in her life. He was Ali Abdul-Wahab, a young civil servant from a distinguished Tunisian family. In autumn 1896, whilst Abou Naddara still thought he was dealing with a 'Mahmoud', Abdul-Wahab had visited him in Paris, and had been struck by the photograph of the 'young ephebe' displayed on his desk, a youthful exception to the host of venerable and elderly ministers, pashas and princes surrounding it. Abou Naddara wrote to 'Mahmoud' suggesting he might like to correspond with the young Abdul-Wahab, who was particularly knowledgeable about Islam. Isabelle wrote to him early in 1897, asking for elucidation of certain points in Islam she had not fully understood. The agenda for the correspondence became the conflict between science and religion. Abdul-Wahab wrote on 18 April that new-fangled theories were taking away all incentives to a just and honest life, and that they promised in return a void ('*le néant*'). So people looked for oblivion in alcohol, or tried to escape this 'abominable existence' through suicide. On the other hand, he wrote, look at the life of people who were guided by faith: 'The unshakeable principles which direct all their acts remind them that this life is essentially transitory, that neither happiness nor misery can last.' In another letter he wrote that he had always had a very unfortunate personality, which saw everything in negative terms and feared for the future. Now he had sloughed off this 'lugubrious nature' – and how? 'Through my limitless belief in Islam. The most radical remedy, the only remedy for my moral malady is this Islamic fervour. It has two bases: impassiveness and resignation.' This 'moral malady', and its cure, must have struck familiar chords for Isabelle.

Another correspondence, also begun in 1896, gave her some practical information about life in North Africa. She had read a personal announcement in a newspaper – 'A young officer in Algeria, bored to death, would like to correspond with a young European girl' – and replied, this time under the (necessarily) female pseudonym of Nadia. The officer, Eugène Letord, was a Frenchman from Lyons, ten years older than Isabelle, and stationed in the South Constantinois in south-eastern Algeria. Through Letord's letters, Isabelle began to acquire quite a detailed knowledge of the areas he was posted to – El Oued, Batna and Bône in the South Constantinois, and Aïn Sefra in the South Oranais – and also some understanding of the workings of the French military there. Letord, temperamentally a loner, had suffered from the desert *cafard* for five years in his southern postings, and reported the rigours and tedium of such an existence to Isabelle, but failed to disenchant her. In fact, Letord now provided an additional incentive to travel to Algeria, since their 'epistolary friendship', as he called it, held the unspoken possibility of a future romance.

During the autumn of 1896, Isabelle translated several Russian poems into Arabic, and sent them to a Russian friend of her family's, Vassily Maseev, asking him to send them on to a famous Russian Arabist for comment. The Arabist was helpful, in a limited way, but it was Maseev himself who wrote her a more interesting letter on 26 October 1896, the same date as Abou Naddara's first letter to her. He wrote in Russian, giving her some avuncular advice:

Undoubtedly, with your exceptional talents, everything you undertake comes easily to you. Without having to concentrate intensively on your studies, you could take up all kinds of things simultaneously, and with your abilities you could succeed in all of them. I would like to give you some friendly advice about the need to concentrate and channel your energies into specific, favourite, areas. By carefully avoiding dissipating your energies, and by concentrating on research in your special field, you will I am sure achieve so much more than many women before you. Husband your spiritual strength economically and you will find good use for your exceptional gifts.

This was sound advice, but it was the advice of an older man, and too sober for Isabelle's present expansive mood.

9

THE MOVE

Nicolas de Moerder had been in Russia for a decade, and was by now head of his section at the Ministry of Foreign Affairs in St Petersburg. Perhaps not entirely coincidentally, he was now in a position to influence the fates of Russian émigrés, including those at the Villa. Vladimir, plagued like his mother with some unspecified illness, and, like Trophimowsky, with a well-founded paranoia, began to be obsessed by the fact that he could not get a full residence permit in Switzerland. He felt this was his one protection against the pressure that Nicolas was beginning to put on him to return to Russia. In Nicolas's view, Vladimir was being a traitor to the de Moerder family as long as he was under Trophimowsky's roof, and he was determined to avenge himself on the tutor by luring him away – particularly since he knew how attached Trophimowsky was to the young man. Vladimir was caught in a kind of fevered terror between the two men, immobilized not so much by a clash of loyalties as by a clash of fears. On 26 February 1897 Nicolas sent him a cryptic, but unmistakably threatening, telegram: LEAVE TODAY MADNESS TO DELAY URGENT TO LEAVE EVERYONE IS WAITING FOR YOU BE CAREFUL GRAVE CONSEQUENCES UNLESS YOU LEAVE IMMEDIATELY.

It may have been this pressure from Nicolas which inspired a new plan at the Villa: to sell up the Villa Neuve, and move the whole of the remaining family to Algeria. The time was propitious: Augustin had recently arrived in Bône, Isabelle had contacts both in Algeria and with magazines in Paris which would publish anything she wrote on the Maghreb, and Mme de Moerder's health demanded a change of air. Above all, the net of the past was closing in from Russia.

Isabelle was no doubt a moving force behind the idea, but it also coincided with a dream of Trophimowsky's: to escape the pernicious influence of modern civilization, and, by settling in a farm in Algeria, once again try to live out his dream of cultivating his garden. The plan was to get Cécile David, the wife of the photographer Louis David, to find a house for them in Bône through her relatives there, and for Isabelle and Mme de Moerder to go ahead and establish themselves there, whilst Trophimowsky and Vladimir stayed on at the Villa until it was sold.

Trophimowsky had an inspiration over who might buy the Villa: a couple called the Cassons, who had introduced themselves to him a few months before. Many years later Mme Casson recalled their meeting:

My husband was a fervent admirer of cacti and had a card of introduction to Monsieur Trophimowsky. We arrived at his house: an old man dressed in almost shabby clothes, but with a venerable face, a real Tolstoy face, welcomed us in a most cordial manner. A young fellow of about sixteen was sawing wood in the courtyard. His delicate, elegant hands and his refined manners should have told us his sex, but we had no idea. It was only on the third visit that Monsieur Trophimowsky revealed the disguise to us. I warmed to the young lady, who was so gifted and so well-educated. She promised to send me her first articles and her first book. She didn't keep her word. A few weeks or months after our third or fourth visit she left for Bône and we never saw her again. Her father [sic] and my husband continued to see one another. The old landowner desperately wanted to sell his villa and the greenhouses to my husband.

The Cassons, however, decided against buying the Villa, and Trophimowsky had to look elsewhere.

Meanwhile in April 1897 Augustin had arrived in Tunis, where he met Isabelle's correspondent Abdul-Wahab. Isabelle – still only known to him as 'Mahmoud', the ex-Russian student – had evidently told him about Augustin's past. He wrote encouragingly to her: 'He has definitely broken with his past and completely given up all forms of alcoholic drink – a decision which he is firmly keeping to. His manner here is both dignified and modest and he is respectful with older people. He spends all his time working and studying.'

This surprising piece of news probably encouraged those at the Villa, and, filled with a new optimism, Isabelle and Mme de Moerder made plans to leave for Bône on 21 May 1897.

10

DAR EL ISLAM

Cécile David told Isabelle and her mother that the house she had found for them in Bône was 'magnificent and pretty', but it did not suit Isabelle, since, as she soon found, it was in the solidly French part of the city, full of settlers and *colons*, and she had not left Meyrin to live in another small-minded, provincial atmosphere. For Bône, of all the Algerian coastal cities to come under French rule, had most faithfully reproduced the temper of existence of a French provincial town. (It has now reverted to its old Arab name of Annaba.)

Since it had been occupied by a detachment of French marines in 1832, two years after the French had first arrived in Algiers, some three generations of French men and women had claimed it as home. They had turned it into a town which could have passed for Toulon or Marseilles, with wide boulevards, elegant hotels, banks, shops, a town hall, a square lined with plane trees and a theatre. Even the patterns of French administration had been repeated, as Bône was classed and run as a 'sous-préfecture', with a French mayor and officials, and, like the rest of Algeria, was answerable not to the Quai d'Orsay – as the later protectorates of Tunisia and Morocco were – but to the Ministry of the Interior. This personal appropriation of Algeria, embodied in the slogan, 'L'Algérie c'est la France', had evolved in an arbitrary way, just as France's whole occupation of the country had done.

Algeria – the ancient 'Numidia' of the Romans, and the second largest country in Africa – had had a long history of invasion by the Phoenicians, Greeks, Romans, Vandals, Arabs, Spaniards and Turks. Each invasion had left traces of the new races and cultures along the coastal areas, and each had pushed the aboriginal inhabitants of the country, the white-skinned, independent Berbers, further back into the inhospitable mountains, the high plateaux, and eventually the desert of the interior. Islam had come with the Arab invasions of the seventh century, and stayed, although the Berbers took what suited them of the religion, mixing into it their reverence for their local chiefs or sheikhs, and scepticism about its more dogmatic aspects. Three Arab and Berber dynasties had then ruled over 'Africa Minor', creating the three countries which, with endlessly contested shifts of boundaries, would become Morocco, Algeria and Tunisia.

Only eleven miles away from Algeria, Spain had ruled over parts of the country for a while; and then, in 1541, the Turks had invaded, establishing what was to be three hundred years of precarious and desultory Ottoman sovereignty over Algeria – and shortly afterwards over Tunisia as well, though never over Morocco. Although nominally under Turkish rule, the Berbers in particular became used to ruling – and fighting amongst – themselves. Turkish rule was tolerated in principle because the Sublime Porte was the spiritual head of the Islamic world. Yet in practice the inhabitants of Algiers managed to assassinate so many Turkish governors that they were eventually given native Deys instead – and even then fourteen out of twenty-eight were assassinated.

During the period of Ottoman rule, the country had developed a thriving piratical trade in response to the action of the Christian powers of Europe in closing their Mediterranean ports to the previously active commerce of Muslim Africa. The Algerian corsairs would not only pounce on any ships bold enough to brave the southern Mediterranean, but even raided as far as the Devon and Cornish coasts – seeing themselves not as pirates, but as pious crusaders for Islam punishing the Nazarenes for rejecting Mohammed. Great Britain, France and even the United States had made occasional efforts to put a stop to the piracy, but all were reluctant to take on a war in such a far-off and inhospitable country. But in 1827, with Turkish power ever more remote, an incident occurred which changed the face of Algerian history.

The Dey of Algiers flicked the French consul in the face with a peacock-feather flywhisk, calling him a 'wicked, faithless, idol-worshipping rascal'. The Dey himself claimed that he was driven to 'two or three light blows with the flywhisk which I was holding in my humble hand' because of the long-standing refusal of the consul to repay a debt, but the provocation served as an excuse for the French to blockade the port of Algiers. When, in 1829, the Algerians fired on a French vessel claiming to be carrying a flag of truce, the French decided that matters had gone far enough. In June 1830 a French force of 37,000 set sail for Algiers, and by 5 July Algiers had fallen to France.

Once arrived, the French had either to pursue their conquest or retreat. Retreat was hard without humiliation: the taking of Algiers had coincided with the July revolution at home, and successive weak and unstable governments began, like many such governments before and since, to find it expedient to divert attention from domestic trouble by a foreign war. However, to stay would not be easy, for the native Algerians, although used to nominal domination by a foreign power, sporadically but fiercely resisted domination by an 'infidel' power. The respected Algerian leader Abdel Kader fought a punishing seven-year war with the French; in 1864 and 1881 there were rebellions in the Sud-Oranais, and in 1871, when the French were particularly weak at home after the Paris Commune and their crushing defeat in the Franco-Prussian war, there were bitter insurrections in Kabylia.

French rationale for being in Algeria at all – always rather nebulous – began to shift throughout the nineteenth century. Many Frenchmen had always been opposed to the occupation of a country five times the size of France and full of desert, but they had been overridden by government expediency, which reflected instabilities at home and the quirks of individuals rather than any coherent policy. The fact that by 1848 most of Algeria was French, for example, was due to the colonizing zeal of General Bugeaud, who was bent on reclaiming 'Africa Minor' for the Mediterranean world, certain that its true destiny was to be reunited with its Latin past after centuries of 'barbarism'. Then in 1860 Napoleon III visited the country with his Empress, developed a romantic liking for the tribal chieftains, and began to see himself, as he wrote in a celebrated letter, as 'the Emperor of the Arabs as well as Emperor of the French'. The Empress concurred warmly, claiming that she was 'mad about the Arabs'.

Orientalists like Chateaubriand and Delacroix had already prepared the imaginative ground for this romantic view of the Arabs; now the territorial conquest followed suit. After the fall of Napoleon III in 1870 and the humiliations of 1871, France began to need Algeria for a different role: to house some 22,000 refugees from the lost territories of Alsace and Lorraine (stock which would produce Albert Camus generations later), and vineyard workers from southern France, whose crops had been lost through disease; and, more crucially, as a territory where France could regain her lost grandeur. It was now, particularly, that Algeria began to seem to the French a natural, preordained extension of their own country, and the Mediterranean all but a French inland sea. The government in the coastal areas was made civil instead of military, and French became the language of government and of higher education. Speaking French, and becoming gallicized, became the only route to advancement for the native population.

The terms of the original treaty of 1830 – that 'the freedom of all classes of inhabitants, their property, their religion and their commerce will be unaffected' – had long since been forgotten. Land had been summarily taken from the local people and offered as bait to French immigrants. The French colonists, like other European colonists, came to consider their rule over others as a worthy duty, a *mission civilisatrice*. This attitude was exacerbated by the social insecurity of the immigrants – not just refugees, but state orphans, political opponents of the government of the day, the poorest peasantry, unemployed urban workers, and ex-Foreign Legionnaires. Most soon took refuge in a bunkered gentility, becoming a class separate both from the native people – a mixture of Berbers, Arabs, Jews, Moors, Turks and some Sudanese – and from the French in the mother country.

Five years before Isabelle's arrival in Bône, even the Prime Minister, Jules Ferry, had deplored the mentality of the *colon* in Algeria: 'We have taken a close look at him . . . We have found him very limited . . . It is difficult to try and convince the European settler that there are rights other than his own in Arab country and that the native is not a race to be taxed and exploited to the utmost limits.' Isabelle's later friend, the French-Algerian writer Robert Randau, wrote of the turn-of-the-century settlers that 'this bunch of *déracinés* is only held together by its need to resist the Muslim crowd, which itself observes the narrow but total discipline of a religion which is both civilization and homeland to them.'

As for the Muslims themselves, whilst some resisted, and some were sufficiently impressed by European know-how and technical bravura to collaborate willingly for the sake of side benefits, others suffered the occupation as the will of Allah. Even the legendary Abdel Kader, defeated by the French in 1847 – he lived out his days in some style in Damascus, a close friend of Sir Richard and Lady Burton – took a philosophical, Koranic view, prophesying that 'you are merely passing guests. You may stay three hundred years, like the Turks, but in the end you will leave.'

Cécile David, for all her zest, was a true *colon*. She had written to Isabelle, 'My dear Isabelle, what a filthy race these Arabs are!' It was this attitude that Isabelle and her mother were turning their backs on when they swiftly left the house Cécile had rented for them, and looked for quarters more congenial to them. They found themselves spacious rooms right in the centre of the old Arab part of town, on the corner of the rue Rovigo and rue Mérabed. They were on the first floor, overlooking Arab courtyards; underneath them was a Maltese family. Around the corner, in the rue Vieille St Augustin, was a Muslim monastery (known as a *zawiya*) of the Rahmania brotherhood.

After the anxieties and alarms of Geneva, this was a period of calm, reflection and work for Isabelle. She wrote to Abdul-Wahab, 'Here I don't move, I don't talk, I study and I write.' The low tenor of her existence was dictated partly by Mme de Moerder's failing health. At fifty-nine, she already looked like a little old lady. A police report of 13 May 1897, a week before she left for Bône, gave a graphic bulletin on her physical state: 'Five foot one, slender, with greyish-brown hair, dark eyes, a blunt nose, large mouth, no teeth, protruding chin, thin face, sickly complexion, a slow and stooped gait, is very ill.' She needed looking after, and for the time being adventurous journeys were out of the question for Isabelle.

Isabelle had hoped to meet Eugène Letord at last, but he had unexpectedly been posted to the other side of the country just before she arrived. She had more success with her other North African correspondent, Ali Abdul-Wahab, whom she invited to come and visit them in Bône. She looked forward to disconcerting the man who still knew her as Mahmoud. Abdul-Wahab later recalled their first meeting, as he disembarked at Bône from the *Ville de Madrid*:

I shan't attempt to describe my astonishment on the quayside when, instead of shaking hands with a Mahmoud, I found myself in the presence of a young girl, very elegantly dressed, whom I greeted with the greatest respect. She looked me up and down for a moment, shook her head, smiled and said with a very frank, slightly mocking air: 'From what I'd heard about you I'd never have thought you capable of such a great respect for prejudice.' All the same, it was a long time before I could get used to the idea of this young and pretty girl giving up the gentler prerogatives of her sex on principle to seek adventures which might have daunted the hardiest of men. It seemed to me so extraordinary that when I got back to my hotel I kept finding myself exclaiming out loud. I left Bône with unforgettable memories of the charming welcome Isabelle Eberhardt's family had given me. My short stay in the town didn't give me time to get to the bottom of the mystery which seemed to attach to Isabelle's life, as I was later able to do, but I did sense she had many troubles, and was suffering.

Abdul-Wahab returned to Tunis after three days, and Isabelle's letters to him now became more self-revealing, particularly since the slower pace of her life was allowing her to take stock of herself. 'Perhaps you've guessed that with me the ambition to "make a name and position for myself" (something in which I have anyway very little confidence, and don't even hope to achieve) is a secondary matter. I write because I like the "process" of literary creation; I write, as I love, because it's my destiny probably. And it's my only real consolation.' She found herself to be a bewildering mixture of elements, and characteristically put it down to inscrutable and 'mysterious' causes. She wrote to Abdul-Wahab:

There are things in me which I still don't understand, or which I'm only just beginning to understand. And these mysteries are very numerous. However, I'm studying myself with all my powers, concentrating my energies on putting into practice the Stoic aphorism 'Know thyself'. It's a difficult, attractive and painful task. What pains me most is the prodigious changeability of my nature and the really distressing instability of my states of mind, which follow one another with alarming speed. It troubles me, and I know no other remedy than the silent contemplation of nature, far from people, face to face with the great Inconceivable, the unique refuge of souls in distress.

Knowing herself was hard for Isabelle. Her real self seemed to her so unfathomable, and so different from everyone else's, that, like many adolescents, but in more acute form, she chose to hide it behind a mask. She wrote to Abdul-Wahab:

For the outside world you and I wear a mask which is impenetrable to all those who, like the vast majority of men, are not like us — we do it out of defiance and out of fear of the banal consolations that people would be sure to heap on us. With you, the mask is of impassiveness, almost of indifference. With me, it's of a certain tomboyishness [bon garçonisme], which explains my continual bantering and baiting. Both of us are very probably sick. We suffer cruelly sometimes, but we want none of the compassion of our pseudo-semblables, so dissemblables.

She had some more literal masks to hand: her cross-dressing and her pseudonyms. Now that she was in Arab lands, she took on far more fully the role of Mahmoud Saadi, young Arab scholar. She already had a command of classical Arabic and a good knowledge of the Koran, and, as a natural linguist, she now swiftly picked up spoken Algerian Arabic. Robert Randau later asked her how she came to learn it. She said, 'I just opened my mouth and spoke it.' In her guise as Mahmoud Saadi, she used to lose herself in the street life in the 500-year-old Casbah, a few streets away from the rue Rovigo, and soon made friends amongst the local Arab students. (It is probable that, like Dmitri in her later novel *Vagabond*, she befriended an Arab student who volunteered to give her lessons in the local Arabic.) She slipped into an easy familiarity with her new way of life, her supple body – never at ease in chairs – half-lying on mats in front of cafés, in the local manner, enjoying the unhurried horizontal daydreaming, the nonchalant unfurling of chance conversations.

Since Isabelle claimed she had been 'born a Muslim', she felt she had no need to convert to Islam, but it appears that her mother, under her influence, now formally converted to Islam from the 'Lutheran' status she had previously claimed on any form. Conversion to Islam is a simple, characteristically unmediated matter: the convert recites in good faith, with the right hand raised, and in the presence of two witnesses, the Koranic credo [*shahada*]: 'There is no other God but God, and Mohammed is his messenger.' With this declaration Nathalie de Moerder took on the Muslim religion and a Muslim name, Fatma Manoubia, in the city built next to the ruins of old Hippone, where the Berber St Augustine had preached and died.

With time on her hands, the twenty-year-old Isabelle now began to write descriptions of the life around her which she had promised to the editor of *L'Athénée*, and her sketches of local life, which she called 'Silhouettes d'Afrique' and 'Visions du Maghreb', were published in the magazine the following year, still under her pen-name of Nicolas Podolinsky. She also wrote asking Augustin, who was in Oran, to send some notes on life in the Foreign Legion for her to incorporate into a story. The notes, which Augustin compiled with a Legionnaire friend (with the felicitous name of Hyacinthe Delastre), were sent on 26 September, and formed the basis for her short story 'Déserteur', which *L'Athénée* published in the spring of 1898. All seemed set fair at long last for an escape from the shadows of the past and for the realization of Isabelle's long-held dreams.

Even Trophimowsky was in an optimistic frame of mind. In Geneva, the Villa Neuve had not yet been sold, but plans were still going ahead to buy a farm in Algeria. The whole family planned to become naturalized French, which would free them from the tentacles of Nicolas de Moerder and of the Russian authorities. Cécile David wrote to Trophimowsky on 3 September enclosing details of land and property in Blidah, and saying she thought there would be no problem over naturalization. Evidently undaunted by Isabelle's refusal of the house, she told Trophimowsky to give her greetings to 'our little mutineer' Isabelle when he next wrote to her. On 19 August Trophimowsky had sent an uncharacteristically buoyant telegram to Mme de Moerder: LIFE IS PERFECT HERE RELAX.

On 30 October Hyacinthe Delastre wrote to say that typhoid was raging in Oran, and when he wrote again briefly on 24 November to say that Augustin was in hospital – albeit 'getting better' – it may have been the final blow to Mme de Moerder's frail system. On 28 November her heart, so often tested over Augustin, gave out, and she died of a ruptured aorta.

❧ II ❧

THE NAIL

Although Isabelle never referred overtly to the circumstances of her mother's death in her writings, a half-fictionalized draft exists amongst her papers telling a story which undoubtedly describes them. The names have been changed, and change within the text. It is not a mother who has died, but (oddly perhaps) a wife, called 'Djénina', and the first-person narrator is a young man. Yet the high content of agony and the date it was written – in the early months of 1898, in Bône – locate its emotional source unmistakably. It is a baleful howl of pain and self-pity, which taps more directly than any finished writing of Isabelle's, and even her diaries, into what she later called her 'abyss of sadness', which she felt was 'unfathomable and unanalysable, without any known cause, and which is the very essence of my being'.

The narrator writes:

As I approached, in the silence of our part of town, voices suddenly reached me: women's lamentations, the lugubrious cries of families in mourning. How can I describe the terrible anguish that came over me all of a sudden: I seemed to recognize the voice of our old housekeeper, Zahra! Everything reeled in my blazing head and I began to run like a madman. I'd scarcely reached our street when I realized that it was indeed Zahra who was weeping, and that it was in *our house* that someone had died. Why in that second did I have the intimate conviction that it was *Djénina* who was dead? Instead of running straight up to the house the increasingly mournful wails were coming from I hit my head violently against the angle of a wall, and there in the corner, not knowing what I was doing, I started to plead with God that it wasn't *her* who was dead . . . I murmured my desperate prayer, almost out loud, leaning my head against the rough wall. My God! Don't let it be *her* . . . My God, don't let it be *her*!

For the first time in ages, I began to recall the once-loved language of my other homeland [crossed out underneath is simply 'my homeland'] . . . And, in my atrocious despair, I prayed, in Russian . . . And yet it wasn't the God of the Orthodox Christians I was invoking, nor that of the Muslims: it was the Unknown, terrible and all-powerful, it was my dark and menacing *destiny*.

Isabelle, or rather the narrator, began running again, and in the courtyard outside the house she met a doctor 'in European dress', who confirmed her worst fears. At first, she could not manage to go up the stairs, but collapsed at the bottom, overcome by weakness and nausea: 'I stayed there inert, without any strength but without losing consciousness: the ghastly thought would not leave me, it tortured my brain unspeakably like a burning nail that someone had hammered into my skull and was then turning slowly, pushing it further in, into the quick of my being.' The doctor helped the narrator upstairs, and she now saw the dead woman:

Her body lay on the bed, arms crossed over her chest, her head veiled with white according to the Muslim custom . . . A curious steadiness came over me: I went up to her and lifted the veil. Her face was as white as wax, her eyes closed, her lips slackened into a slight smile. A great aura of celestial joy and peace seemed to radiate from her. Her forehead was framed by charming henna-tinted curls, and they had put a red and blue velvet *chechia* on her head and a blue silk scarf fringed with silver. I fell to my knees beside her: she was already fixed in the icy stiffness of death. Oh, how to find words for the atrocious suffering of that hour, as I lay mute, unable to cry, and almost prostrate in my terror! In the darkness falling on me from all sides, only the *burning nail* continued to penetrate my brain, in a continuous, awful blaze: she is *dead, dead*.

The agony then turned to anger:

Crazily, with clenched teeth, I cursed life, and God, and love. I cursed my existence. Why did that gypsy, my mother, make love to Mikhail Zemlinsky, the madman, the outcast? Why, by what right did she bring me into the world for so much suffering, for so much agony, so pitiless and so pointless? Oh, how I hated the Universe, and God, in that moment! I didn't even want to deny his existence, I accused him, furiously, of all the ghastly injustice of his odious creation! I didn't even beg for death, the supreme redemption.

The narrator turns on the doctor in blind fury. He replies quietly that her death was instantaneous, she was simply struck down. 'Struck down! Can't you see that it's God, God the tyrant, the eternal Evil, who struck her down. Can't you see that?'

Isabelle's worst, most intimate fears came out, raw and pell-mell: her bitter accusation against her mother for her weakness in succumbing to 'the madman, the outcast, Mikhail Zemlinsky' — a thinly veiled

Trophimowsky, with no trace here of the fantasized Muslim – and for bringing her accidentally into the world, and a chilling apprehension that the universe was perhaps not ordered for good but for evil. Perhaps she was even subconsciously transforming into metaphysical form her worst doubts about her father: the horror may have been not that God/the father did not exist, but that He/Trophimowsky was indeed there, but a tyrant, and evil.

At the funeral, the body, covered in a shroud of orange silk, was carried to its Muslim grave on the wooden stretcher that bears any Muslim, rich or poor. From the balcony, the narrator watched the procession leave: 'As long as I live I shall see the long orangish thing disappearing around the corner of the road, in between the white shrouds and the multi-coloured burnouses.' In real life, René Doyon (an early biographer of Isabelle's) tells us – although the source is lost – that 'Vava arrives a few hours after the funeral; the state Isabelle is in makes him stiffen; when his daughter cries out that she wants to die with her mother, Trophimowsky hands her a revolver, and when she talks of suicide, he points to the balcony.'

Later in Isabelle's draft the narrator becomes undisguisedly herself. She voices not only her suffering, but also her black sense that she was born to suffer, that she would always be hounded mercilessly, as if by ancient, vengeful Furies:

Suddenly all the appalling *injustice* of my life appeared to me, in a sort of terrifying synthesis of all my unhappinesses . . . and of my ultimate abandonment from that hour onwards. I realized that I was cursed, from the day of my birth, destined to suffer, doomed to solitude and despair. Ah! if happy people, those whom deaf and blind and probably unconscious fortune favour were to read these lines they would no doubt seem to them 'composed' or artificial. And yet these are the cries of a desperately unhappy soul, victim of a sort of blind curse, and above all *undeserved*! I glimpsed the whole atrocious cruelty of my destiny, of this shadowy *fate* which seemed to pursue me, everywhere and at all times, implacably.

Even if Isabelle herself felt her 'abyss of sadness' to be 'unfathomable', she leaves the reader in no doubt that its genesis was in the unwelcoming, ambiguous circumstances of her birth.

ISLAM

Isabelle's turmoil and despair gave way to a numb state of shock over the next three months. She did not attempt to go back to the Villa with Trophimowsky, but stayed in the place where she had been hurt, like a wounded animal. She did change her lodgings, leaving the previous house, with its now empty room next to her own bedroom, and its images of death and pain in the turn of the staircase or in the view from the window. She chose a small, plain white room to live in and went to ground there during December, January and February, nursing her wounds. The December weather was dark and stormy, with violent winds whipping the grey Mediterranean up against the harbour rocks. In sheets of notes dated 'Annaba 1898', she wrote she had 'passed from *mobility* and quick-wittedness to a resigned *immobility*', with the energy to do only the bare necessities to keep alive each day. 'Except for *indispensable* work, I do nothing. What's the point?' Even writing seemed pointless, since 'the old tunes would come back to haunt me more insistently and sadly.' She avoided company, spending the evenings of early spring sitting out on her balcony gazing out over the harbour on to the 'distant horizon' and only leaving her lair for solitary and nostalgic walks to the bridge in the Casbah which overlooked the bay, or for even more melancholy visits to her mother's grave. She could not begin to make plans for any future beyond the next day. The very concept of planning had been dealt a mortal blow for her by her mother's death. Her struggle to come to terms with the whole 'atrocious cruelty of my destiny' was particularly acute since she saw her plans to live in Algeria and to bring the rest of the family with her as the one lifeline out of an otherwise hopeless situation. Now that her lifeline had been severed, she was what she called 'adrift', *à la dérive* – a phrase she chose a few months later as the first title for her novel, which subsequently grew into *Vagabond*. At first a wistful description of her lack of moorings, it became in the months following her mother's death a key to a new state of mind: that of submission. This deliberate acquiescence in the workings of fate, a conscious decision to allow herself to 'be carried along, adrift, by the mysterious waves of the ocean of life', released her from her brooding inertia. 'Days passed like this, in a kind of mournful and bitter dream, until one evening, finally, I found *peace in my heart*.' The peace came from an 'absolute submission to the unknown decrees of Fate', now that she had been chastened by 'the blows of undeniable realities'. 'What strange peace and pride these final resolves give us, even the most desperate ones, even ones like mine which are the total negation of all hope, of all earthly *expectations*!' Now Isabelle began to exchange the moral currency of the European – hope, expectations, directed will – for that of a more ancient culture: submission, acceptance, living from day to day. 'My innate, dormant fatalism has been gradually awakened in contact with Muslims, who are resigned in advance to the inevitable defeat of human hopes.' The Arab word for submission is *Islam*, and it was the life-saving acceptance of *submission* which sealed her allegiance to the Muslim faith. Islam, in both its meanings, had rescued her from the trauma of her mother's death. *Mektoub* (it is written) and *Insh' Allah* (Allah wills it) became touchstones of salvation for her, as well as embodying what she now felt to be the nature of reality. The paradoxical, familiar move had been made: a free-thinking, independent young rebel, reared on scepticism, now wholeheartedly embraced one of the most dogmatic of religions, the simplicity of the creed making it an effective ballast against the restless complexities of her character.

Yet she could not stay inert and resigned for ever. Not only was she 'slipping into poverty for want of working', but she was still young, and life forces were beginning to gather in her again. There was also a world outside her walls in the grips of its own upheaval which was about to impinge on hers, and to challenge her to stand up and be counted as a Muslim.

In March 1899 Bône was experiencing stirrings of Muslim student revolt against the French administration. Isabelle's friendships with the local Muslim students had made her aware of the groundswell of resentment against colonial rule, and in early March matters were beginning to come to a head, with Muslims turning against the Christians and Jews, who, they claimed, had insulted them. Isabelle was sympathetic to their cause, but wrote on 2 March, in some unpublished journal notes which she began to take on the incident, that it would be foolhardy for the Muslims to respond to the provocation: 'We're doing everything we can to prevent a general revolt, which would be fatal to the Muslims . . . They would be sure to shoot down the first *roumi* [the Arab word for Christians] who got on the wrong side of them with some crude insult (in the noble custom of those who wish to "civilize" Algeria!).' However, she decided in advance that

if the fight becomes inevitable, I won't hesitate for a single instant, because it would be cowardice . . . And that makes me smile: perhaps I shall be fighting for the Muslim revolutionaries like I used to for the Russian anarchists . . . although with more conviction and with more real *hatred* against oppression. I feel now that I'm much more deeply a Muslim than I was an anarchist.

The simmering revolt broke out in the evening of 14 March in the Arab quarter. 'All night long, soldiers and police patrolled the streets, clicking their steel heels on the paving-stones of the old Moorish streets. In the cafés there is nothing but clandestine, furtive talk. In the *zawiyas* [which became the focus for discontent] everyone is whispering of an armed revolt.' In the barracks, the native soldiers had the sense of impending action and 'a certain effervescence reigns.' The next day a line of Muslims from the *zawiya* of the Aïssaouas filed through the streets chanting their hymn, and the police tried to disperse them. Isabelle, in another group of Muslims, heard the chant interrupted by police warnings.

In a flash, there was nothing but a terrible commotion, an infernal tumult. The police drew their weapons. All the students were armed with revolvers and daggers. The *khalifa* of the Aïssaouas, Ribah Bellefia, stood up and said 'In the name of the merciful God! Our brothers are fighting. Let's go and help them!' We left in a group, but we were immediately caught up in the fighting and had to use our weapons. Faces were pale and long black eyes shone.

A ragged Bedouin sitting astride a windowsill harangued the crowd to 'exterminate these sons of bitches who are insulting Islam!' and then quoted a verse from the Koran which inflamed the crowd instantly: 'And do not say to anyone killed in the path of God: he is dead! No, he is alive!' Isabelle, who had written only careful and conciliatory advice in her diary only a few days before, was now galvanized out of her inertia. The proper response of a Muslim to a

challenge to the faith was to fight even to martyrdom, but Isabelle did
not disguise the fact that her response was more suspect: a sensual
pleasure in bodily violence for its own sake: 'My chest was pounding
and my head spinning, deliciously . . . I saw Bellefia in front of me
brandishing a truncheon . . . At every moment it slashed into the
surrounding police, cracking into skulls and arms raised in self-
defence. Ribah Bellefia seemed transfigured: he seemed to me to have
an ineffable mystical beauty.' A friend of hers was covered in blood
and trying to fend off four policemen with his short Moorish dagger.
Isabelle picked up a fallen sword and went to his aid. 'For the first
time, I felt the savage intoxication of battle, bloody and primitive, of
males body to body, wild with anger, blinded by fury, drunk on blood
and on instinctive cruelty. I knew the consuming voluptuousness of
streaming blood, of the atrocious brutality of *action* triumphing over
thought.' Action triumphing over thought had a particularly seductive
appeal for Isabelle at this time, locked as she was in the treadmill of
her thoughts, and the few moments she spent caught up in the Bône
riot sealed her compatibility with Islam. The violence had brought the
blood coursing back through her after months of immobilized grief,
and the fact that it was all done for a greater cause legitimized the
physical thrill. Now she had experienced both Islam's spiritual solace
and its (Koranically strictly defensive) licence to arms. In some atavistic
way, both powerfully appealed to her. She noted approvingly that
'the Arab only drops his haughty calm in moments of battle . . . but
then he's cruel and pitiless.'

In the Bône skirmish the Muslims were outnumbered and out-
armed, and when the troops arrived Bellefia ordered everyone to
disperse. Most got away, including Isabelle, but many were arrested.
Isabelle made her way back to her rooms with her head spinning, but
with caution, taking detours along the way to avoid being tailed. By
the time she arrived home she had to face a new dilemma: she realized
she now had to leave Bône. The police and military were especially
vigilant over visiting foreigners in Algeria, whom they were prone to
suspect of being spies. They kept detailed records on their files of
anyone who might be thought to be politically provocative, and
Isabelle's sartorial tastes and foreign nationality had probably alerted
the authorities to her from her first weeks in Bône.

Returning home at midnight on 15 March, she realized that the
French authorities would almost certainly be alerted on the grapevine

to her presence on the Muslim side of the disturbance, and that she might now be *persona non grata* in Bône. She began to make plans to leave. She would wait the next morning for word from a Muslim friend, who worked at the town hall, to say whether she was going to be arrested or not, and if so, when. If they were not coming for her that day, she would leave on the nine o'clock steamer to Marseilles in the evening. If they were coming earlier, she would have to leave before that, and planned to head east, across Tunisia, to the Libyan border. Whatever happened, she wrote in her notes, this would be the last day she would spend in Bône.

Neither the military nor the police came to arrest her the next day, so she was able to leave that evening for Marseilles. However, from now on it was on the local police records in the administrative area of Constantine that Mlle Eberhardt, of Russian origin, not only dressed as a young Arab, but also sympathized with Arab elements hostile to the French.

In the event she took some comfort from the fact that she could not return to Bône. Her enforced departure, four months after her mother's death, offered her a welcome opportunity to stand back from her first, traumatic contact with Algeria and to take stock. It also encouraged her to do her duty by attending to matters at the Villa Neuve, which were now in a terminal state of decline. She wrote:

I certainly love this barbaric country, profoundly love it . . . But curiously it seems to me that exile would do me good, that I'd love these places more completely from a distance, places where the main act in the strange drama of my life has unfolded . . . Oh, there's no doubt that wherever I go I'll take with me in my innermost heart the indelible mark of Islam and of my intensely sad love of my elected country . . . and the incurable regret of having been happy . . . for so little time.

13

THE HYPOCHONDRIAC

When Isabelle arrived back in Geneva at the Villa, she found the garden a melancholy wilderness, and Trophimowsky and Vladimir living alone in cloistered morbidity. Trophimowsky had been, in his own words, 'severely shaken' by Mme de Moerder's death, and had begun to go into a slow decline. Now Isabelle found him in poor health, coughing a lot in between his constant smoking, and so morose that he could scarcely bring himself to shop for food. Vladimir was in a worse state. He had turned the corner into madness, provoked by an incident which had occurred a fortnight after Mme de Moerder's death. He painstakingly delivered an account of the matter to the police afterwards, his beleaguered personality oblivious to its farcical elements.

On 14 December 1897 he had been summoned to the office administering residence permits. He hoped it would be to issue him with the long-delayed full Swiss residence permit from the Russian Ministry of the Interior, but to his horror found instead his brother Nicolas waiting for him, accompanied by the Russian consul, the Polish Count Prozov. After trying for years to get Vladimir to return to Russia, Nicolas had now come in person to 'abduct' him and take him back 'forcibly'. They knew Vladimir suffered from a 'chronic illness', and he felt that they played on it mercilessly, 'trying to push me to the limits of my strength and sanity'. They taunted him with being a coward and a 'toady', and prevented him from leaving the office – 'At this moment the clock chimed midday, the time when, if I don't eat immediately, my chronic illness undermines all my mental and physical strength.' He remembered the sequel only in cameos: Nicolas and he were alone in a café; Nicolas was telling him, 'You have inherited your mother's money, and she's disinherited me. You're coming with me now by hook or by crook. From today you belong to me body and soul.' A car was waiting outside, with two

Russian detectives in it 'supplied by the Russian government' . . .
Vladimir broke free, running down the street until, with the help of a
bookseller who knew him, he ended up under the protection of the
mayor, who put a guard of two policemen on the Villa for the
night.

From then on Vladimir's precarious sanity was lost. Neighbours
used to hear him sobbing from the upstairs windows, or, equally
alarmingly, singing hymns. They knew in their minds what had
happened: the old ogre, Trophimowsky, had driven him insane.

Trophimowsky's and Vladimir's demoralized state was compounded
by their lack of income. Mme de Moerder – 'my sainted mother',
according to Vladimir – had indeed cut both Nicolas and Nathalie
out of her will, and left her money to Vladimir, Augustin and Isabelle,
but it was proving difficult to get the funds out of Russia. Trophimowsky – and Isabelle, when she returned, broke, from Algeria – began
to borrow money against promises of the trust money to come,
Trophimowsky from a solicitor called M. Samuel, and Isabelle from
moneylenders in Paris. Trophimowsky dictated a letter for Vladimir
to sign, addressed to the Moscow Magistrates' Court, requesting an
advance from his legacy. The court replied on 13 April, refusing the
request, under the terms of an almost suspiciously propitious new
clause of 23 March. But Vladimir never received the letter. On
the day it was written, he put his head in a gas oven at the Villa,
turned on the tap, and snuffed out his life.

Trophimowsky, evidently at his most terse after the deaths of those
closest to him, and with no one else to turn to, sent a blunt telegram
to his botanical acquaintances, the Cassons: MY CACTOPHILE IS
DEAD. COME OVER. Poor Vladimir was only 'my cactophile' to
Trophimowsky, even in the moment of his greatest grief. A few days
later M. Casson accompanied Trophimowsky to the simple funeral,
and the 'silent hypochondriac', as Mme Casson called Vladimir, was
laid to rest in the small, hillside cemetery of Vernier.

Isabelle wrote to Abou Naddara in Paris, telling him of Vladimir's
death. He replied that 'the world lives in such an unhappy state that
we should congratulate those who die. Your brother, whose story you
told so eloquently that I wept, suffered so much in this sad vale of
tears that death alas! is a release for him.' She wrote of herself as an
'orphan' now, but Abou Naddara replied that she was not, 'because
you have an affectionate father in the noble person of your tutor,

whom you've made me love and bless through your eulogies of his great virtues and superior qualities.'

Isabelle was now left alone in the degenerating Villa to look after her 'affectionate father', whose health continued to deteriorate.

14

RACHID

But Isabelle was not devoting all her energies to looking after Trophi-mowsky. During the spring, perhaps even before Vladimir's death, she had become involved with a young man who rapidly became an aspiring suitor. He was Ahmed Rachid, a young Turkish diplomat working as a secretary in the Imperial Ottoman Embassy in Paris. As a career diplomat, he was not necessarily tarred with the brush of Sultan Abdul Hamid II's reactionary Ottoman regime, but it was still an unusual choice for Isabelle, who had been more used to consorting with the Young Turks in Geneva who were trying to depose the Sultan.

There is no record of where and how the two met. It may have been in Bône or in Geneva, but Rachid's earliest surviving note to 'my sweetest' Isabelle from a boulevard St Michel café shows him in love with her by the end of May. His duties in Paris, and the fact that Trophimowsky did not yet know of the relationship, made it difficult for them to meet, but he began to take any opportunity available to take the overnight train to Geneva to see her, even if it was just for a few hours. He was ardent and needy. He had been drifting slowly but surely towards a kind of suicide until she came along, he wrote. 'My heart was empty, but now everything has changed. It's a pleasure for me to come, to love and be loved. It's you who have attached me to life again, and I thank you for it.' They were both in unhappy periods of their lives, but by 3 June he was writing, 'All our dreams will come true as long as we are patient. We both deserve a better fate.' One of his dreams was of getting a posting to North Africa, which he knew was dear to Isabelle's heart, and of living there together in the sun as man and wife. His next posting was due any moment, and he had high hopes of it being to Tunis or at least Madrid. When it was announced on 16 June, it was, with familiar diplomatic contrari-ness, for the Hague in Holland. Rachid tried to look on the good side, and yet knew Isabelle would be disappointed:

I've spoken to several people who have lived in Holland, and they have a lot
of good things to say about it. Yet however agreeable a life we live in Europe
we shall still miss the Orient's sun. I can manage without it, as long as we
can fulfil our other dreams, and meanwhile try and find some way of getting
to the Muslim countries, perhaps to Egypt, land of pharaohs, which I know
you'd love to study. My greatest joy is going to be to see you happy. But you
are pessimistic, as usual.

Indeed the prospect of moving to Holland did not appeal to Isabelle,
whose own dreams had for so long been focused in the opposite
direction.

Yet they shared other ambitions. Rachid was generously keen to
see Isabelle succeed as a writer, and whilst he was in Paris, he
tried to help her get commissions from magazines, notably from the
magazine *La Fronde*, run by the well-known feminist Séverine. In his
rather abrupt French, he wrote to her in mid-June envisaging their
future together:

I'm looking forward to taking you for walks in the Dutch forests, and to the
moaning of the ocean waves as they break endlessly on the shore, and to your
soft voice telling me how much you love me. What beautiful dreams. Will
they come true? Yes, I think so because I don't think there's anything to stop
them at the moment. It's so good to think of, too good even. So, my adored
darling, what will the future hold? In a few years I'm sure that you'll be
well-known in the writing world. For the moment, I'm feeling untranslatable
things which my pen is powerless to describe. I'd like ten years of my life to
tell you what's in my heart. The heart that belongs to you. Only to you, and
forever.

He was due to leave for the Hague within the month, and pressed
Isabelle to come to see him in Paris for a couple of days before a visit
she was planning to make to Augustin in Marseilles. He said 'the old
man' need not know: she could send a letter addressed to him for
Augustin ('our brother') to send on. His imminent departure was
adding urgency to his romance: he wanted to marry Isabelle as soon
as possible, so Trophimowsky now had to be told of his suit. Once
told, Trophimowsky played the traditional *pater familias*, writing the
young man a formal letter requesting confirmation of his intentions
and of his posting. Rachid replied respectfully, eagerly writing that he
planned to come to Geneva shortly to have the honour of meeting
him personally and 'of embracing you as a son embraces his father'.
But Trophimowsky decided to make independent enquiries through

Abou Naddara about Rachid's character. At Isabelle's request the old Egyptian bustled over from his rooms in Montmartre, just behind the newly mushrooming domes of the Sacré Coeur, to the Ottoman Embassy next to the Etoile. Dressed in his full oriental robes, he peered through his gold-rimmed spectacles at the Ambassador, his Excellence Munir Bey, and demanded a character reference on the young man. The Ambassador was able to assure him that he held Rachid in high regard, that he was 'a young man whom everyone likes', and that he had indeed been given the post of Second Secretary at the Ottoman Legation in the Hague. If Trophimowsky found this reassuring, Rachid did not. He was ruffled, and wrote to Isabelle, 'I know it's not your doing, but you must admit all the same that in acting like this the old man is starting off on the wrong foot, and insulting the people he's wanting to find out about.' He wrote a little peevishly that whilst he would not for all the world want to disturb the peace of such a venerable old man, Isabelle might perhaps acknowledge that there were other men in the world whose feelings and loyalties needed to be taken into account.

The relationship was evidently given Trophimowsky's blessing, and matters began to move towards marriage. Isabelle wrote to her old correspondent Eugène Letord at the end of June to tell him the news. Letord was at first dismayed, 'entirely selfishly', since he thought they might have to stop their correspondence, but then came around to worthier feelings: 'As I read, and sensed the contentment in every line, I began to share it with you. This event is going to give you a companion for your whole life, and deliver you from the cheerless existence you were beginning to lead alone in the world. When I read that you wouldn't stop being my friend I nearly leapt up on my chair for joy!' On 5 July Rachid wrote to say that he was planning to come to Geneva overnight in a few days and wanted to take Isabelle back to Paris with him, where they would be married in Muslim fashion, which only needed the blessing of the embassy's *imam*. Isabelle's hair was still cropped like a boy's, and Rachid added a plea: 'A request: let your hair grow as I've let my beard grow. I'll receive news of this with the most grateful thanks.'

Perhaps Isabelle felt this as an implicit call to heel, and resented its wider implications for her freedom, for by mid-July, when they were to have married, she was backing away from the idea. In fact, from the start she had not been entirely wholehearted in her feelings towards

Rachid, in spite of her letter to Letord, and he had occasionally picked up on it. He had complained in early June of her lack of letters, compared to his profusion: 'In between hundreds of things I have to do, although they are admittedly mere formalities and nonsenses, I find the time to let you know I'm alive.' Now, in July, he was writing, 'If ever you weren't sure of yourself – of being mine alone – mine and only mine – tell me now. I would certainly be unhappy not to be united with you, but at least you would spare your life and mine. When a woman wants to deceive a man, she can always do so. I am jealous, you know. It's perhaps a fault but I am and have to tell you so.' Isabelle had evidently been trying to safeguard her future independence in her last letter to him, and he interpreted her words bluntly: 'What you are really saying is: "Today I love you as a lover, but who knows what may happen later, when I have you as a brother? It's quite possible that I would let myself be taken by anyone – particularly anyone *dark-skinned* – clever enough to catch me."' These were conditions Rachid could not accept. For her part, Isabelle perhaps sensed that, however much she was in need of a port, she was in danger of sacrificing something more important to her, which she was only on the threshold of savouring: her independence. Her vagabond fantasies could not easily be reconciled with being a diplomat's wife, especially amongst the Dutch forests and moaning waves. The plans for marriage came to a halt, as did the letters, although for a few months Rachid and she still remained friends.

POISON II

By the autumn it was clear that Trophimowsky was very ill. He had been a broken man ever since Vladimir's death, and now he had contracted cancer of the oesophagus, or 'smokers' cancer', as the Cassons put it. He would not recover, and did not want to do so. In a letter he dictated to Isabelle in December 1898, addressed to his Moscow bankers, and trying to ensure Isabelle and Augustin's financial security after his death, he confided: 'After [Mme de Moerder's] death I was severely shaken, but when I lost her son, who was everything in this world to me, I was finished.' He added: 'I'm longing for death, as the peace of mind I never found on earth, hoping as I have done foolishly, by tradition, for something good to come from humanity.' Ironically, just as Mme de Moerder had fallen back on 'well-organized social life' when she was ruffled, now Trophimowsky in his dying days was showing a sudden regard for tradition. (His words are reminiscent, too, of his mentor Bakunin's 'profound disgust with public life' just before his death: 'I have had enough, and after having spent my entire life in the struggle, I am leaving it.')

Isabelle now devoted much of her time to looking after the old man. Four years later, in a revealingly ambiguous phrase, she wrote that she stayed in Geneva during this period 'to accomplish my filial duty towards my great-uncle'. It was now just a question of waiting for the end. Even Augustin was making an effort. Trophimowsky wrote in the same letter to his bankers that Augustin was 'making a point of trying to replace Vladimir in my affections'. However, Augustin's presence was only sporadic, since whenever possible he used to go off to Marseilles, where Hélène Long was happy to have the opportunity to console him.

Isabelle found distraction from the melancholy Villa with her Russian student friends in Geneva, and in her writing. Her friend Vera Popow, a medical student who was aiming to go back to Russia once her studies were completed to help those suffering in Siberian camps, was a calming and strengthening influence at this time (and was to be the model for the character of Vera in *Vagabond*). However, it was only Trophimowsky's illness which kept her in Geneva now, and for the time being she put her fantasies and her spare time to good use, embarking on her first novel, *Rakhil*, on 15 November.

She wanted the story to be 'a plea in favour of the Koran and against the prejudices of the modern Muslim world'. More effusively, she envisaged it as 'a song of eternal love, beautiful in form, with melodious sentences and glittering images to intoxicate the heart of a sensualist, or anyone in love with art, which amounts to the same thing'. Several months later it had become an 'imbroglio' which was boring even her as she wrote it. Her 'song of eternal love' now looked more like a 'loathsome collection of badly-edited police files', she later wrote in her diary, reflecting, in a rare moment of self-irony, that 'there's no doubt that if my book produces the same effect on its readers as it does on me at the moment, no one would read beyond the second page'. The story, centring around the love affair in Bône between a Jewish prostitute, Rakhil, and a wealthy young Paris-educated Muslim, Mahmoud, introduces a theme which would recur in Isabelle's writing: the corruption of an old culture by sophisticated but empty modern ideas. The villain is 'nihilism': 'Algerian, Tunisian, Egyptian or Turkish students absorb modern civilization as if by contagion in Europe, contaminating themselves by contact with its most unhealthy and vile aspect: the appalling moral and religious nihilism most people have.' This is the fundamentalism she was setting out to preach, but it is the character of Mahmoud who redeems it as a narrative, and who is the real subject of the story. He is a dilettante intellectual, infected by the ideas of his time, but also paralysed by them, incapable (like Gide's Arnaud in *Les Faux-Monnayeurs* thirty years later) of 'raising himself up to a point where he could fulfil his own concepts of grandeur'. Isabelle's emotional sympathies in the story are with the exploited Rakhil, but it is no accident that she gives Mahmoud her own Arab name: she was exploring her own dilemma through the selfish and alienated rebel Mahmoud, the harbinger of a twentieth-century malaise, caught between two systems of values.

*

Such were Isabelle's preoccupations as she watched the old ex-nihilist slowly dying. By the new year, the last of the century, Trophimowsky's throat was so engorged with cancer that he could barely eat or speak, and he was taking chloral daily as a painkiller. If Augustin and Isabelle were not around, he would summon M. Casson and painstakingly scrawl out on a slate instructions about the care of his cacti. In a letter of February 1899 to his bankers in Moscow he asked them to look after 'Isabelle Nicolaievna Eberhardt' with 'the same solicitude you showed her ineffably unhappy mother', and asked them to open two new accounts, one for Isabelle and one for Augustin, and to transfer his own debentures into them. He also took a last, bitter swipe at Nicolas for 'assassinating his own brother'. The suicide had now firmly become murder in his head.

To add to Trophimowsky's misery, Augustin decided to abscond again. Now all of twenty-seven, he ran away from home once more on 13 April. The police were called, and Isabelle no longer had the patience to protect her brother. She declared that he had always been a weak character and had caused endless trouble. He had frequently left the 'paternal home', taking sums of money belonging to others in the household as he went, which he then spent on loose women in the quaintly and probably accurately described *maisons de tolérance*. The police officer felt that this was as far as the matter needed to be taken, and wearily concluded that the intimate life of this family had already wasted enough of his time.

On 25 April Augustin, in a sentimental impulse to see his mother's grave, left for Bône. He arrived on the 5 a.m. boat and turned up unannounced on the doorstep of a friend Isabelle had made in Bône, Koudja ben Abdallah. Meeting him for the first time, Koudja was astonished at this 'spitting image' of his sister. He accompanied him to Mme de Moerder's grave, where Augustin wept copiously, and promised that he would eventually return to Bône to live with Isabelle for good. Koudja wrote to Isabelle: 'I fear greatly for him. I've noticed from what he says that he is not very attached to life.' Although Augustin took the boat back to Marseilles that evening, claiming that he had to get back to look after 'the old man', it was another fortnight before he actually appeared at the Villa.

By now Trophimowsky was suffering constant, terrible hallucinations. According to Mlle Guillermet's second-hand and eager account, he saw 'menacing spectres which seemed to haunt his delirium, and which he reached out pale-faced to thrust away'. (She was not at all surprised that this 'vile seducer' had met such a gratifyingly appropriate fate.) He died on 15 May 1899. Mme Casson claimed that 'he ended his life in great privation, and my husband was one of the few who saw him to his final rest. Isabelle Eberhardt was not present in his final moments. In any case she wasn't seen in the days preceding his death or at his funeral.' His funeral was, as he had requested in his will, a very simple affair, and he was laid to rest alongside Vladimir's grave, in 'the cheapest possible coffin'.

Although Mme Casson claimed that Isabelle was not seen at the Villa in the days before Trophimowsky's death, a different version of events emerged two years later, in an anonymous letter which claimed (amongst other charges against Isabelle) that she had poisoned Trophimowsky with a fatal dose of chloral. The truth of the matter, like the truth of the General's death, lies buried; however, the anonymous letter writer's other information is heavily biased against Isabelle, and a more charitable interpretation would be that if she did give him an overdose, it was to put him out of his misery, and perhaps at his own request, since he 'longed for death'. Isabelle herself was silent on the matter, as with so much at the Villa that had been difficult to speak of, or come to terms with. From now on she consigned 'Vava' to the idealized realms of gentle old philosopher in her few subsequent references to him, just as she would consign her mother in her diaries to the spectacularly idealized notion of 'the White Spirit', the all-good, all-suffering (and implicitly insubstantial) maternal image.

*

The thought of staying any more nights than necessary in what Isabelle later called the 'ill-fated abode', hung with death, was a chilling one, and she and Augustin tried to expedite all the formalities so that they could leave as soon as possible. Trophimowsky had bequeathed the Villa Neuve to Isabelle and Augustin for their lifetimes, but after their deaths the property, or the proceeds from its sale, was to be used for a charity in memory of their mother. The patrician in him had flickered briefly as he entrusted, in a supremely unanarchic gesture, the execution of this extremely impractical plan to the Grand Duchess Elizaveta Feodorovna of Moscow, a member of the same Imperial family he had spent so much of his life trying to subvert.

In the event there was no attempt to meet the conditions of the will.

As soon as Trophimowsky died, 'legitimate heirs' from Russia came in for the kill to take posthumous revenge for the acts of a quarter of a century before, which had been festering, but not forgotten, ever since. Trophimowsky's will was contested by the Russian consul in Geneva, acting on behalf both of Trophimowsky's own family in Kherson and the remaining de Moerders in St Petersburg. Perez-Moreyra, who had had no contact with those at the Villa for the past ten years, in spite of the fact that he and Nathalie had had two children in the meantime (Raphael, born in 1892, and Camille, born in 1896), now appeared in Trophimowsky's lawyer's office, having lost none of his flair for intimidation. He staked his claim on behalf of Nathalie and took the opportunity to demand that the police show him their file on Trophimowsky, hoping to get the elusive proof he was sure existed that he had poisoned the General. More, Nicolas de Moerder had just made contact with him for the first time, since they had a common cause against the old tutor, and Perez (who was now a bank manager with the Crédit Suisse) threatened the police with dire consequences from the Russian Ministry of Foreign Affairs if they did not do as he wanted. The police refused to be bullied, but even if he had seen the file, he would have found no proof, only the ambiguities and contradictions which pervaded everything to do with the de Moerders and Trophimowsky, including their deaths.

Isabelle and Augustin, anxious above all to get away from the Villa and all it represented, gladly relinquished its sale and the task of dealing with the daunting legal problems ahead to M. Samuel. They gave him power of attorney to deal with their affairs, and made plans to leave Geneva on 4 June, less than three weeks after Trophimowsky's death. On the day she left Geneva, Isabelle made a last pilgrimage to the two graves on the slope of a hill in the tiny Vernier graveyard. She noted the Italian inscription on a nearby tombstone: 'Gia non si deve a te doglia ni pianto/ Chi so muori nel mondo nel ciel renasci' – 'Now no more grief and pain is owing to you/ I know you die in this world to be born in the next.'

TWO

ADRIFT

In travelling to Africa to find a psychic observation post outside the sphere of the European I unconsciously wanted to find that part of my personality which had become invisible under the influence and the pressure of being European.

CARL JUNG 'North Africa',
Memories, Dreams, Reflections

REBIRTH

Some debentures of Trophimowsky's own, which he had left to Isabelle and Augustin, now provided Isabelle with the wherewithal to do what she wanted for what seemed to her the foreseeable future. The sudden almost complete severing of the bonds to her past life brought an unforeseen elation; she felt a brimming, if guilty, sense of release at being free of the tensions she had carried for so many years. As a result, for the next few months her actions were more reflex reactions against what had gone before than considered plans. The Villa Neuve had been almost a prison – now she wanted unbounded freedom. Geneva had been full of spying and prying neighbours – now she wanted voluptuously to lose her identity. Geneva had been cold and claustrophobic – now she wanted the sun, the purging heat and the limitless desert. Her feelings were conveyed obliquely, but unmistakably, through her description of Rakhil's, written a few months later: 'Through all the fibres of her body she felt a new, naive and infinite physical delight: the joy of existing. All the shadows which had kept her soul in mourning since her childhood had dissipated and it seemed to her that she had just woken up from convalescence to a radiant morning, after a long night of heavy sleep, fretted with anxious and delirious dreams.' In Isabelle's description of Dmitri Orschanow in *Vagabond* there are also echoes of her own feelings: 'He despised himself enormously for feeling so high-spirited so quickly, when he . . . was on his way to see the ruins of everything that he had loved so much, to see his father buried, the house and garden sold.' Isabelle's high spirits were unstable, and punctuated by a penchant for graves, but they came from a deep sense of rebirth.

Now she could go back to North Africa on her own terms. She chose Tunis as the starting-point for her odyssey, since Ali Abdul-Wahab was there, and it was the traditional gateway for adventurers going to the Sudan or to the Algerian Sahara. Tunis was a magnificent city port layered with history familiar to Isabelle from Trophimowsky's lessons. Egyptians, 'egoistic and ferocious' Phoenicians (as Isabelle called them in her schoolgirl notes), Greeks, Romans, Vandals, Jews, Arabs, Negroes, Turks, Italians and Spaniards had all had a hand in shaping the city, which included ancient Carthage, founded by Queen Dido as she fled Phoenicia, who was given as much land as she could encompass with an ox-hide, and, by cutting it up into tiny strips, encompassed a great deal. Known as the 'white city', Tunis was also lush with Arabic-Berber mosaics and painted plasterwork, 'adorned with much painting and carving' as the happily named Leo Africanus had written three centuries before. Tunisia itself had been under the rule of the Ottoman Empire since his time, but in 1881, when some petty cattle thefts by the Khmir tribe had given France the excuse it was waiting for to invade the country, it became a French protectorate, in an effort amongst other things to put a stop to the thriving piracy of its corsairs. Turkish power was spent and offered no resistance, and Lord Salisbury had given the wink to France in 1878 that Britain would condone France's 'free hand' in Tunisia in exchange for French acquiescence in the British lease of Cyprus and in Britain's handling of the Egyptian question. (In 1890, he said, referring to the whole of North Africa, 'We have given the Gallic cockerel an enormous amount of sand. Let him scratch it as he pleases.') But whereas Algeria was seen as an integral part of France, Tunisia remained ostensibly governed by the native Regency of the Beys, who, like all the indigenous officials in Tunisia, down to the local sheikhs, governed 'under the watchful eye' and 'discreet supervision' of French officials. The Bey was 'advised' by the French Resident-General, but the fact that the Marines, and the Ministries of Foreign Affairs and Finances, were run directly by France, and that the 'general in command of the French army relieved the Minister of War of his responsibilities', indicated to what extent the Regency was a puppet regime. In fairness, the French at first, like many previous invaders, also enriched the land, building railways, expanding agriculture and mining minerals. But it was not the local population on the whole who benefited, particularly if they remained Muslim, as the vast majority did; and they were crushingly and shockingly taxed.

When Isabelle left Geneva, she took the overnight train to Marseilles, staying in the Hôtel Bauveau. Next day she took out money from her bank and arranged her visa at the Russian consulate. The

1. Isabelle dressed as a sailor, photographed by Louis David in Geneva in 1895. Note the motto on the hat: 'Vengeance'.

LE CHEIKH J. SANUA ABOU NADDARA

Interprète Honoraire du Ministère des Postes et Télégraphes,
Vice-Président d'Honneur de la Société Archéologique
Scientifique et Littéraire de France
Directeur et rédacteur en chef du " Journal d'Abou Naddara ",
et de l' " Attawadod ", Revue Internationale illustrée,
Correspondant Parisien de Journaux d'Orient.

6, Rue Geoffroy-Marie, 6, PARIS

LE CHEIKH J. SANUA ABOU NADDARA

2. The headed notepaper of Sheikh James Sanua Abou Naddara.

3. Isabelle dressed in 'Arab' clothes, photographed by Louis David in Geneva in 1895.

. The marquis de Morès as a oung man and in middle age.

5. Isabelle in Tunisian garb, 1895.

6. The oasis at Biskra, ca. 1900.

Sheikh Mohammed El Hachemi, naib of the Qadryas in El Oued, and his brother Mohammed El Taìeb, who headed the sect in Ouargla.

El Oued, 'city of a thousand domes'.

9. Isabelle dressed as an Arab girl, *circa* 1897.

10. A Moorish café on the outskirts of Oran at the turn of the century.

11. Isabelle on Randau's horse 'Ziza' in the *bled* outside Ténès, 1902.

12. The staff of the *commune mixte* in Ténès, 1902. Slimène Ehnni is standing amongst the local chiefs, fourth from the right. The administrator Bouchet is seated, second from the left in uniform.

13. A group of foot soldiers from the 7th Regiment of the Algerian tirailleurs.

14. Algerian soldiers under French command filing past in the foothills of the Aurès Mountains *circa* 1900.

15. Brigadier-General Hubert Lyautey in 1903: a studio photograph taken in Algiers.

16. Lyautey dressed as an Arab in 1880.

17. General Lyautey and his staff at Aïn Sefra in 1904.

18. Isabelle in 1904, showing the physical ravages four years had wrought.

19. Isabelle in the military hospital at Aïn Sefra a few days before her death.

20. A body, claimed to be that of Isabelle, being carried from the rubble after the flash flood in Aïn Sefra. (The authenticity is doubtful, since the army was in charge of the operation, but it was published in the original version of her diaries.)

21. A portrait said to be of Isabelle, by the painter Pruna.

following two days, her brief travel notes tell us, she spent in Toulon and St Mandrier, 'with sailors from the ship *Admiral Duperre*', which was in port.

This bare statement hides Isabelle's particular weakness, one which would later be interpreted as promiscuity, and which did indeed have a lot to do with sex: she was irresistibly attracted to the seedy areas of towns. She was particularly drawn to ports, with their wayward, bustling, provisional life, their sense of people always on the point of setting off for the unknown, their coarse virility, their smells, their raucous gaiety, their snatched, rough couplings, and above all their suffering. Like Dostoevsky, she only felt really alive where there was suffering, and where circumstances forced people to live, in a raw way, by their instincts. The edge that suffering gave to life was something she instinctively sought out, to rouse herself from her underlying melancholy, just as she sought out other extremes – lush colours, desert landscapes, brutal, uncommitted love-making. With the sailors in Toulon and St Mandrier, she was probably dressed in her loose workman's clothes of blue linen jacket, trousers and cap. If she made love with the sailors – and she probably did far less than the scandalized bourgeois later implied – it was as a girl, but as a girl who was their physical equal. Dressing as a man allowed her into these areas which her class and her sex would normally have denied her, and gave her other things she wanted: she was in control (or at least, she thought she was) of how and when she revealed her sex to men; and she could get the thrill of passing for 'rough trade' while at the same time maintaining her independence. She could, in other words, get sex – and life – on her own terms, without responsibilities, without babies, without sentimental ties, just as her compatriot Marie Bashkirtseff (with whom Isabelle has a great deal in common) had yearned to do, writing in her diary in 1879, 'What I long for is the freedom of going about alone.'

On 9 June Isabelle was back in Marseilles for a meeting with M. Samuel, who had arrived that day from Geneva, and the following day they were joined by Augustin. On the 12th she and Augustin made the forty-two-hour crossing to Tunis, on, as it happens, the *St Augustin*, and they were both met by Ali Abdul-Wahab. After a few days Augustin left for Marseilles, while Isabelle found a vast, shabbily magnificent old Turkish house in the old Arab part of Tunis, Bab-Menara, almost on top of the hill overlooking the bay, in the rue

Bou-Khrous. The area was quiet and full of old houses, which were inhabited but 'ferociously closed to the outside world'. Isabelle installed herself there with a black spaniel, whom she called 'Dédale' after the maze of picturesque streets characteristic of the city, and a seventy-five-year-old Moorish servant called Khadidja, deaf and bent double with age, who had spent her life working for the best families in Tunis, and whom Ali had probably engaged for her. (Ali's family was prominent in Tunis, and had a street named after them.)

Isabelle called the grand house her 'Palazzio', and enjoyed almost a month of reverie there in the restoring silence of its rooms. It was a time of retreat, similar in its inaction to the weeks after her mother's death. She stayed on her small Arab bed every afternoon in the heat of the day, in her huge, ornate and permanently shuttered room, lost in thought and drinking in the 'atmosphere of the old Orient' as she gazed at the rich, colourful old porcelain mosaics that lined the walls, and the golden dome on the ceiling, surrounded by exquisite lacy-patterned cornices. Khadidja used to crouch in a corner, sliding the black beads of her rosary up and down one by one, muttering through colourless lips the ninety-nine Arab names for God – happiness, the one and only, the merciful – ending in the hundredth: God. Dédale 'stretched himself out in a leonine pose, resting his tapering muzzle on his sturdy paws and attentively following the languid flight of the occasional fly'. Days passed by 'deliciously languid and sweetly monotonous', with only the five daily calls to prayer of the muezzin interrupting the stillness.

Isabelle wrote about this time in essays which were published in Paris four years later in the famous *Revue Blanche* under the title 'Heures de Tunis'. They are short, picturesque sketches of the life around her, with a finely observed sense of its delicacies and satisfying, daily sensuousness, but with the thread of her fascination with death running through them. Arab cemeteries held a particular appeal: 'I have always loved to wander in the egalitarian dress of the bedouins in Muslim cemeteries, where everything is peaceful and resigned, and where none of the things that make European cemeteries so lugubrious come to disfigure death.' Indeed Arab cemeteries were a long way from the sombre emptiness of the Vernier cemetery. Each Friday, for example, women and children would come with sprigs of myrtle to visit those who had 'entered into the mercy of God', the women sitting in white-clad, chattering groups on the tiles of the tombs, drinking coffee and eating sweets under the fig-trees while the children played. An Arab town was surrounded by its cemetery, so that you had to pass through the dead to get to the living. These images of death integrated naturally into life were a balm to Isabelle. The last of the stories in 'Heures de Tunis' deals with a doomed love affair between a fine, pensive young Moor, who sat in his carved wood stall in the perfume *souk* reading Arab poetry, and a beautiful young Moorish-Algerian prostitute. The love affair is thwarted by his father, and the girl is banished and dies. Her grave, which the young man discovers and visits, is in the Muslim cemetery in Bône, high on a hill above the harbour. 'Nothing lugubrious and nothing sad about this flower-filled cemetery, with its bushes and vines . . . Everything breathes a great, august calm and resignation, and an unshakeable, consoling conviction.' The cemetery was of course Mme de Moerder's, and the girl bears part of her Muslim name, Manoubia.

North Africa gave Isabelle another image to mirror another preoccupation, that of rebirth: the sunset and the sunrise. She was mesmerized by the 'delicious, iridescent play of light at sunrise, and these purple-golden evenings, which inspired the ancient Arab storytellers and poets'. It was the sunrise above all which appealed, the moment when 'there is something infinitely light in the clear, still-fresh early morning air, something which seeps into the soul and body, and intoxicates the senses, a joyful moment of rediscovered youth and the rebirth of hope.'

In the last essay, she dwells on an incident which she returned to later in her diaries: a moment when she was wandering through the streets in the very early morning, before daybreak, gripped by an anxiety she could not explain. A shutter clattered open above and the voice of the muezzin rang out calling the faithful to prayer, the 'secular affirmation of divine omnipotence': 'God is almighty! Allahou akhbar!' rang out in a clarion voice, followed by other, responding tones, and then by the dawn chorus of birds from a nearby garden. 'Prayer is better than sleep!'

She loved the muezzin's fine, transcendent regularity, just as she loved the secretiveness of Arab buildings, the way they were boxes within boxes, protecting their intimacy with a subtle system of exits and entrances. She loved the Arab character, 'proud, impenetrable and discreet', with its 'harsh majesty, born for dreaming and war'. These three and a half weeks in Tunis were spent sloughing off her troubled European identity and absorbing 'through all the fibres of her body', like Rakhil, her new Arab persona. The seeming contradictions in the Arab character responded perfectly to her own: peace and adventure, dreaming and war, religion and sensuality.

Locally she was known as the 'young man with the dog', as she used to take Dédale for walks up into the surrounding hills, or down to the shallow lagoon, El Bahir, the Lake of Tunis, which opened out on to the gulf and the sea. She enjoyed wearing the 'egalitarian dress' of the Bedouins, but also the richer finery of the Tunisians. She would wear a burnous, the fine white woollen cloak favoured by Tunisians and Algerians – each one traditionally made from the wool of seven sheep – worn over a thin silk *gandoura* (a large voluminous shirt), under which was a light blue, long-sleeved shirt and waistcoat, tied with a red- and green-striped belt. Under this were baggy trousers, white stockings and yellow slippers. She now had her head shaved completely, Muslim fashion, and wore a tasselled fez. The colours, she wrote, were not garish, but rich and 'very tasteful'. And, with her height, her lithe figure, her habit of passing as a young man, her lack of female coquetries, in spite of her eyes – which are variously described as black, grey, green and even yellow, and which had a notable dark, liquid lustre, very like the Arabs' own – she was taken amongst superficial acquaintances for a young man. Si Mahmoud Saadi had come into his own.

OASIS I

By early July Isabelle was ready to set off from Tunis to find the desert. She would travel westwards into Algeria, and try to reach the southern oasis of Ouargla, on the northern border of Tuareg country. On 7 July 1899 she was up until 2.30 in the morning with an Arab friend, possibly a lover, savouring the seedy dockland area of La Goulette. At eight next morning she set off for Algeria, taking the train from the Place de la Gare du Sud, stopping for lunch in Beja and dinner in Guelma. She arrived at El Khroub in Algeria at 11.15 that evening and spent the night in a hotel near the station.

Next day she made the four-and-a-half-hour train journey down to Batna, spending the night at the Hotel Continental. On the 11th, she set off at three in the morning, just before dawn, to make the fifteen-mile journey to Timgad by mule, accompanied by a guide, Salah, whom she had engaged the day before. Salah's guidance was not all that it might have been, and they lost their way, ending up for part of the night in a religious penitentiary in Lambessa, due south instead of east of Timgad. Next morning they found Timgad, but later that night the expedition was fully redeemed for Isabelle when they made the last stage of the return journey to Batna at full gallop, by moonlight. The evening was spent with Salah and a *spahi*, one of the native cavalry soldiers trained by the French. They started off in the *village nègre*, went on to supper in the *spahi* café, then drank the thick, bitter local coffee with an Arab friend of Salah's, and finally paid a nocturnal visit to some artesian wells which were being built at night, because of the heat, south of Constantine. On the 13th, she and Salah rode off for Biskra, and then for Sidi Okba, sleeping the night there on mats in the local sheikh's courtyard, Arab-fashion. The next day they went to the mosque and the café, where Isabelle had long conversations with a local Arab *caïd* (judge) and teacher.

Isabelle's Algerian Arabic was colloquial enough by this time for her to negotiate her way easily through these parts, but she was also following a trail which was well trodden by the French army, which had military posts from Batna down to Ouargla in the south. The presence of the French army over the past half-century had brought not only drink and brothels to these Muslim regions, but also the French language, which was spoken to some extent by most Arabs who had dealings with the French – the *spahis*, local officials and teachers.

After Isabelle had spoken with the *caïd*, she went on to meet the brigadier of the Touggourt *spahis*, Smaïn ben Hattab. As an Arab officer within the native section of the French army, Brigadier Smaïn was evidently aware of what European adventurers looked for in any country which came under the notional rubric of 'oriental', and took it upon himself to introduce Isabelle to the more sybaritic aspects of Arab life. He took her to see some of the legendary young dancers from the Ouled Naïl tribe, who worked as dancers and prostitutes until they could collect the money for a dowry, and who performed dances in which they fluttered their hands like the wings of a hunting hawk; then he gave her some *kef* (hashish) to smoke with him. Not yet banned in the country, as it was to be a few years later, *kef* took its name from the Arabic word for the sensation it produced, *kayf*, eloquently described by Sir Richard Burton in his account of his voyage to Mecca as 'the savouring of animal existence; the passive enjoyment of mere sense; the pleasant languor, the dreamy tranquillity, the airy castle-building'. It was Isabelle's first recorded encounter with narcotics, although she may well have tried *kef* in Bône two years before, and may have dabbled with opium in Geneva with Augustin, before she began to disapprove of his way of life. Certainly, like Trophimowsky, she was already an inveterate cigarette-smoker – and had had since childhood a penchant for 'airy castle-building'.

*

Smaïn's attitude to Isabelle was revealing, since he was treating her to men's pleasures, as if she were the man she purported to be. Yet he probably did it tongue-in-cheek, deferring with Arab discretion to how she wanted to be seen, and at the same time enjoying the titillating charade, which must have greatly relieved the boredom of military life in the arid *souf*. Isabelle retained a trace of European naivety in failing to realize that the Arabs' acceptance of her disguise often reflected their face-saving tact, rather than the success of her own camouflage. She was certain, for example, that Salah and her subsequent guides took her at face value as Si Mahmoud Saadi, the young Tunisian journeying from *zawiya* to *zawiya*, in the long tradition of students in search of Koranic truth; but the highly realistic Randau later maintained (and Isabelle eventually realized) that the Arabs with whom she was in contact for any length of time always knew perfectly well that she was a woman, and a European, but went along out of discretion with how she chose to present herself. It was a tact described in general terms by the pragmatic British traveller Gertrude Bell, making her first voyage to the Middle East this same year: 'You will find in the East habits of intercourse less fettered by artificial chains, and a wider tolerance born of greater diversity . . . a man may go about in public veiled up to the eyes, or clad if he please only in a girdle: he will excite no remark. Why should he? Like everyone else he is merely obeying his own law.' (Indeed the Arabs' 'wider tolerance' of the velleities of sexuality and passion had become an incentive for many nineteenth-century individualists and outsiders – including Burton, Flaubert, Gide and Loti, as well as Isabelle herself – to come to 'the orient' to 'obey their own laws', rather than the increasingly institutionalized European conventions governing sex.)

Of course, Isabelle *could* pass as a young man, as Mme Casson's testimony had shown in Geneva, and her whole demeanour could allow her to pass superficially as a young Arab, 'incognito amongst the local people', as she wanted to. This alone was a unique feat, comparable only to Burton's entering Mecca disguised as a Muslim dervish. Isabelle had a certain animal adaptability, a lack of the characteristic primpings and awkwardnesses of the European in more primitive, ancient cultures – what Jung called 'that faint note of foolishness which clings to the European' – which enabled her to begin genuinely to live the life of the people as she travelled.

Yet it went deeper than her surface manner. Disguise for her was not just a way of tricking herself into a different society, not just a colonial, scholarly nosiness. It also represented an identity she genuinely wanted to assume. Her whole background had predisposed her to want to *become* 'the Other' – not as an amusing ploy, but because she found it deeply seductive. Other more or less contemporary travellers – Kinglake, Doughty, Bell, Bird, Kingsley, North and even Burton – were at heart very much in the colonial mould, with a strong sense of their own national identity, and usually superiority, which prevented them ever wanting to become 'the Other'. However much Isabelle may have been deceiving herself in thinking that her disguise was universally effective, the will to be fully assimilated was there: she wanted to 'blend in with the local people's life, which is the only thing that's really characteristic of a country in our time, when the privileged classes aspire to nothing but drab uniformity', and to know 'the soul of a country, of a race'. It was partly this to which her travelling companions instinctively responded.

*

Yet in her thirst to lose herself in another way of life, Isabelle showed signs of another European naivety: she failed to give due heed to the fact that slowly, and usually unknown to her, she was acquiring a reputation. Because of her recent past, she needed to feel that North Africa was virgin territory, an anonymous vastness. But increasingly French military and police reports, and the word of mouth of the local people, began to precede her.

On 15 July Isabelle visited the head of the Arab Bureau in Biskra, Lieutenant-Colonel Fridel, to get permission to travel south. South of Biskra the French administration ceased to be civilian, as it had been in the coastal areas of the Tell since 1870, but was in the hands of the military 'Arab Bureaux', as these French establishments were incongruously named, which had the sole power of allowing strangers to travel further south. Although in male Arab dress, Isabelle had to announce herself as a girl to the authorities because of her passport. Fridel was taken with this charming and knowledgeable young *originale*, and invited her to lunch at his house, and later to dinner at the Hôtel de l'Oasis. At dinner she met a certain Captain Adolphe-Roger de Susbielle of the French army, who was on his way back to the Touggourt garrison, and who eagerly suggested that she should join him and his convoy the following morning. Since Isabelle wanted to go to Touggourt, this seemed an irresistible invitation, although she had her reservations about the captain's forward manner and evil-tempered features. In fact, de Susbielle had a chip on his shoulder, and was all too aware of the discrepancy between his illustrious ancestry and grandiose aspirations, and his own diminutive moral and physical stature. In spite of the best efforts of his family, which was studded with generals, he was still, at thirty-seven, only a captain, for his superiors had noticed that he was lazy, philandering, arrogant and sadistic. The army reports on him even as a cadet had noted his 'bad character and detestable turn of mind'.

Later that evening Isabelle met up with a local Arab and with Brigadier Smaïn, who had followed her from Batna, and the two men alerted her both to de Susbielle's 'bad intentions' towards her, and to his notorious cruelty towards the Muslims. Next morning, when de Susbielle came to collect her, Isabelle declined to travel with him after all, fielding the excuse that she was waiting for some money from her brother, which had in fact arrived that morning. He begged her to hurry and catch up with him, and, like a fairy-tale wolf, said he would be waiting for her at Chegga, on the road to Touggourt. Isabelle let two days elapse, then set off with Salah and another guide from Bou Saada.

On the way to Chegga she found a courtyard in which she was sleeping infested with scorpions, was unable to find any food except bread for two days, and suffered from intense fever and thirst throughout the journey. However, she met Abd-el-Kader ben Aly, the sheikh of a tribe of Chaamba (nomadic Tuareg from southern Algeria); 'a model of good grace', he volunteered to take her on to Ouargla with his caravan without any payment. They arrived at Chegga to find that de Susbielle had moved off, but a little further on they found an order from him forbidding her to stay there for more than twenty-four hours. Piqued by her rebuff, he had retaliated by using such authority as he had against her – for the first but not the last time.

Isabelle's journey down to Touggourt was, like the Arabs' own, a hand-to-mouth affair. Apart from a shortage of water, she endured a fairly constant fever and occasional vomiting and vertigo. Her horse suffered from thirst, and the donkeys got ill. There were quarrels with people encountered along the way, provisional friendships struck up with fellow-travellers, a night spent for the first time lying out on the desert sand, wrapped only in her burnous. She and her guides tried for an hour, successfully, to find the only good well in Ourlana by the light of matches. Her guide from Bou Saada tried, unsuccessfully but divertingly, to light a cigarette with a shot from his gun. The journey progressed like a trail of ants, full of small incidents and encounters, as those going up to Biskra crossed those going down south.

They arrived in Touggourt at eleven in the evening on 23 July. The 135-mile journey had taken them eight days of travelling, and Isabelle slept the whole of the next day. Brigadier Smaïn turned up again the day after, probably following her both for his own amusement and to keep a weather eye on her. In his capacity as an epicurean guide, he took her to a brothel in the evening so that she could watch the lascivious dancing and preliminaries to love-making. Isabelle claimed that 'artist's curiosity' took her on this kind of foray. The voyeur of 'Sepulchral Sensuality' was finding her new disguise particularly congenial.

Next morning she was summoned to appear before de Susbielle in his office. The two-hour meeting was at first 'violent' and then more courteous, in an icy way. The captain refused 'glacially and politely' to give her guides permission to take her down to Ouargla. Isabelle then set off to find the Chaambas who had offered to take her there, but by ten that evening she found that the sheikh had already left, assuming she had made other arrangements, and leaving profuse greetings for her. Next morning she went back to the Arab Bureau to ask permission for her guides to take her to the Souf, the vast area of white, scrubby sand dunes pitted with salt lakes to the east of Touggourt, which stretched up to the Tunisian border. This permission was forthcoming, largely because the Souf was a marginally less dangerous area for travellers than the south, which had been the sandy grave of several wide-eyed European travellers who had misunderstood the ways of the local Tuareg.

From Touggourt to El Oued was sixty miles, and it took Isabelle and her guides five days to make the journey. It was slow travelling, filing along the narrow, shifting dune valleys, or climbing their vertiginous and dangerously thin ridges. A whole day was spent with a sheikh at Ourmès. Although the Arab Bureaux had bureaucratic authority over travellers, real power lay, as it always had since the country had become Muslim, in the hands of the local religious leaders. Wherever Isabelle went the sheikhs seem to have accepted her wholeheartedly, and it was this, rather than the Arab Bureaux's say-so, which was her real passport in these volatile and dangerous areas; and the way in which she was passed along a line of hospitality not only safeguarded her but made it possible for her to undertake a journey which no previous European traveller had accomplished with such ease. Her talks with the religious sheikhs – whom the French called *marabouts*, a blanket term taken from the Arabic word for a frontier hermit – were lengthy and engaged, centring around the corruption of Mohammed's *hadith* (sayings) which Isabelle felt centuries of orthodoxy had bequeathed to Islam. It was on the basis of her good faith and her relatively scholarly knowledge of the history of Islam and Koranic dogma that she was so readily accepted. Unlike Richard Burton on his journey to Mecca, or Jane Digby who disguised herself as a Bedouin but remained a Christian, or Lawrence in Arabia, or even the wilfully ascetic Father Charles de Foucauld in Morocco, Isabelle was not an 'infidel' in these lands, whatever her other faults: and it was the one credential that mattered. Her journeys, like those of the Arabs themselves, followed the oases and springs, but they traced just as much a route from *zawiya* to *zawiya*, drawing physical refreshment from one and spiritual from the other.

Isabelle and her small convoy arrived in El Oued at sunset on 3 August 1899. She wrote about the moment two years later in an essay, 'Au pays des sables':

There are certain special times, certain mysteriously privileged moments when, intuitively and fleetingly, a country will reveal *its soul*, in some way its own *essence*, when we see it in a unique and clarified way, which months of patient study could neither improve on, nor change. Yet in those special moments the *details* necessarily escape us and we can only catch an overall impression of things. Is this due to our particular state of mind at that moment, or is it a special attribute of the places, caught on the wing and always *subconsciously*? I don't know . . . But my first arrival in El Oued was a total, definitive revelation of the harsh and splendid country which is the Souf, of its particular beauty, of its immense sadness.

She watched the sun setting over the innumerable little domes of El Oued, turning them pink in the fading sun, and dominated by the minaret of Sidi Salem, all set in the 'somnolent waves of the great, grey, ocean of sand'. El Oued, the 'grey town lost in the grey desert, participating fully in all its flamboyance and pallor, like the desert and in the desert, pink and golden in the magical dawn, white and blinding in the flaming heat of the day, purple and violet in the radiant evenings . . . and grey, grey as the sand it came from under the wan winter skies!' The cemetery featured too: 'Then, near us, there were graves upon graves, another whole village, that of the dead, adjoining that of the living.' During this metamorphosis, this apotheosis of the town, its domes now flaming in the last rays of the sun, there was complete silence, not a sound to be heard, nobody to be seen. Then, at the point of sunset, came the voices of the muezzin, chanting from all the mosques 'Allahou, akhbar!' and from all the seemingly deserted little valleys and dunes a mass of people emerged, all dressed in white, all filing down quietly to the mosques and *zawiyas* for prayer.

Isabelle spent three days in this oasis town, which was to prove more fateful to her than she could have guessed. Later evidence suggests that she met up with an Arab poet from El Oued with whom she had been in correspondence, and who now became her lover, but that he was old and alcoholic and she swiftly turned to 'more energetic native lovers'. The story was no doubt largely true, although embroidered, since she only had three days to accomplish all this. Leaving El Oued, she and her guides joined a caravan led by two French officers, Lieutenant Toulat and Major Mauviez, travelling back to Batna, where the officers were stationed. The party included nine camels, two Chaamba, a *spahi* and a Negro, probably from the Sudan. The journey took thirteen days, and was fraught with the usual fever, difficulties in finding water, and quarrels along the route. One of the officers' camels died of sunstroke, and one evening, when the officers were out, Isabelle had to prevent the *spahis* from almost massacring the local people, who were no doubt taunting them with being puppets of the French.

By 19 August they had arrived in Batna, where Isabelle threw money out of the windows of her room one day in an exuberance of freedom and scorn for materialism – which not surprisingly made a lasting impression on those who witnessed it. It was here in Batna that she finally met up with Eugène Letord. This first meeting, over dinner at the Hôtel Continental, sealed their friendship, and if it was also amorous, it was not urgently so, for they were to meet only intermittently from now on. Nevertheless Isabelle said later that Letord was the only European she had ever found attractive.

*

Meanwhile, nine days earlier, on 10 August 1899, a significant event had taken place in Marseilles: at six o'clock in the morning, Marie Madeleine Long, known as Hélène, had finally lured Augustin de Moerder to the Town Hall and taken him as her wedded husband, in the presence of her parents and the necessary witnesses. Four years before, Hélène Long had written the illiterate letter to Isabelle deploring Augustin's absence; now she was reaping the questionable reward for having waited patiently in the wings.

Isabelle returned to Batna on 28 August, after some further travels in the region, to find Augustin's telegram telling her the news. He added that he and Hélène were coming to Bône on the 30th, and hoped she would meet them there. Isabelle set off at once by train to meet them, visiting her mother's grave as soon as she arrived in Bône. Next evening Augustin and Hélène arrived, and, from Isabelle's curt recording of the fact, it seems there was no love lost between the two women. Augustin's choice of such a prosaic wife, 'Jenny l'ouvrière', as Isabelle called her disparagingly, had, it seemed to her, sealed his rejection of their poetic, adolescent dreams.

She spent the next day with Arab friends from her previous stay in Bône, and then left for Tunis on 2 September. Five days later she went over to Marseilles to discuss the continuing lack of a buyer for the Villa with Augustin and M. Samuel, returning after two days to spend the autumn in Tunis, and meditate on what to do next.

TAX AND SEX

Travelling incognito, a Muslim amongst Muslims, so that her companions 'stretched out and slept', their guard down 'thanks to the absence of women', Isabelle was dismayed to observe again what she already knew from her first stay in Bône: how badly the occupying French behaved towards the native people. The French soldiers had been comrades-in-arms of the local *spahis*, who had fought so bravely on their behalf in the Crimea, in Mexico, Italy and France, yet even they, Isabelle noted with despair, treated the *spahis* with contempt. This makes her next step even more surprising.

In the autumn of 1899 she took off by train for Sousse and Monastir, on the south-eastern coast of Tunisia, 'without knowing anyone, without any aim in view, completely unhurried and above all with no fixed itinerary. My mind was calm, and open to all those much-loved sensations of arriving in a new country.' But when she arrived in Monastir she met up with a shy, slender young *khalifa*, Si Larbi Chabel, whose job was to collect the *medjba*, a poll tax which the French authorities imposed on the local peasants, and she decided to join him in his work, as a way of getting to know the countryside and people. He was a fundamentally good-hearted young man, but he, like the *spahis*, was reckoned by the local people to have sold out to the French, and to be operating against the Muslims' best interests. For Isabelle to ally herself with him shows how the writer and observer in her trumped her commitment to the Muslim cause, since she spent two months in his company and managed to tolerate the piteous scenes they provoked as they went about their business of tax-collecting. Those who had failed to pay their tax arrears were convened before them publicly in their villages. If the failure was due to them being too poor to pay, they were sent to prison and sentenced to forced labour. If they admitted to possessions – some hovel, a goat or a few sheep – they were freed, but the red-cloaked *spahi* soldiers with whom Isabelle and Larbi travelled would arrive shortly afterwards to take possession of them. 'And yet these men dressed in splendid colours come from the same people whose misery they know only too well for having shared it. But the *spahi* is no longer a Bedouin, and sincerely believes himself to be very superior to his brothers in the tribes, because he is a soldier.' Isabelle's own role was to read out the names of the accused one by one from a list and summon them for questioning. Not surprisingly, 'everywhere we went amongst the dark, intractable and poor tribes, we met with a hostile reception.' Isabelle admits that 'Si Larbi's good heart bled for them, and we were ashamed of what we were doing – he out of duty and me out of curiosity – as if we'd committed some bad deed,' but she brushes it off in the next sentence: 'All the same I spent some enchanting hours down there.'

She had promised some travel notes about southern Tunisia to a Paris journal, and also some articles for publication in Russia through the good offices of her Russian correspondents Maseev and an old friend of her family's, an elderly teacher called Reppmann. Yet at first her note-book stayed virtually empty: 'Once again the soothing, free and easy Bedouin life has gone to my head, and lulled me into indolence. Writing . . . why bother?' It was above all the daily rituals of nomadic life that appealed: the setting up of the long, low goatskin tents, the waking in the early mornings to bitter coffee brewed over a stove. 'I felt a delicious sensation of liberty, peace and well-being which with me is an insepar-able accompaniment to waking up to the familiar sights of nomad life.'

*

Towards the end of her time in the Sahel, Isabelle did write an account of the episode, which was published eventually in *Notes de route* as 'Notes sur le Sahel tunisien'. In it she claims that during all the weeks they spent with her, Si Larbi and the *spahis* believed that she was a young man: 'Si Larbi never suspected that I was a woman, he called me his brother Mahmoud, and I shared his nomadic life and his work for two months.' To all of the young men she was, she wrote, 'Si Mahmoud Saadi, the little Turk [a change of nationality now that she was in Tunisia] playing truant from his French college'.

Once again, Isabelle was probably deluding herself in thinking they believed she was a man. But it is interesting to note that she felt she had given these young men no clues at all to her real sex, even though she had lived with them constantly for two months. Of course, many of the clues had been eliminated over the years: her looks were hardy and boyish, her movements unfeminine, her head shaved, and her loose Arab clothes a good camouflage; but what about that other feature of femininity, menstruation? The fact that it would have been hard to hide from such close living companions, bedding down together in goatskin tents, suggests that Isabelle might have been medically amenorrhoeic – probably through some degree of anorexia – as Joan of Arc is reputed to have been. The circumstantial evidence for this is strong, for not only did Isabelle never have children, in spite of a free and often indiscriminate sex life, but she only once seemed to take the possibility into account, when she wrote off for the neo-Malthusian literature at eighteen. The unusual freedom from constraint she felt in her actions, including her love-making, derived obviously from her upbringing: she said later, 'I wanted to be sure that for me at least freedom was not a vain word, and I took it in its entirety.' But perhaps it also grew from her physical make-up.

Certainly, through Trophimowky's teachings, and perhaps also as a defence against him, she had never acquired the usual cultural notions of femininity – and her defence could have expressed itself physically, in an anorexic resistance to menstruation. Or her periods could have been intermittent, influenced by this time by her way of life: her cigarette- and *kef*-smoking, her lack of interest in food except as minimal sustenance, her irregular hours, and the physical demands she made on her body may have been enough to render any menstruation at the most irregular. Even her physical strength may have contributed to amenorrhoea, as often happens with women athletes. (Ancient medical wisdom had already made the connection: 'Such failing of the menses happens because of the power and quality of strength, which digests well and converts the nourishment from the limbs until no superfluities remain, as it so happens among strong, mannish women who are called viragoes.') There is no sure answer now, but if Isabelle did have an abnormal menstrual pattern it would have obviously contributed to her strong sense of being different from the rest of humanity, a lament which runs through her diaries.

However, there is another reason which has been suggested, chiefly by Françoise d'Eaubonne in *La Couronne de sable*, to explain why Isabelle never had children, and why she disguised herself as a boy – and that is that she wanted to be made love to *as if she were a boy*, that is exclusively through anal intercourse. The theory also maintains that this is why she preferred to make love with Arabs, on the basis of the cliché that Arabs are more used to *Vénus inverse* with both sexes than Europeans are. D'Eaubonne suggests that anal intercourse was a deliberate, although subconscious, attempt to avoid the shackles of child-rearing, given her mother's unbeguiling example.

All kinds of small clues suggest that this explanation is too neat and theoretical – apart from the fact that the mechanics of such an intimate deception tax most imaginations. The fact is that whilst Isabelle wanted to take the freedoms men had – including that of 'sowing wild oats' – and felt herself socially a man to an unusual degree, sexually she felt herself a woman, something to which all of her close relationships with men testify. Isabelle's later writer friend Robert Randau was never her lover, but he was a relatively acute observer of human nature, and he wrote that 'she was a woman above everything else.' (He might have added 'and in spite of everything else'.)

Although Isabelle said later, to Randau, 'I'm much more of a woman than you imagine,' something about her was plainly more masculine than most. It was, however, not a predilection for anal intercourse, nor was it lesbianism. In all her references to the sexual act, in *Vagabond*, her stories, or her diaries, it is face-to-face love-making, with a man, which is being described or implied ('I long to hold my master in my arms, close to my heart').

Isabelle's sexuality was 'masculine' in a different way, and even then only according to the European bourgeois code of the time – which is why she preferred making love with Arabs, or in working-class areas: she wanted a very physically active role in it, and to be able to make love without any responsibilities, even without love, just 'for the love of making love' as a biographer, Claude-Maurice Robert, wrote. (Her later biographer, Cecily Mackworth, who was still able to talk with people who had known Isabelle, told me that lovers of hers would say she was 'indefatigable'.) In Isabelle's own mind, her downfall lay not in any unnatural sexual orientation, or even in promiscuity, but in periodically falling prey to a literally violent lust, which would sometimes tip over into brutality. (There had been a hint of this sado-masochism in the way she had thrilled to the bloodlust in the air in the Bône riot.) It was this which sometimes made her feel ashamed afterwards of her sensual life, seeing it as separate, unworthy part of her, something which would lead her to beat her breast in her diary at being 'debauched' and 'depraved'. Isabelle undoubtedly reveals her own nature in describing

Dmitri's reactions to scenes of lust in *Vagabond*: 'This atmosphere of brutal orgy did not displease him. How he had despised himself long ago for this taste for brutal sex which he knew so well, and which often led him into adventures of which he was ashamed afterwards.'

Herein probably lies the explanation for the conflicting evidence there is about Isabelle's sex life, which had been at its most abandoned on her trip down to El Oued. On the one hand those who knew her always protested that her behaviour was always seemly, never promiscuous; and on the other rumour had it that she indulged in wild orgies and was highly promiscuous. The reason was that she led a divided life: those who lived alongside her knew that she went for long periods without sex, as she had in the Sahel, if you call two months long, but from the sleazier parts of town would come rumours from people who knew she had indulged in orgies of *kef*-induced eroticism – harmless enough, but since those in the know would have implicated themselves by being too specific, the rumours inflated into knowing, vague insinuations. In a draft of an unpublished story, 'La Zaouïya', Isabelle describes the way she saw this dichotomy herself, writing of 'that strange *second life*, the life of voluptuousness, of Love. The violent and terrible inebriation of the senses, intense and harrowing, contrasting with my everyday existence, so calm and pensive . . . what intoxications! What drunken love under this hot sun!'

Robert Randau intuitively suspected these two sides of Isabelle, although he did not quite understand them, writing that 'with this Russian, the suggestion of passion always led to a panic reaction; most often love for her was a form of intellectuality.' Equally, he wrote later of Isabelle that 'carnal needs were making more and more regrettable incursions into her interior self, where until then the cerebral life had held complete sway.'

Isabelle's sex life does not of course 'explain' her character, which more than most was rich in contradictions. If her physique or her sexual preferences dictated to some extent the form of her life, then to an equal extent other parts of her life impinged on the sexual. Whatever her precise physical characteristics, whatever the traumas of her past, whatever her lusts, part of her impulse to live as a man came from the observer in her, from her writerly core. And there is a sense in which from now on she was living out in reality to an extraordinary degree the omniscience and androgyny that many writers take on in their imaginations.

℀ 4 ℀

PARIS: FIN DE SIÈCLE

Returning to Tunis from the two months of tax-collecting, Isabelle found some harsh realities of her own to face. Her lack of vigilance over the Villa had had its effect. Since it was unsaleable until the legal problems over the inheritance had been sorted out, Samuel had had the house locked up and shuttered. This had been enough to alert local thieves to the fact that it was empty, and soon it had been duly stripped of whatever was left there of any worth. Samuel claimed he could do nothing about petty theft or damage unless Isabelle and Augustin were prepared to pay for a guardian to live in permanently, which they were in no position to do. He himself was about to move to Berne. The money that Trophimowsky had left them both had now all but run out, and Isabelle was having to consider her position soberly. The legal fees were mounting and nothing could be done to realize the one asset they had, the Villa, without incurring further heavy fees.

Isabelle began to feel conscience-stricken about the *dolce far niente* of the past six months. She had meant to write more than she had, enough to begin to carve herself a literary career, but 'Rakhil' was still only half-finished, and her travel writings were languishing. In her journeyings with Salah, she had more than once got 'plastered' with him in inns, and this, together with her frequenting of seedy areas, was, she realized, causing people to judge her as merely a 'drunken, plate-smashing degenerate'. 'I assume for the gallery the borrowed mask of the cynic, the debauched layabout. No one yet has managed to see through to my *real* inner self, which is sensitive and pure and which rises far above the degrading baseness I choose to wallow in, out of contempt for convention and also out of a strange desire to suffer.'

Now, as the century was drawing to a close, a reckoning was approaching. Her blithe hurling of money out of the windows in Batna that summer was something which had lodged vividly in the memory of the locals. (Ironically, it was to stand her in good stead later on, for all the wrong reasons.) Now that she was broke once again, she was ruing it. She needed to work more practically and urgently. She decided to go to Paris and make contact with Bonneval and other magazine editors, and with anyone else who might prove helpful, like Abou Naddara.

Her friend Ali Abdul-Wahab was planning to go to Paris towards the end of the year, and they planned to meet there. But first she needed to see Augustin in Marseilles to discuss their affairs. She left Tunis for Marseilles in early October 1899. Once there, in a two-day spate of letter-writing she sent off letters to Ali, Si Larbi, Lieutenant Toulat and other friends, then to her Moscow bank, to Nicolas in Russia (soliciting his help over the legal impasse), to her Russian lawyer, her Swiss lawyer, the Russian consul in Geneva and (unaccountably) the US consul in Tunis. She stayed, not with Augustin and Hélène, but in a cheap hotel. Augustin, always easily influenced, now saw Isabelle through his wife's eyes, as an eccentric and rather embarrassing presence. Hélène wanted Augustin to give up his past erring ways and become the respectable person she felt he ought to be with his education. Everything in Isabelle influenced him dangerously, she felt, towards the wayward side of his character. Fortunately, Hélène soon found that her sister-in-law seemed as eager to avoid her company as she was hers.

Feeling in need of likeminded company Isabelle wrote to Vera Popov in Geneva asking her to come and stay for a while. 'Pop' arrived on 20 October, and for three days they talked endlessly as they visited the city sights together. Isabelle told Vera of her frustrations with her writing, and, more generally, as they visited the churches of Notre Dame de la Quai, St Victor, or the Château d'If, she lamented on the *mal du siècle*, the joyless inanity of the surrounding society as she saw it – its frantic pursuit of pleasure, the godless void at its centre. Vera encouraged her to write about just that, since it might get her out of her impasse with her writing, and was obviously close to her heart. Vera returned to Geneva, and within four days Isabelle completed the article, which she called 'The Age of the Void'.

Although it is a lugubrious, haranguing essay, it is a valid enough diagnosis of looming twentieth-century ills, and Isabelle's most unequivocal statement of her views on society. Using a visit to the theatre (no doubt with Vera) as the starting-point, she writes of her dismay at the greedy faces and glazed eyes of the audience, particularly the women, 'bourgeois women used up prematurely by a petty and narrow-minded life, with no range to their minds, dwarfed and all looking oddly alike'. She takes modern society to task for perverting all man's natural instincts:

Civilization, that great fraud of our times, has promised man that by complicating his existence it would multiply his pleasures ... Civilization has promised man freedom, at the cost of giving up everything dear to him, which it arrogantly treated as lies and fantasies ... Hour by hour needs increase and are nearly always unsatisfied, peopling the earth with discontented rebels. The superfluous has become a necessity and luxuries indispensable.

Widening the vision, she sees current European society as surpassing Moloch or Baalim, or Rome's decline, or Byzantium's depravity, or even the Middle Ages in moral turpitude: 'Never has any society known the terrifying cult worshipped by modern civilization, abjectly on its knees in front of the menacing spectre of nothingness.' Now in full apocalyptic vein, she conjures up 'tomorrow's black masses, born of today's grey masses' marching lemming-like towards the abyss of their own making, thanks to wilful ignorance of human priorities: hope, love, sacrifice, pity, repentance. Atheism above all has produced this wrong-minded society 'condemned to devour itself in sterile and ugly misery', for even in the worst of past times, people acknowledged 'dualism in natural forces: the struggle of the principle of light against that of darkness'. Now, there is no such framework for mankind to strive within, only a 'void of which it believes itself to be a part', 'glazed boredom, which is the shadow of the void projected on to the things of life' and 'terror, which is the vertigo of the abyss'. Many people 'to get the agony over with' prefer to 'hurl themselves into death'. The end of the essay rallies to a heavy-handed optimism, hoping that 'a new, radiant dawn may arise above the smoking ruins of the old, fallen world ... purified by blood and suffering'. 'From every ruin,' she concludes, 'life springs up again and everything that dies is born again.'

Isabelle dated the piece 9/11/1899, signed it 'Mahmoud Saadi', and sent it off to L'Athénée in Paris, where it was published in March 1900. She also sent a translation of it to her Russian correspondent Reppmann, a kindly old man who was troubled by it: 'Your article made me feel sad: such pessimism at such a young age! Of course it can be explained by the sort of life you've had. This is why I'm sixty-eight years old, but I'm still an optimist and idealist; I'm beginning to think it's a lack of observation and intelligence!' Isabelle also asked him if he would lend her money, which he rather sadly agreed to do. With this, and the proceeds from some private tuition she had been giving to a young Arab boy in Marseilles, Isabelle set off for Paris on 20 November 1899, intending to see in the new century in the vibrant and humming city.

Paris and Isabelle might have got on well at this time, since its social and artistic life was coming out into the cafés and streets from its previous, more rarefied, salon existence, and Isabelle might have been a natural *boulevardier*. However, Paris was also a more full-blown version of all the things she had deplored in 'The Age of the Void'. It had become notably theatrical ever since Victor Hugo's funeral in 1885, when the city had been burying not only a man but also prematurely but consciously, a century. Baron Haussmann's 1880 facelift for Paris had set the stage for such self-awareness, with its bold new star of wide boulevards cutting through the previous pell-mell city streets. The great exhibition of 1889 had bequeathed the city both Edison's new electric light, which began to light the cafés, theatres and *bois*, where women now sauntered to preen themselves, and the Eiffel Tower, which gave the city a new symbol and focus. The artificiality of this street life was not for Isabelle, and she no doubt found the Eiffel Tower, as Dumas *fils* and others did, a spectacularly pointless 'Tower of Babel', a monument to blind hope in progress for its own sake.

When Isabelle arrived in Paris, she found a room in the *pension* Louna, a boarding-house for students in the rue Cadet in Montmartre, not far from Abou Naddara. Ali Abdul-Wahab arrived a few days later, but on 16 December Isabelle wrote a curt 'terminal row with Ali' in her notebook. Although she had planned to stay 'months and months' in Paris, her row with Ali precipitated a sudden decision to leave the city. Since she was also carrying a *fin-de-siècle* melancholy of the kind that had driven Gauguin to write on a canvas two years earlier 'Where do we come from? What are we? Where are we going?' – and then subsequently take an (unsuccessful) dose of arsenic – she may have also decided, like him, to flee the new century which seemed to be announcing itself in such a brittle way.

On 17 December she took the express train to Marseilles and installed herself again in the Hôtel Bauveau. It was at some point during the next ten days that she met someone whom, she felt, 'fate had placed in my path just at the moment of a crisis', and it was with this someone that she set off on 29 December by train to Livorno, through Genoa. They left Livorno at midnight on 31 December 1899, arriving in Cagliari, the capital of Sardinia, on 1 January 1900. Although she does not name him, the person she had met was Abdul-Aziz Osman, a young Tunisian who had been sent into exile for his political views by the Bey of Tunis – in spite of the fact that he was related to the Bey through his mother's family. Isabelle and he shared a common passion for Islam, and both were adventurous and radical. Although they were to share their lives for the next four and a half months, and although Osman, by his own account, fell deeply in love 'body and soul' with Isabelle, she never had any romantic illusions about him. She treated him as a close friend and was fairly sure that, despite his protestations of eternal love, and of her image being engraved for ever on his heart, he would forget her when their paths ceased to cross. This much was true, but it was to be Abdul-Aziz who determined the next stage of that path for her.

❧ 5 ❧

JANUARY 1900

The day she arrived in Sardinia was an auspicious date: the beginning of a new century. Isabelle opened a new diary with a flourish in the most elegant version of her measured, graceful handwriting: 'Premier Journalier. Cagliari, le 1er janvier 1900'. In fact, it was not her first diary, as she had mentioned an 'old diary' of hers to Augustin as far back as 1895, but it is the first of four surviving ones. The previous ones she probably destroyed. She chose the word 'journalier', instead of the usual 'journal', catching its connotations of both 'day-labourer' and 'everyday'. It reflected her current philosophy of taking each day as it came, rooted in the Muslim requirement to trust in God to provide. The choice of such a pristine date was irresistible, particularly given the coincidence of the ties to her own past life ending, with Augustin's marriage, in such close harmony with the nineteenth century itself. She was also influenced by her current reading: the Goncourts' *Journal*, which opened on a date that was both personally and publicly auspicious – the day Louis Napoleon had seized power, and their first novel was published. Unlike theirs, her diaries were a very private affair, charting the moral progress of the intimate, inner self she felt not even Augustin knew. They are allusive and obscure: she wrote that 'a stranger reading the pages of these diaries would find them most of the time virtually incomprehensible', and to Augustin a year later, 'I am the only person who will ever find my own diary of use in evoking dead sensations and things . . . My diary is just a series of allusions to people and events which do not actually feature there.' Since she turned to it for consolation, or to check her 'moral progress', it only shows the melancholy, introspective side of her character, the disembodied 'diary self' which often tends to materialize in diaries.

From the chronological and geographical eagle's nest of Cagliari on the first day of the century she reviewed her life and looked forward with stoic pessimism to what lay ahead. 'I am alone [*je suis seul* – she writes of herself in the masculine gender, occasionally slipping into the feminine], sitting facing the grey vastness of the shifting sea . . . I am alone . . . alone as I've always been everywhere, as I'll always be throughout this delightful and deceptive great Universe . . . alone, with a whole world of disappointment and disillusion behind me, and of memories growing daily more distant, almost unreal.' Her only consolation is that the trials of the past months have strengthened her morally: 'I feel my soul tempered for good now, and indestructible from now on, resolute even through the worst storms, devastations or loss.' She thinks back longingly to the desert travels of the previous autumn, to the 'bitter-sweet happiness that used to flood through my orphan's heart during my chaotic encampments, amongst my chance friends, the Spahis or the nomads, none of whom suspected the hated and rejected personality that fate has saddled me with to my cost.' Now, as always, she feels she wants only one thing – 'to reclothe myself in that cherished personality, which in reality is the true one, and to go back to Africa again. I long to sleep in the cool, deep silence under the dizzying shower of stars, with nothing but infinite sky for a roof and warm ground for a bed.' She loved this life because it was the very image of what she felt was her true predicament: 'to be free and without ties, camped in life, in this great desert where I shall never be anything but a stranger and an intruder.' This was, she felt, the only happiness fate had in store for her, since 'for me real happiness, the kind that the whole of humanity runs panting after, is denied' – although whether it was her physical or psychological make-up which denied her ordinary happiness she does not say. Her commitment to Islam is the only thing which provides a spiritual home, and the only thing for which she longs one day to 'spill the hot blood that runs through my veins'.

As January wore on, Isabelle's thoughts turned more towards the past, and particularly to the Villa, with its good as well as bad moments. 'I say the good as well, because I mustn't be unfair to the poor old place, now that it's all thoroughly dead and gone. I mustn't forget it contained Mother's kindness and gentleness and Vava's good intentions – never realized . . . Since I've finally left that house, where everything had died a death even before it conclusively fell into ruins, my life has been nothing but a quick, dream-like flash through various lands, under different names and different disguises.' The past had, she acknowledges obliquely, imprisoned her: 'One thing delights me: the further I get from the limbo of the past, the more my character is strengthening in just the way I wanted it to. What's developing in me is the most stubborn and indomitable energy, and an upright spirit, two qualities which I value more than any other and which are, alas, very rare in a woman.' She had a specific use in mind for these qualities: she wanted to 'become somebody . . . and through that alone, to achieve the sacred goal of my life: revenge!' (The motto on the sailor's hat in David's picture was indeed no accident.) 'Luckily the whole of my past life and adolescence have taught me that peaceful happiness is not made for me, and that, alone amongst men [*sic*], I am destined for a relentless struggle against them, that I am, if you like, the scapegoat for all the sins and misfortunes which precipitated three people to their dooms: Mother, Vladimir and Vava.'

At the same time as she was writing these words, laden with the spectres of what had gone before, she was also making notes and plans for a collection of her stories – with, she hoped, a preface by Bonneval – which would include a story called 'Apostolat', which she drafted in Cagliari. (Although she was never to write it in that form, echoes can be found in *Vagabond*.) The plot was to be about a group of Russian agitators trying to spread the anarchist word amongst workers in St Petersburg. A young figure called Kyrillov emerges who, in *imitatio Christi*, takes the sins of the others on his shoulders and is sent to a forced labour camp, although he is technically innocent. She ends with the phrase 'whoever suffers, but is innocent, should not be pitied.' At this stage she seemed to feel that she, too, was taking on the sins not only of a family but almost of a century, and one remembers how as a child she was often seen carrying things which were too heavy for her.

⚘ 6 ⚘

ADRIFT

Isabelle left the Sardinian winter, as balmy as a Parisian summer, at the end of January, without having mentioned in her diaries her companion, Abdul-Aziz Osman. She travelled to Marseilles and on to Geneva, to engage once more in the 'sinister and relentless battle being waged over a tomb which has been sealed for eight long months'. She asked the Moscow Bank to send her copies of the letters Trophimowsky had sent before his death, which he had fondly imagined 'completed the organization of the future of those of Nathalie Nicolaievna's children remaining after Vladimir's death'. When Isabelle read these short, well-intentioned letters she must have groaned inwardly at how many loopholes there were through which her expected inheritance could flow away. Trophimowsky's strong suit, had never been organization. The Villa itself, which she went back to see, confirmed her forebodings: it was now only 'the ill-fated abode, shuttered and silent, lost in the undergrowth, as if plunged into a funereal and morose dream'. There was nothing to keep her in Geneva, and everything to suggest that she must urgently look to her own resources for the future.

She returned to Paris, and stayed at the *pension* Louna again throughout the spring, together with Osman, amongst a group of students many of whom, men and girls, developed a crush on her, and wrote her teasing letters after she had gone to tell her so. She was living 'daily' and 'intimately' during this period with Osman, although she told him she only stayed his mistress 'out of pity'. We only know this from a love letter he wrote her on 2 May, the day they parted, which he wanted her to carry with her on her travels. Isabelle herself still did not refer to the affair, except in her diary entry of 2 May where she makes a passing allusion to the 'Tunisian with the shadowy, velvet eyes, whom I loved but who misunderstood me'.

In her room in Paris, Isabelle had pinned up a cheap road map of

Bône that Koudja ben Abdallah had sent her as a souvenir. The cemetery where her mother lay was marked 'cimetière indigène': the two words gave her an 'inner shiver, a reminder of the dead past, which is for me one of the essential conditions of moral health', and she felt they would be a moral touchstone throughout her life. If only she could stay true to the lessons learned from grief and suffering, epitomized by the three graves in Bône and Geneva, she felt sure she was capable of great things. 'Thank heavens for sadness and melancholy, the divine inspiration of my spirit!' for they gave her intimations of the 'great soul' she often felt incubating inside her. (Her feelings echoed those of Dostoevsky's 'underground man', that suffering is to man's advantage, and that life is a quest for self-definition in which pleasure is of no use.) She saw death as having a mystical link to life, a link which was a key to understanding the puzzle of the universe. 'Thank heavens for the silent tomb, which is not only the gate to eternity for those who go through it, but also the gate to salvation for the chosen few who know how to interpret its mysterious depths.' But she felt an unwelcome dichotomy within her: 'Away with that vulgar and sensual side, which shouldn't be a part of me! It comes over me when I'm confused, and it is my undoing.' A month later, at the end of March, she felt that her life in Paris was a 'sombre dream', and she was invoking the great ideas of the past, and of Islam – 'which is peace of mind' – to focus 'this inexplicable drama called my life, which I have to keep on acting out'. The more fragmented her life became, the more she sought the healing unity of a single idea, an absolute, whether it was the image of a tomb, the idea of Allah, the simplicity of the desert, or the sun, the great monolithic healer and symbol of renaissance.

Meanwhile 'The Age of the Void' had appeared in *L'Athénée* on 3 March, and Bonneval wrote encouragingly a week later asking for further material, sure, he said, that 'you will send us something sensational'. (Isabelle also sent off an 'Algerian story' to *La Fronde*, the feminist magazine edited by Séverine, although it was never published there.) 'Adrift' as she was, Isabelle was in need of a mentor, and the kindly Abou Naddara gave her an introduction to someone who seemed set fair to become that mentor, and even to determine the direction of her life – the well-known Russian traveller and writer, Lydia Paschkoff, at present in the Crimea. Lydia was not only a seasoned traveller in the near oriental countries, but she also considered herself to be a worldly woman, and her contacts in Paris would, Abou Naddara felt, be useful to Isabelle. Her first letter to Isabelle, written from Yalta on 18 March 1900, exudes slightly scatty advice:

Mademoiselle, I understand you, and I absolutely sympathize with your taste for travelling. To travel is to chase after a *dream*. And what are we doing here if it's not dreaming! I speak of intellectuals. But alas! the body is an encumbrance. You will see this for yourself, because you have arrived in France (as I did in 1889 from Egypt) to try to get into journalism, which I'm finished with, for Abou Naddara and I know it only leads to *vegetation and cheap publicity*.

Journalism, she writes, cannot provide a living for a woman in France, unless she is French, has a lover working on a magazine, or a husband who will support her. Even George Sand, she writes, would have got nowhere without Sandeau, Musset, etc. She herself, she ventures, scorned all such routes. Her advice was that Isabelle could make a name for herself in Paris, but not a living. The one thing she might try to do was to get commissions from various people to travel, and she suggested Isabelle approach the explorers Prince Roland Bonaparte (the President of the influential Geographical Society), Count Leonti-eff, Prince Henri d'Orléans and the Prince of Monaco, all of whom might help with funds: 'Only you have to present yourself in such a way that you don't seem an adventuress.' She goes on to warn Isabelle that the French 'in spite of everything are very *pot-au-feu*, and like the little woman to cook. The woman of letters is a *useless* phenomenon to them.' Lydia's letter ends peremptorily: 'Write to me; how old are you? Avoid the *Libre Parole* like the pest. It's important to be *friends* with the Israelites; they are intelligent people.'

Isabelle evidently wrote back telling Lydia about herself and her background, a revealing story which we see only in its mirror image, in Lydia's reply to her of 7 April:

Dear Mademoiselle, I knew your mother at her sister-in-law's house (the wife of General Moerder, commanding the regiment at Preobrajensk – the one who was *née* Countess Apraxine). Your mother was very often in Pawlowsk and loved horses. Your old friend [Trophimowsky] is well-known here in Yalta. He used to be the admirer of General Charemberg's wife. He was not understood here. Which means nothing since in Yalta they think nothing is worthwhile except the systematic exploitation of the people who are stupid enough to come here. Now let's talk about you. Everything you tell me worries me. You have the same dreamy and passionate character as I have; the same impatience, the same taste for the desert and for the adventurous life. I've paid heavily for this passion for danger and a life of liberty. Like Lady Stanhope and Lady Ellenborough [Jane Digby El Mezrab], I loved the Orient; like them, I lost my fortune there. Yes, it's charming to be on horseback. As the Arab poet says, there's no joy greater than to have a good horse, a good saddle and countryside all around where one is free to prance about. But in order to live that life, I neglected my own fortune. I was a cicada and the Yaltian ants win the day in our prosaic century.

She advises Isabelle to sacrifice a year to Paris, to get established, but to

avoid the Russians. You have an excellent reason: your mother has married a Muslim, and became a Muslim. Russians will only do you harm. Be on your guard with them and keep apart from them. *You are a Turk*. Muslims adopt each other amongst themselves. Believe me I think of you as an adoptive daughter. Work for friendship between Muslims and Christians, it's the obvious choice for you. You are on your own, it's that which is tough, and looks bad. To everyone you want to meet, write a letter in advance to ask for an appointment. Tell them you have just come back from the Sahara, where you travelled in men's costume, and that you are the daughter of General de Moerder's wife and of the Turkish doctor. Use the name your father gave you. You must always tell things as they are: *the truth*.

This unwittingly ironic statement shows how Isabelle was now presenting her parentage – her father was not only a Muslim, but specifically a Turk.

She was so keen on being Turkish at this point that in May, when she left Paris for Marseilles, she wrote to Abou Naddara – who, to confuse matters further, signed his letters to her 'Your Egyptian papa'! – asking if he could get a Turkish passport for her. He wrote back saying that not a day passed without her name reverberating in their house – 'so you must have a telephone continually ringing in your ears' – but that he could not possibly agree to her request.

I know no one at the Turkish Consulate in Marseilles, and even if I had friends there, I could not tell them that you have Turkish parents, nor that you are Mahmoud Saadi, because I *cannot* mislead a representative of the Sultan, that would be an immense faux pas. Anyway, I don't think it would make any difference in these areas, where a *boy*, as you know, is in just as much danger as a girl. I beg you not to throw yourself into dangerous adventures without proper reflection. I assure you that you're as dear to me as Louli and Hilmi [his children], and it's this paternal affection which makes me speak so frankly.

The correspondence between Lydia and Isabelle developed into something quite sentimental during the spring and summer of 1900, as they found they had so much in common, including their dislike of Paris – 'a factory', Lydia wrote – and the Great Exhibitions, and an interest in mysticism (in Lydia's case 'occultism', although she complained airily that she had 'no friends in the other world: those of my relatives who have died were vastly below my intellectual level'). Lydia admired Isabelle's 'courage and aspirations: these sentiments are not understood by the bourgeoisifying bourgeois of our time.' Soon Isabelle was calling herself Lydia's 'child', and Lydia was assuring her of her 'maternal' feelings for her, and writing that she loved her as 'the evening star of my life'. By June Lydia was suggesting that the two of them should set up in Alexandria together for the winter: 'We could live with just one lamp and one casserole.'

Meanwhile, however other events had been taking shape in Isabelle's life, and as soon as it became clear that she was going to go her own way, the friendship lost its urgency. In the event, Isabelle followed up few of Lydia's introductions. Apart from anything else, she had no suitable clothes to wear to see the princely explorers, and was not enough of an exhibitionist to follow Lydia's advice and wear her Arab clothes just for effect.

THE DE MORÈS CONNECTION

Lydia had advised Isabelle to 'avoid the *Libre Parole* like the pest', for it was a virulently anti-semitic and nationalistic newspaper with the slogan 'France for the French', which had had a hand in provoking the Dreyfus affair. It had been founded and edited in 1892, two years before Dreyfus was arrested, by Edouard-Adolphe Drumont, an ex-historian who had caused a national stir with the publication of his anti-semitic book *La France juive* in 1886. One of the daily paper's editors was a man called Jules Delahaye, who was linked through one of the most bizarre episodes in the history of the Sahara to Isabelle's lover, Abdul-Aziz Osman. Although it had taken place four years before, it bears relating in full because it was this episode which not only set the scene for a great deal of what happened to Isabelle subsequently in North Africa, but also in due course nearly cost her her life. Moreover, the tale, an extraordinary black farce, graphically highlights Isabelle's own achievement in travelling in these desert regions.

*

In the spring of 1896 a swashbuckling adventurer called Antoine de Vallombrosa, the marquis de Morès et de Montemaggiore, had taken it into his head to forge single-handed a route through to Lake Chad in central Africa on behalf of the French. After its humiliating defeat at the hands of Bismarck in 1871, and the loss of its interests in Egypt to Britain in 1882, France needed a victory to regain her pride, and de Morès was determined to be the man to give it to them.

As an extreme nationalist, de Morès had been particularly incensed by Britain's takeover of Egypt. France had had a stake in the country for almost a century, ever since Napoleon's Egyptian campaign of 1798-9, which in spite of being a military disaster, had left a legacy of French influence which culminated in the building of the Suez Canal in 1865. To de Morès, Egypt should have been a cornerstone of the French Empire, a rival to Britain's Indian Empire, just as Napoleon had envisaged. Now, the Third Republic, which he despised, had actually handed over Egypt to her rival. He scorned the government's reasons for doing so: the interests of its wider diplomacy against Germany, and of an unwritten agreement of 1878 with Britain that in exchange France would be allowed a free hand in Tunisia. (Leeway which France took in 1881, when it made Tunisia a protectorate.)

As a monarchist, de Morès, like many other monarchists, had been deeply frustrated by his party's own powerlessness since the end of the Second Empire. The monarchists had ceded power tactically to the Republic in 1871, judging it best to let it do the unpopular task of raising the taxes for the war indemnity, before making a bid for power once the donkey work had been done. But they had miscalculated, for the country rallied to the government they saw steadily, if prosaically, working at restoring France's position. The monarchists were left without a role, which was all the more frustrating since they were split amongst themselves, having three, equally reluctant, candidates in the field as a future monarch. Powerless at home, they set their sights on foreign conquest, with their battle cry the opening up of a trade route from Algeria to the Sudan. It was a fantasy, an *idée fixe*, and not a realistic plan, partly because the 'trade' route could not do any viable trade: building railways or establishing caravan routes to transport Sudanese gum arabic or castor oil to France and French items to the Sudan which the Sudanese neither wanted nor could afford was not going to rebuild the Empire. But that was not the point: they could consolidate their nationalist dream of France stretching uninterrupted from west to east, from Senegal to the Red Sea, just as Cecil Rhodes and Britain dreamt of British Africa stretching from north to south, from Cairo to the Cape. And they might even succeed in winning back Egypt for the French.

Inevitably, French and British dreams would collide, and they did so two years later at Fashoda: just as de Morès was setting off for Lake Chad, the young Captain Marchand was embarking on an epic journey from the Congo to raise the French flag over the Egyptian Sudan. (In 1888 Marchand reached Fashoda, where he met Kitchener in a famous encounter which brought France and Britain to the brink of war.)

Although other European powers – Belgium, Germany and Portugal – were also carving up Africa in the last two decades of the century, de Morès and the other monarchists reserved their spleen for England, who, they were convinced, was part of a sinister Anglo-Jewish pact to do France out of its share of Africa. De Morès wanted to counter this alleged alliance of small-minded shopkeepers of Englishmen and Jews with an alliance of his own: a grand Franco-Islamic pact, which would be idealistic, not materialistic, based on faith, not commerce, and validated by history. Many French nationalists at the time agreed broadly with his views, but few broadcast them as blatantly as he did, and no others were so touched with megalomania that they believed they could cut a swathe through Africa alone, gathering Franco-Islamic acolytes as they went.

In his chequered career, de Morès had frequently sought out battles. He was an aristocrat of French and Spanish parentage, who had made and lost fortunes in America mainly – ironically, as it turned out – through abattoirs and shipping meat. He had killed a grizzly bear in single-handed combat in America, some tigers in India, and three men in duels in different continents for having crossed him. Even his face, with its square jaw, waxed moustache and hooded eyes suggested swagger.

The French government had been alerted to his intentions and wanted nothing to do with him. French officers in Algeria had tried to dissuade him from a journey which could only lead to his death, either from the treacherous terrain or the treacherous Tuareg. The marquis scorned their advice. He was certain he could subdue the Tuareg by charisma, and in a memorable phrase in a letter to a colonel, he wrote, 'Tuareg? Wonderful men!'

He arrived in Tunis with his rich American wife in March 1896 and gave a conference which drew a crowd of 2,000, including some from the French residency. He conjured up a vision of a Muslim uprising in Egypt and India against Britain such that from 'Dunkirk to the valleys of the upper Nile officers will go off to serve to the cry of "France and Liberty!"' He said he was going to send 'a sort of declaration of war to the Queen of England'. The French administration judged coolly in their reports that 'on the whole de Morès, by his expositions of paradoxical ideas and improbable facts, gave the impression of a fanatic lacking any sane judgement.' No more was heard of him until 23 April, when he announced that he had changed his planned itinerary. The military attaché at the residency, Lieutenant-Colonel Rebillet, was detailed to find out more about de

Morès's intentions, and to try to prevent him setting off. Rebillet noted the marquis's 'absolute lack of any preparation and total ignorance of the most elementary things concerning the Sahara'. He had a naive confidence in a talisman some tribesmen had given him, thinking he could charm his way through the Sahara with it. He also warned Rebillet darkly that he belonged to a 30,000-strong society pledged to total solidarity, which would avenge him 'spectacularly' if he should die. 'The heads of Rothschild and of the Prince of Wales will answer for mine,' he told him. The residency refused him formal permission to go, and strictly forbade him to travel through southern Tunisia because the Tripolitan frontiers were unestablished and insecure. He agreed to go through the south of Algeria instead, but had no intention of doing so. The French authorities were given the order to 'take no responsibility for de Morès; just stay neutral and keep an eye on him.' General de la Roque, commanding the Constantine division, privately 'feared the fatal ending threatening such an ill-organized expedition'.

In May de Morès arrived in Gabès by boat, ready to set off. Through the caïd of the Nefzaouas, who presented himself roguishly for the task, he unwittingly engaged a guide who was a 'known bandit', and who only attached himself to de Morès to ensure his doom. The French may simply have watched as de Morès so unerringly brought about his own downfall, as they had no reason to regret it politically, but it is possible from the evidence that they had given the nod in the first place to the caïd to do away with him. So in May, a singularly bad time to travel, de Morès set out from Gabès in Tunisia, heading westwards towards the Algerian border. His caravan was large and well stocked with all the European paraphernalia which would ensure he would be a prime target for robbery: tins of food, jewellery, gifts, guns from Bond Street suppliers. He travelled with some twenty men, forty camels and an interpreter.

De Morès was in splendid spirits on the journey, laughing and joking with the servants who surrounded him, confident in his charm. He had a magnificent tent to himself and, a Negro servant noted afterwards in awe, a completely made-up bed, cutlery and a table. He also had another even larger ceremonial tent, which he used only twice, for entertaining local chiefs. The caravan stopped in Hassi Mechiguig on the borders of Tunisia and Algeria, then moved on to the large plain of El Ouatia, where there was already a large encampment of tribes. De Morès was soon surrounded by Tuareg and

Chaamba, making protestations of devotion. Confirmed in what he saw as his rapport with these 'wonderful men', he blithely dispatched his Tunisian guides and his camels, since the Tuareg had promised him better ones. He paid for them, sight unseen, and then gave the Tuareg leader, Bechaoui, a present of his own Winchester from Holland & Holland, New Bond Street. In three simple strokes, he had put himself at their mercy. Day after day, the promised camels failed to arrive, for it suited the Tuareg to have de Morès amongst them, unable to leave, and forced to bribe them with gifts to bring the camels. After four days, de Morès, realizing the extent of their treachery, threatened to go back to Tunis. The next day the camels arrived, mangy and inadequate, and the party set off for Ghadamès, where it had been forbidden to go, accompanied by some twenty-eight Tuareg and Chaamba hangers-on, who attached themselves uninvited to the party – an occupational hazard of desert travel. Rightly uneasy at being so outnumbered, de Morès dismissed all of them, although three continued to accompany him 'for a little while'. A little further on, still within sight of the dismissed Tuareg, the three dismounted from their camels to 'bid him goodbye'. One of them held out his hand, and whilst de Morès was bending down to shake it, a blow from a Targui sabre hit him across his face and wrist. The marquis tried to stop his camel to defend himself, but – camels having notoriously independent opinions – failed to do so. De Morès, infuriated, shot it between the ears, ensuring neatly that the dying animal fell right on top of his only remaining repeating rifle. In the meantime suddenly increased numbers of Tuareg and Chaamba began to rain blows on his head and shoulders. He finally disentangled himself, dripping blood, from his camel and faced his aggressors. He still had his revolver, and managed to kill or wound five men with the five bullets left to him – an extraordinary feat considering his condition. The Tuareg ran off 'appalled' to rejoin those they had left behind. De Morès and his interpreter tried desperately to get his rifle out from under the camel, but failed, and the Tuareg were soon back in increased numbers. One Chaamba, El Kheir ben Abdelkader, crept round behind a jujube tree which de Morès, miraculously still alive, was leaning against. Using a gun the marquis had given him, he shot a bullet through the back of his neck, which came out through his throat, finally killing him. His interpreter and guide were also killed, but the Negroes were spared. The Tuareg and Chaamba then spent some five hours battling amongst themselves over the booty. It was later discovered that El Kheir had already murdered a sheikh to whom he was serving as guide. (The fact that the sheikh had been on his way back from a pilgrimage to Mecca made no difference to the Tuareg, of old Berber stock, who never felt themselves bound by the dogma of Islam.)

*

This was the terrain Isabelle was dreaming of reaching in Paris in the spring of 1900, when she was cursing the city for its over-sophistication and longing for the simplicity of the desert. The heads of the Prince of Wales and of Rothschild did not fall to avenge de Morès's murder, and, although the affair was to remain politically sensitive to the French over the next few years, the only person who took up the cudgel on de Morès's behalf was Jules Delahaye of the *Libre Parole*. Although he had not known the marquis well, Delahaye claimed he had been charged with avenging him by de Morès's widow, who lived in style in the boulevard Suchet in Paris, next to the bois de Boulogne. Delahaye took on this thankless task with fanatical devotion, spurred on by his conviction of a Jewish conspiracy. Ten years after the assassination he produced three turgid volumes on the affair which tried to prove that French government agents – Jewish-French agents – had engineered the marquis's death. This was the man who was a close colleague of Isabelle's lover, Abdul-Aziz Osman.

For Osman, de Morès's appeal lay in his committed espousal of the Islamic cause. Osman's grandfather was a general who had fought in the Crimea, his mother's family were related to the Beys, and he himself had served for eight years in the French army. But he saw himself now as a 'soldier for Islam', and became such an activist for the Muslim cause that in May 1899 the Bey had ordered him into exile in Kerkenna, in eastern Tunisia. As they handcuffed him, he told his friends that if he disappeared on the way they were to tell the French who was responsible – 'René Millet, the Resident Minister, already accused of Morès's murder'. He managed to escape from exile, and went into hiding in France in July 1899. It was six months later that he met and courted Isabelle. In the circumstances, it is no wonder that Isabelle does not mention her companion in Cagliari and Paris by name, even in her private diary. Isabelle, forged in the anarchist crucible, was notably discreet where political secrets were involved.

Osman told Isabelle the story of de Morès, and of how he was involved in helping Delahaye to bring the culprits to light. He had personal friends amongst the sheikhs of Algeria and Tunisia, and had already served as interpreter for Delahaye in Algeria. He knew Isabelle wanted some means of getting down to the Algerian Sahara, and they talked together about how it could be done, so that she would not only have friends amongst the sheikhs when she arrived, but also be paid to go down there. His particular friend was the *naïb* of Ouargla, Si Mohammed Taïeb ben Brahim, the head of the religious brotherhood of the Qadrya there. But there was another possibility: he and Delahaye were trying to organize an expedition, which the marquise would sponsor, to interview the sheikh of Nefta, Si Mohammed Taïeb's father, who, they thought, had inside information on the de Morès murder. They wanted to see him in Algiers, since Osman had been exiled from Tunisia, but since the sheikh was elderly, it might not be possible for him to travel out of Tunisia. This is where Isabelle would come in, for she would take Abdul-Aziz's place as interpreter if the meeting had to take place in Tunisia. Meanwhile, they would wait for word from the sheikh.

This was why Isabelle decided to leave Paris for Marseilles and then Geneva on 2 May, to attempt to get her affairs in order so that she could leave, at short notice if necessary.

❦ 8 ❦

ROOM TO LET

By the time she left, Isabelle was beginning to be reconciled to 'this Paris which I've begun to love deeply', describing it as 'decked out in radiant colour. Everything is shining and seems festive.' She was in such improved spirits that she even found Marseilles and her brother's household more congenial, particularly since the couple were expecting a baby, and Augustin had 'got out of the appalling state I had left him in last time'.

However, while she was in Marseilles she received a letter from Osman giving her the news of the reported sudden death by assassination of his friend Si Mohammed Taïeb, which seemed to put paid to one of her routes down to the desert. He wrote that 'if only he's still alive, all the Qadryas would make it their duty to ensure you arrived safe and sound by his side – but if he's *dead*, who will guarantee your safe passage? I'm very much afraid that you might find yourself in a difficult situation in the desert. If he's been assassinated, what would become of you, my poor darling, alone in the desert and penniless?' He suggested she should wait to hear news from the sheikh of Nefta. But he had a warning: he had written to a newspaper editor in Paris recommending her, in an attempt to get her a commission to report on her imminent journey. The editor had since proved to be on Millet's side, and 'since the Morès affair is the government's nightmare, your arrival in Africa might be signalled in advance and you might hit up against all kinds of administrative and other obstacles in your path.' This lodged in Isabelle's mind, and began to put her off going to the desert on Osman's terms. Although she had had perforce to understand the world of political intrigue, she had a deep-seated hatred of it, and would not have wanted her arrival in Africa to be of any political moment.

In mid-May she went up to Geneva, on what was to be her last visit there, and stayed with student friends at 12 boulevard La Cluse, and then in the rue de l'Arquebuse. She visited the two graves again, in melancholy mood, and reflected how her diary so far was 'merely an endless record of the unfathomable sadness there is at the bottom of my heart, at the bottom of my life'; and, once more, that the only consolation to be found was in her 'increasing Islamic resignation'. In mid-June she noted that she would never be attracted by the 'serenity of achievement', but would only ever be drawn to people who suffered from 'that special and fertile anguish called self-doubt, or the thirst for the ideal'. Outside the window of her small, bare room, with its camp bed, few papers and even fewer books, was a sign which, she thought, epitomized her life: room to let. 'Nothing, in my chance lodgings, could express more clearly my deep solitude, my absolute abandonment in the middle of the vast universe.' She spent an anxious and miserable night, but the next morning hit on a phrase which gave her a clue to what she might do next. Whilst she was writing the euphonious and liquid words 'dans un ksour de l'Oued Igharghar lointain', she suddenly realized that instead of depending on Osman and the marquise's commission, she could simply head for Ouargla, the southern oasis she had failed to reach last time, come what may. There was nothing to stop her: she had just enough money to get there, and her needs would be small – determinedly, philosophically small – once she got there.

On 8 July Isabelle heard the news that Augustin's daughter, Hélène Nathalie, had been safely delivered at one o'clock that morning. She was relieved: perhaps it was a symbol that the clouds which seemed to have hung over her and Augustin in the past years were at last lifting. She decided to wind up her affairs in Geneva as soon as possible, go down to Marseilles to meet her new baby niece, and then set off for Africa. The Villa was still a stalemate, and the 'cruelty and arrogance' of Nicolas, Perez-Moreyra and Nathalie, together with the deviousness and greed of the lawyers, only convinced her that this city held nothing but bad luck and hostility for her. The only consolation was that Samuel, who had proved to be a swindler, now had nothing more to do with their affairs.

Her last few days in Geneva were spent in long, intense and nostalgic talks with her Russian friends, particularly with Vera and an Armenian friend, Archavir Gasparian. He and Isabelle shared a sombre, poetic view of life and a certain intellectual fastidiousness, allied to an abandoned enjoyment of the senses. It led them to different conclusions: Archavir felt that in life you should explore and multiply your needs in order to set about using all your available energy in satisfying them, whilst Isabelle felt that needs should be reduced to a minimum to avoid the painful, embittering effects of disillusion. She was, characteristically, interested in fulfilment through reduction, simplicity, authenticity. He looked for it in expansion, diversity and high expectations. Their common ground was in agreeing that the independent ability of each individual to satisfy his own needs was the starting-point of moral growth.

At midnight on the night before she left Geneva, Isabelle walked about 'like a shadow' in front of her lodgings, conscious of the fact that she would probably never return. The next day was grey and stormy, and she wrote plaintively in her diary 'Where am I going? Towards my destiny!' In the early hours of the next morning, she arrived in Marseilles to a superb sunrise which reminded her of Africa. Reading the signs now – the sunrise, the successful birth of her niece, the departure of Samuel from the scene – she felt a cautious optimism that perhaps fate was only unkind to her and Augustin in small things, but in larger matters had their interests at heart. She was aware of the importance of the next step: 'This journey could turn either into a ghastly shipwreck of my whole future, or a steady progression towards my salvation, both material and moral, according to whether I can manage everything properly or not.' She was determined to work at her writing in a more disciplined way, as Vera had chivvied her to do. In the week she spent in Marseilles she stayed with Augustin and his family in their new home in 12 boulevard Mérentié. With her new resolution in mind – and perhaps because of her continuing lack of communication with Hélène, in spite of the new baby – she finally finished 'Rakhil' after four years of writing and re-visions, and a novella called 'El Moukadira'.

Her dream was now to create a 'solitary owl's nest' for herself in Ouargla, 'far away from people'. 'I want to isolate *my soul* for months and months from all human contact . . . I must also force myself to create an inner world of thoughts and feelings which will console me in my solitude and poverty, and in the absence of aesthetic pleasures, which are too much of a luxury in my present situation. I must, at all costs, put into practice my theory of diminishing my needs as much as possible.' She planned to be in the desert for at least six months, to finish her accounts, in Russian, of the Tunisian Sahel, and then to think about following the French troops, taking 'detailed notes', if they began to move into Morocco, as it was rumoured they might.

Then she would return to Paris, if the Villa had been sold, and attempt to establish her writing there with the fruits of her desert labours, in a much more professional way than before. Such were her dreams and good intentions in July 1900.

On 20 July she was once again contemplating a last night on another camp bed, this time in Augustin's house, towards the top of the steep hill that climbs up behind the harbour in Marseilles. She stood looking out of the barred sitting-room windows of the house on to the peeling plane trees which lined the small residential street on either side, and listening to the warbling of the household canary as it petered out in the setting sun. She spent another fretful eve-of-departure night, then set off in the heat and the sun of the following afternoon for Algiers, on board the *Eugène Pereire*.

Augustin came to see her off, and she watched him standing on the quayside in his staid black frock coat, trousers and felt hat, symbols of his 'definitive dedication to the calm and sedentary life'. She wrote in her notebook, 'I am setting off for the unknown. He is staying behind. And we look at each other, separated already by the ship's rails, and think how strange our destinies are, and also alas! how futile all human plans are. What of all those beautiful azure dreams we dreamed together in the old days in the land of exile, when we first opened our eyes to the bitter reality of life?' The ship's siren croaked, rending the air, the quay seemed to be moving away, there was a sudden great stirring in the dull, blue-green water, and they were off. Isabelle watched Augustin's 'dear silhouette' on the quayside until it disappeared from view. She stayed leaning against the rails for another hour, watching Marseilles retreating into the distance, and reflecting that she was leaving it, as she had Paris, just when she was beginning to warm to it – or was it that she loved them *because* she was leaving them? She realized the pattern ruefully.

She resigned herself to going down to the captain's table for a meal, feeling, not surprisingly, odd and out of place in her 'Muslim fez'. 'They all look at me as if I'm some curious animal.' After dinner, she went up on deck again to find it empty of passengers, who had been driven inside by the breeze. She stretched out on a bench, looking up at the ship's two funnels and beyond them at the shower of stars. Rocked by the ship's motion, she fell peacefully to sleep. 'I feel alone, free, and detached from everything in the world, and I'm happy.'

THREE

SOUTH

Savoir se libérer n'est rien; l'ardu, c'est savoir être libre.

ANDRE GIDE,
L'Immoraliste

OASIS II

From the moment Isabelle arrived in North Africa, it felt like a homecoming. At the last minute she had chose Algiers rather than Bône as a starting-point, mainly because her 'friend Eugène' was there, and when she arrived in the afternoon of 22 July 1900, he came at once to see her in her room. Letord was also at a crossroads in his life: his father had died suddenly in Lyons in March, he had taken some weeks' leave to go back and comfort his mother, and now he had to decide whether to go back to France and civilian life, or to stay on in the army in Algeria, where he had just been promoted to captain. If he went back to Lyons, he had told Isabelle in a letter in the spring, he would set about getting married as soon as possible, having 'had enough of the bachelor life'. Although he was, Isabelle wrote, the only European man she ever found attractive, and although he was a loyal friend to her, often lending her money in hard times, their paths were beginning to diverge. He was coming thankfully to the end of his time in the desert, and Isabelle, full of hope, was just beginning hers.

As soon as Eugène had left, Isabelle went out alone into the streets – coming back for her fez, so that she would not be 'cut off from Muslim life' – and savoured the Arab bustle, or the 'vieux train-train du tabadji arabe de la rue Jénina' as she wrote, echoing its sounds. There was the peaceful freshness of the white lace-patterned arches in the Djemaa-el-Kebira, a visit to the bluish *zawiya* at the top of the hill, where she drank some jasmine-scented water, an encounter with a venerable old man from the mosque with 'no misplaced or indiscreet curiosity', and a meal on the corner of the street she was staying in. 'I felt *intensely* the joy of returning, of being back once again in this land of Africa, which I'm attached to not only by the best moments of my life, but also by that strange attraction I felt for it even before I saw it, years ago in the monotonous Villa.' Later, in the vast mosque of Djemaa Djedid, where she went with her servant Ahmed to join in the evening prayer, the *icha*, she felt a lyrical thrill as the clear young voice of a novice alternated his responses with the grave, cracked, quavering tones of the old *imam*. 'I felt an almost ecstatic feeling tightening my chest and surging towards the heavenly regions that the second voice seemed to be coming from in a tone of melancholy joy, serene, at peace, and utterly convinced.' The experience was enriched by an involuntary memory, as her mind flashed back to the time in Tunis when she had heard the voice of the muezzin calling the morning prayer, 'Prayer is better than sleep.'

On the way back to her room that night she noticed a shopkeeper lying on an oval mat outside his shop, making long-drawn-out, abstracted, 'infinitely slow' movements. From her own experience she recognized the effects of *kef*, and, drawn to share the man's languour and detachment, and to merge into the life around, she bought some *kef* and her first small pipe. She spent four more days in Algiers, and the 'many moments of intense life, of fully oriental life' worked their magic on her: 'Je renais, une fois de plus, à la vie.'

Early in the morning of 27 July she set off for the south, intending to head for Ouargla. Travelling third-class in trains through Constantine to Touggourt, on railways built by the French, with local labour, she passed through the jagged Kabyle mountains, streaked with silvery-ochre patches where the Arabs had made the odd field, then through the 'lugubrious' oasis of Ourlana with its enclosed gardens, giving off a thick smell of saltpetre, humidity and fever. From Biskra she travelled on to Touggourt with a guide, Habib, and slept out on the warm sand under the bright light of a sky thick with stars. She had felt a surge of joy in Algiers at the spiritual soul of the country; now she felt the same for its physical features: 'O Sahara, menacing Sahara, hiding your beautiful, grave soul under your bleak, desolate emptiness. Oh yes, I love this country of sand and stone, this country of camels and primitive men and perilous vast salt-flats.'

By the time she reached Touggourt on 31 July, she had decided that she would not head for Ouargla after all, but would instead base herself in El Oued, the oasis town that had so captivated her the year before. She felt it would be less risky from the point of view of her health since typhus, scabies, malaria and syphilis, hazards throughout Africa, were virtually endemic in the southerly regions. En route to El Oued on 1 August, by mule and camel, she felt pleased with this decision: 'How glad I am I left Europe and decided – yesterday

– to choose El Oued as my base. If only my health holds out, I must stay as long as possible in El Oued. Above all, I pray this time won't be wasted, from all points of view, but particularly from that of my moral and intellectual development.' She suffered from constant slight fever on the three-day journey, but through it she drank in the light-play and sounds of the desert, and the 'ineffable delicacy and purity of the tones'. She saw a new moon flood one half of the sky with a diaphanous bluish-white light, whilst the other was still golden from the setting sun, and heard a cold wind ruffling the desert dunes, sounding like the sea.

At sunset on 2 August she arrived in El Oued and spent the night in Habib's family's house. She rose at 4.30 and rented herself a house in the town from a *caïd*, across the square from an old fortress, then dropped a note at the Arab Bureau announcing her arrival and asking to be received by the head of the Bureau, Captain Cauvet. Cauvet, who astutely preferred to see newcomers in their own surroundings, went round later that day to call on her. Although the forty-year-old bachelor had been away from El Oued when Isabelle was there the previous year, he already knew a lot about her, unknown to her. He had been told on his return about this cross-dressing girl with a mysterious background, reputedly rich, perhaps aristocratic, who had swiftly exhausted the sexual energies of the local El Oued poet, and who had a taste for native lovers. With such advance publicity, Isabelle's designation of her base as her 'solitary owl's nest' was likely to prove naive.

Gaston Cauvet was a cautious, intelligent, and mildly eccentric man, with piercing eyes and exuberant whiskers which cantilevered sideways into the air. In his quiet way, he took a more than soldierly interest in the life around him: he was something of an amateur artist, and had taught himself Arabic and Berber. (Six years later, internal army reports described him as 'one of the most distinguished' of the officers serving in the Sahara, and twenty years later he wrote a book which is still the definitive work on the camel.) He was a man of independent judgement, but since he stood on the sidelines himself as far as passion was concerned, he took a dry view of other people's baffling fleshly excesses. He found Isabelle 'quite well-educated', and in a report to his superiors a few months later, he wrote that

apart from the eccentricity of her manner and her dress (she dresses like a young native man from the Tell, with a *chechia* [a red skullcap] with tassels, a French-style jacket and trousers, and an Arab chaplet), there is nothing that she has been reported as having said or done that has not been perfectly correct. From what I've seen and heard it seems that Mlle Eberhardt professes quite advanced ideas and is involved in the contemporary feminist and socialist movements.

However he added witheringly, 'Physically she is a neurotic and un-hinged, and I'm inclined to think that she has come to El Oued principally to satisfy unhindered her dissolute tastes and her penchant for natives in a place where there are few Europeans.'

Cauvet bore Isabelle no personal malice – he was relatively kindly disposed towards her – but the harshness of his view is revealing. On one level Isabelle was simply taking liberties of which he disapproved: she was indeed a sensualist, and on her previous journey to El Oued had taken Arab lovers when the impulse took her, in a bonanza of freedom. But on another level his view was coloured not so much by the reality of Isabelle's life as by the particular nature of the colonial predicament in Algeria. Most of the colonists, 'building a future in a blind alley', in the historian Jacques Berque's vivid phrase, were living the half-truth that they were the country's benefactors; most of the native Algerians of all races were living the half-truth that they were submissive. Something of a voluntary apartheid had grown up to protect the uneasy, and essentially false, status quo, and within it sexuality, that wild card and last private sanctuary, became even more highly charged than usual. Fear of the endemic syphilis kept the French away from inter-marriage – and away from the potential sexual revenge of the Muslims for their lost lands, values and hierarchies – but fear of breaking down their 'differentness', on which their power depended, also played a role. In this context, for a European woman to have sexual relations with Arabs was not just unseemly: it also threatened the precarious fiction of European dominance and Arab submissiveness on which the colonial venture in Algeria was built. (It was particularly inflammatory in Algeria, which was the most extreme case of European colonization of a Muslim country.) Cauvet's momen-tary venom in his confidential army file was a foretaste of the kind of closing of ranks which would gradually bear in on Isabelle's 'vast horizons'.

Cauvet had arranged for a 'discreet watch' to be kept on Isabelle from the moment she arrived in El Oued, in spite of the fact that she had come 'as a tourist' the previous year, and so was known to some extent. She knew that now this was her real life and not an escape, her behaviour would be commented on, but she had no idea of the extent to which she was from now on systematically under surveillance. To her cost, she also forgot that there was already someone in the army with an old score to settle against her.

On 4 August she wrote blithely:

Here I am, finally arrived at the goal which seemed a little fanciful while it was still a project. Now it's done, and I must act with all the energy I can muster . . . and set to work on the story of my travels, with Marseilles as its first chapter. I'm far away from people, far from civilization and its hypocritical shams. I'm alone, on the soil of Islam, in the desert, free and in excellent conditions. Apart from my health, the results of my enterprise now depend only on me.

IDYLL

It was probably on her way down from Touggourt that Isabelle first met Slimène Ehnni, a young Arab officer from the *spahi* regiment in El Oued. They quickly and discreetly became lovers, in the way that Isabelle had taken Arab lovers on her previous trip to these regions. Yet something in Slimène seemed to Isabelle exceptional, and quite different from anyone she had met before. She instinctively trusted him, in a way she had not done since her adolescent relationship with Augustin, and the trust began to lead to what she soon felt was the 'great love of my life'.

Slimène – Isabelle usually used this French version of his Arab name Slimane or Seliman – was dark-skinned, with open, regular features, large, liquid, sulphur-coloured eyes, and a fine moustache. His health, even at twenty-four, was not robust, and he suffered from a battle wound in one leg. Although he was a Muslim, he was committed by his background to French rule in Algeria, keen both to improve his education in Western terms whenever he could, and for promotion within the regiment. His story shows in miniature the ways in which seventy years of French occupation had modified a large section of the native population.

The *spahis* were a relic of the long Turkish occupation, a cavalry regiment of native soldiers which the French had taken over in 1842 and gallicized. They were recruited as part of the French army, with incentives of training, uniforms, basic pay, French nationality and increased status *vis-à-vis* their own countrymen – a kind of Gallic Ghurkas. It was through the *spahis*, and later the *Sahariens* and the more lowly foot-soldiers, the *tirailleurs*, that the French had acquired the reputation of having their conquered nations do the conquering for them. Young men from good families tended particularly to volunteer, since half of the officers in the *spahis* were taken from the native ranks, and since every recruit had to provide his own mount.

(Brigadier Smaïn had been such an officer.) Slimène's family had been one of the first to respond to the recruiting call.

His father's ancestors came from a family in Constantine headed by Sidi Mabrou, his mother's from the Chaoui tribe in the Khencela district in the Aurès mountains, between Bône and El Oued, and it was to his mother's ancestry that he owed his dark skin. His father, Ali ben Mohammed ben Hani (or Ehnni), known as Boudjemah, had joined the 3rd Regiment of the *spahis* in 1853, only twenty years after the French had first arrived in Algeria. He had left the *spahis* nine years later with a 'certificate of good conduct' and joined the French-founded police force in Bône. (The *spahis* tended to take over an informal policing role in their areas, as on Isabelle's tax-collecting trip.) There he became an inspector, then an official interpreter. In 1870 he was naturalized French, and in the same year personally procured 258 voluntary enrolments for the French army from local men in Bône, who were being recruited for France's disastrous war with Prussia. In the following year he recruited over 400. (It was *spahis* like these whose mistreatment by French soldiers Isabelle had so deplored.) By 1882 he had become a Commissioner of Police. He died in 1889, and his wife, Slimène's mother, Hemmouna bent Lakhdar, died four years later. Three of Slimène's uncles had fought for France in the *spahis*, and been decorated for their efforts, and two of them had been killed in action. Slimène's two older brothers had served in the *spahis* before him. It was a family which had taken great pride in its service to the colonial army, and for whom honour, bravery and authority were important words.

With this background, Slimène had become an *évolué*, a gallicized Muslim. He had been born on 12 June 1876, a few months before Isabelle, and his father's naturalization had automatically conferred French nationality on him. At seventeen, Slimène had joined the 3rd Regiment of *spahis*; in January 1895 he had been made a corporal, and by the time he met Isabelle he was a sergeant.

Isabelle was careful not to mention Slimène too much at first, even in her diary, knowing how awkward it would make her life if it became known that she was having a regular affair with a native soldier. When Captain Cauvet had visited her for the second time, she had asked if she might borrow an army horse for her daily rides, and he had agreed. Since Slimène was in the cavalry and had access to a horse, she took to meeting him late at night outside the town, when they would ride over the dunes to spend the early part of the night together in the surrounding small oases. They often went to the palm grove of Bir R'Arby, a long, narrow crater of sand, with wells and tall palm trees on one side, like feathery quills in the greenish light of the moon, and melons, watermelons and basil growing in between. The water from the wells was clear and fresh: the goatskin bucket clattered to the bottom, and the primitive pump-handle made a grinding squeak as they drew the bucket back up, dripping with water. Isabelle would fling off her *chechia* on to the sand, and plunge her head into the bucket, drinking the water avidly 'with that feeling of almost agonized sensuality which cold water gives one here'. Then they would make love, and lie for a while on the sand.

Once, they went to another grove, where the well happened to be empty, and sat beside it in dejected mood. Part of Isabelle's depression was apprehension – which she later considered 'prophetic' – about the 'really terrible possibilities that might happen' if the few people who might know of their meetings were indiscreet. But beyond that she recognized a generalized sadness, a well of inscrutable melancholy, 'unanalysable, without any known cause, which is the very essence of my soul'. A month later she described it as an 'inexpressible desire for a something which I can't explain, a nostalgia for an *elsewhere* which I can't put a name to'. Slimène, his 'soul still young', believed in eternal love, and was already talking in terms of seven years time. Hearing him talk like that, she felt much older than him, much more cautious as yet about thinking that a love affair might last. 'On that score there is not only absolutely no illusion left in me, but also *no desire* for illusions, no urge to try to make these things last which are only sweet and good because they're ephemeral . . . But then, these kind of things are so personal, so much *my problem*, that it's impossible to explain them clearly, or above all to make anyone else understand them.' They lay down on their burnouses underneath the palm trees, their heads on a pillow of sand.

Isabelle was more sensitive to the potential dangers of their association than Slimène was. Slimène was proud to have such a dashing European girlfriend, and enjoyed being teased by his fellow-soldiers. He wrote about Isabelle to a soldier friend in Biskra, who replied, 'We all wish you good luck and happiness with this Turkish noblewoman [Slimène had evidently also been told of the 'Turkish' father]. At last there are better times ahead for you, my dear friend.' By 17 September the news had reached a *spahi* friend in Touggourt, who wrote in French, which Slimène and all *spahis* learnt as a matter of course: 'I hear you're luckier than I am and have managed to find yourself a mistress in the sand dunes. I congratulate you from the bottom of my heart, because it's no fun without a girlfriend in these little villages.' Another friend from Touggourt wrote, 'From what I hear on the grapevine it seems you're not languishing and that you're managing to pass your time quite agreeably in the middle of your sand dunes. Lucky devil.'

August and September in the 'town of a thousand cupolas' drifted by in a haze of heat which stifled work. Isabelle deplored the inertia that seemed to take hold of her each time she moved to a new place, and noted ruefully that seeing Slimène every night meant that the siesta played 'too much of a role' in her life. An inordinate amount of the rest of the time seemed to be taken up by 'taking administrative measures against the flies'. She decided that a horse of her own was a necessity in the south, and when a small sum came through from Augustin, she bought one, named him Souf, and became very attached to him. He was spirited and frisky when saddled, and 'sweetness itself' at home. He lived in the courtyard, but followed her around like a dog outside, roaming around freely, nuzzling his 'beautiful, intelligent head' against them, and nibbling their hands.

By October the mornings were beginning to get cold. She changed her lodgings, moving to a house in the old Jewish quarter in the north-east of El Oued, near a mosque. There she settled down to a quiet, domestic life with her 'honest, placid, *kef*-smoking servant Khalifa', a daily orderly, Biskri, who helped her with the animals, and the animals themselves: Souf, a goat – her 'capriform rodent' – chickens, pigeons and rabbits. Slimène now lived there whenever he had free time. The house was plastered all over inside, even on the floor, unlike the poor Arab houses which had sand floors. Her large main room contained her tin trunks, a wobbly table, an iron chair, her blue woollen mattress with a tent-cloth draped over it, and her 'famous African leather cushions'. On the wall were photographs of her friends and family, including Trophimowsky and baby Hélène, her bridle, decorated with amulets, her spurs, her revolver and Slimène's, a rifle, and a red burnous with gold braids down the front. Only one thing threatened their bliss, Isabelle told Augustin tongue-in-cheek in a letter of 10 November 1899: recently they had all started to drink, servants and all, and had to be prised out of the local bar every day. But all this had stopped now, since she had come home once 'so smashed' that she had broken down the door. Khalifa had mended it, and afterwards they had all returned, chastened, to a more sober life. This minor matter apart, she assured Augustin, she thought perhaps that she had found her port, as he had found his. She described Slimène to her brother: 'He has a gentle, gay character, and hates noise, outings and night clubs. He loves his home, which he defends jealously against incursions from the outside. Slimène is the ideal husband for me, weary and sickened as I've been by the desolate solitude in which I've always found myself, whatever company I've been in.' They were thinking of 'regularizing' their relationship, since in the present situation, although Cauvet was lenient with them, they were at the mercy of the 'first Arab Bureau captain to come along who doesn't like my face'. In her diary, she wrote, 'I'm becoming daily more attached to Slimène and he is really becoming a member of my family, or rather *is my family.*'

By 10 November, Isabelle no longer saw El Oued as a stepping-stone on the road to Paris and literary fame, but as an end in itself, the Dar El Islam. 'I'm seriously thinking of attaching my existence to this lost oasis, which I'm growing increasingly fond of,' she wrote to Augustin. To do this she had to ensure a livelihood for the future. Slimène had no capital, and earned a basic three francs ten centimes a day from the army (for comparison, they paid Khalifa ten francs a month). But she felt he had a good chance of becoming an interpreter, which would mean 'comparative riches and absolute security' for them. For her part, she wanted to spend whatever accrued to her from the 'ruins of the Villa Neuve' on a nearby garden with a well in it, so that she could make it into a market garden and grow vegetables and date-trees. The old Trophimowsky dream was surfacing, in more mellow form.

Isabelle's love for Slimène played the major part in her contentment: she quoted approvingly his description of their 'nights of love and absolute security in each other's arms'. But her new sense of appeasement also had a spiritual source. Through Abdul-Aziz Osman, she had been put in touch with two local sheikhs of the Qadrya brotherhood. They were the colourful brothers of Sidi Mohammed Taïb ben Brahim, Osman's friend who had been killed in battle, and to whose protection Osman had wanted to entrust Isabelle the previous spring.

They were two of the eleven sons of the recently deceased Sidi Brahim, the Grand Master of the brotherhood of Qadryas in Nefta, southern Tunisia, whom Isabelle had been going to visit as interpreter. Sidi Brahim had told his sons to go out and found new *zawiyas* (monastery-cum-lodges) of the Qadrya order, which they had duly done, four of them doing so in the area around El Oued. Sidi El Hussein (ben Brahim), now the eldest son, had a *zawiya* in Guémar, ten miles to the north of El Oued, and Sidi El Hachemi headed a lodge five miles to the south of the oasis town, in Amiche, near another brother, Sidi Elimam. Isabelle was welcomed by them, doubly recommended by Osman and by the fact that Slimène was himself a member of the Qadrya order. Some time in early November she herself was made a *khouan*, or initiate, of the Qadrya lodge by Sidi El Hussein, an unprecedented honour for a European. They gave her the black rosary or chaplet of the order, which Cauvet had noticed in his report, and this, together with the particular *dhikr* or ritual prayer of the order, would identify her to fellow Qadryas wherever she went in Algeria, enabling her to count on their practical and spiritual help.

The Qadryas were a Sufi order within Islam, with a mystical tradition which other orders, like their rivals the Tidjanyas, did not have. They were the first and oldest of the Sufi orders, with adherents stretching throughout the Middle East, India and further east. The order had taken its name from its founder, the prophet Abdel-Qadir ben Abdallah el-Djilani, who had migrated to Baghdad from his native Persia in the eleventh century AD. The original Sufis sought a return to fundamental Islamic values, emphasizing the individual's union with God, after the centuries of corruption and orthodoxy which had followed Mohammed's death. Like any mystical religion, traditional Islam had been characterized by its rejection of anything which interfered with each man's direct experience of God, such as priests, money, worldly goods, bureaucracy or institutions. (Although in Islamic Sufism, as in Islam generally, carnal love was not an impediment to a pure love of God, but a step along the way, an intimation of divine union.) Named after the simple woollen garments they wore, the original Sufis drew on mystical elements familiar from other centuries and other religions: from neoplatonism the withdrawal from the objective world, from Buddhism the rosary and the spiritual stages along the road to God, from Christianity an uncompromising monotheism and its monastic (though not its celibate) strain. For the Sufi, the stages along the road to union with God come in two parts: stations and states. The stations are earned rites of passage; the states follow, as gifts of grace from God. The core of the seven stations, which vary in different texts, consists of: conversion, abstinence, renunciation, poverty, patience, trust in God, satisfaction. The ten states are: meditation, nearness to God, love, fear, hope, longing, intimacy, tranquillity, contemplation, certainty. The goal is to destroy the illusion of self, to pass into the consciousness of survival in God, and to make a good death. By the end of the nineteenth century in Algeria, the Sufi orders had become less single-minded, and more of a social, tribal grouping sworn to help each other as a practical measure in hostile desert conditions. This meant that not all Qadrya-initiates were mystics, but the path was well trodden and signposted for anyone who was so inclined.

The extent to which a quest for the mystical influenced Isabelle's life from now on can only be inferred, as she never referred to Sufism in her diaries and rarely (with one memorable exception) alluded to the mystical experience beyond the vague, atavistic yearning that is present in her make-up from her earliest writing. However, the written record is not the only criterion of existence, and the mysteries of induction into the mystical life were traditionally secret. Isabelle, no stranger to secrets, would never have been accepted as an intimate of the sheikhs if they had not judged her to be discreet. (They knew her to be a woman, but this was no bar to the Islam which had developed in Algeria, in which the wives and daughters of 'marabouts' had occasionally taken over their mantle in the absence of a son and heir.)

Isabelle's initiation by El Hussein (which she mentions briefly in her letter of 10 December to Augustin) put her in a position to be close to the mystical life, and the mystical search for authenticity and simplicity exactly coincided with her own quest. Trophimowsky's teaching had unwittingly paved the way, giving her a background history of the great philosophies and religions. Even his anarchist ideas had an echo in Sufi teaching, which opposed orthodoxy and authority: both favoured direct, individual action, anarchism politically, Sufism spiritually. Temperamentally, too, Isabelle would have found the mystical road compelling. The Sufi journey towards destroying the illusion of self held particular appeal for someone who had found her selfhood so confusing and painful, and the Sufi goal of a good death, and of daily preparation to meet it, was highly compatible with Isabelle's own raw, long-standing awareness of its proximity. The possibility of mysticism, and of many of the formal stages along the way to it, are woven into the pattern of her life from now on, and sometimes surface visibly. Yet, much as she responded to the quest, it was almost certainly an unfulfilled mysticism, diffused by the high degree of incident in her life, which she allowed to sidetrack her, and impaired by her urgent personal *need* for a revealed destiny in order to be able to make sense of an otherwise baffling life.

*

Ramadan came, the month of fasting for Muslims. Isabelle would spend the days in menial tasks or in riding out to talk with the sheikhs in their *zawiyas*. Whenever possible, the nights were spent with Slimène. In the evenings, from the terrace of their house they would watch the sunset, sometimes pale and veiled, sometimes as spectacular as fireworks, purple, orange, pink, violet then suddenly, as the sun dropped, uniformly grey over the dune-horizons. Slimène and Sidi El Hachemi's right-hand man, the local schoolmaster Abdelkader ben Saïd, would sit cigarette in hand, waiting for the moment of sunset which released them from the fast – which included smoking – and Khalifa and Aly, their servants, would be waiting to stuff their pipes with *kef* or *ar'ar*. Isabelle liked to tease them, swearing that the minaret of the local mosque was still pink with light. They cursed her, and Abdel-Kader teased her back, calling her 'Si Mahfoudh'. For her part, she would prolong her fast, riveted by the dying fall of the sunset. Sometimes she would go and wait for Slimène to come out of his barracks, wearing his red *spahi* cloak and boots: 'I never saw the red shadow coming out without a certain shiver, a sweet thrill inside, voluptuous and strangely sad.'

Sidi El Hussein used to visit them several times a week, and became a father-figure to them. Soon, Isabelle wrote to Augustin in her November letter, his brother Sidi El Hachemi, 'the most incredible mind I have ever met', would be returning to Touggourt from Paris, and she and Slimène would be going to join his brothers and a mass of the faithful who were riding out to meet him there in a desert *fantasia*, perhaps the most brilliant of desert events. She wrote proudly that 'you will see there a cavalier mounted on a fiery little horse, wearing a gandoura and white burnous, with a high white veiled turban, a black rosary around his neck, and his right hand bound with a red cloth to hold the bridle better, and it'll be Mahmoud Saadi, adoptive son of the Great White Sheikh, son of Sidi Brahim.' The day before El Hachemi arrived, Isabelle and Slimène rode up to Touggourt with El Hussein to await him, along with an escort of hundreds of men and women, all decked out in their ceremonial costumes, the numbers growing by the minute. The sound and smell of gunpowder in the air and the raucous noise of pipes and drums accompanied them as they slowly advanced on the road to Touggourt, where they met up with El Hachemi and his entourage. In contrast to the colourful crowd, El Hachemi was wearing the austere, undecorated green silk robes, green turban and long white veil appropriate to a descendant of the prophet El Djilani. The crowd hailed him with cries of 'Ya [O] Djilani!' 'With an impassive manner', Isabelle wrote in her *Cahiers*, he attempted to control his spirited white stallion. The surrounding sterile dunes seemed to be breeding flocks of people by the minute. At one moment Isabelle looked up and saw above the sea of heads the faded red, green and yellow banners of the Qadryas being unfurled at the top of a dune: it was Sidi Elimam coming to meet his brother, with a contingent of *khouans* not only from his own order, but also from the Ramanya, Taibia and Aïssaouas brotherhoods, all of whom traced back their allegiance to El Djilani. Horses reared and whinnied, frightened and excited by the gunfire, by the presence of the late Si Mohammed Taïeb's black stallion, and by the acrid smell of the smoke hanging in the air above them. Only the camels, decorated heraldically, stayed aloof. Si Elimam, a 'giant', with startling blue eyes, advanced with his entourage behind his three banners, chanting a prayer. When everyone was gathered together, they all moved on into a vast plain dotted with tombs, where the horses and riders, quickening to the sense of empty space ahead, finally let rip in a headlong gallop, racing, Isabelle wrote, 'as if to the ends of the earth'. Later, a group of twelve horsemen gave an impromptu display in a circle created by the crowd, simulating an attack, wielding inlaid rifles and shrieking a staccato war cry as they feigned a charge and then emptied a salvo of bullets into the sand.

Isabelle's pride in taking part in the *fantasia* was well justified, as it was an extraordinary feat of both horsemanship and assimilation. Even her hero Loti, a superb horseman himself, had not managed to participate in one, to his chagrin; and it is possible that Isabelle still remains the only European woman to have done so.

The *fantasia* lasted for over two days, and for two more days Isabelle was almost deaf from the noise. But this potent combination of peace and adventure was what she had come to these southerly oases for. She wrote to Augustin in December: 'Finally the horizon has cleared for me and there are no signs of any stormy weather in the near future.' On 1 December she wrote in her diary: 'I've found domestic happiness, and far from diminishing, it seems to grow and grow each day.' However she did add: 'Only politics threatens it . . . But alas! *Allah alone knows what is hidden in the sky and the earth!* and no one can predict the future.'

DANGEROUS LIAISONS

Isabelle's intuition was right: politics, on a network which stretched back to Russia, and touched on some of the most sensitive current European issues, was about to catch up with her.

Just over a month after she had arrived in El Oued, on 7 September 1900, an anonymous letter had been sent from Paris to General Dechizelle, the general commanding the Constantine subdivision of the French army at Batna. Isabelle was never to know of the letter's existence. It ran as follows:

I, a Friend of the Army, have the honour to inform you of the following facts: towards the beginning of last July a young woman – illegitimate, and of very suspect morality – Isabelle Eberhardt, born in Switzerland but of Russian nationality, disguised as a man and calling herself Mahmoud Saadi, installed herself in El Oued in order to spy on the activities of the officers of the Arab Bureaux on behalf of the Paris journal *L'Aurore*, with the aim of aiding and abetting the relentless press campaign against the officers of the Arab Bureaux in particular and of the Army in general. The better to gather her information, she caught the eye of a *spahi* sergeant, one Slimane, who is, it seems, serving in the Arab Bureau in El Oued. This woman is dangerous from all points of view. She is in extremely bad odour with the authorities in Geneva, where she was born, as well as with the Russian authorities, since she has come under grave suspicion firstly of poisoning, in connection with the death of an old man called Alexander Trophimowsky, a friend of her mother's, who was her benefactor during his lifetime, and secondly, on the subject of 140,000 francs which were stolen from this poor old man, and which disappeared from the Villa where he lived in the suburbs of Geneva after his death some year and a half ago. This theft was committed at the expense of the legitimate heirs. Moreover this woman is the subject of secret enquiries by the Russian and Swiss authorities.

Sir [*mon Général*], the friend who is addressing this letter to you tells you all this so that you may know what kind of a woman you are dealing with. In any case, Sir, commission an enquiry on the subject of her activities in El Oued and you will find it edifying. This woman also has a profound hatred for France and would like nothing better than to excite France's Arab subjects against her. In order to gain the Muslims' trust, she passes herself off as a Muslim, which is not true. I remain, Sir, your obedient servant, a true Friend of the Army.

This letter was calculated to cause maximum possible alarm to the general on several counts. The position of the French army locally in the Saharan regions was, as we have seen, already sufficiently delicate for any incident – or any 'unhinged' person – to be able to detonate trouble for the French. But there was worse paranoia still in the upper echelons of the ruling Third Republic in France about the Algerian situation, for it had assumed a symbolic weight bearing little relation to reality.

If the colonial venture in North Africa had become something of a symbol of reclaimed virility for the Republic, it was even more so for the monarchists, as de Morès had shown. The monarchists still had grand designs for a Franco-Islamic pact in Algeria and Tunisia. However, in the four years since de Morès's death, the position of both the monarchists and the army had changed considerably, thanks to the Jewish issue.

Since they had 'old money', the monarchists could afford to be romantic about a natural alliance between peasants, aristocrats and Catholics against the 'decadent' influence of capitalism, as represented by the Republican government, the Jews, and the English. (This had led to the curious position of many monarchists calling themselves socialists, amongst them de Morès.) They resented Jewish influence not only abroad, but also at home, where they claimed that the Germans were conspiring to maintain their humiliating hold on France by infiltrating German Jews into high positions in the government and army. It was through the monarchists' machinations, channelled through their standard-bearer, the anti-semitic *Libre Parole*, that a wealthy Jewish officer called Alfred Dreyfus had been selected as a hapless victim and accused of treason, and the whole of the notorious Pandora's box of the Dreyfus case had been opened.

In the growing general anti-semitic climate of 1894, the army had not thought twice about sending Dreyfus off to Devil's Island. But pressure for a retrial had grown, and by 1900 it was clear to most of the public that the army and the War Ministry had made a scapegoat of him, and covered up the true traitors, a major and colonel from within the Ministry. The pending acquittal reflected badly on both the *Libre Parole* monarchists and the army. Partly through Zola's championing of his case, and partly through a public backlash, Dreyfus had become almost a national hero, and certainly a litmus test of a good citizen. The monarchists found themselves hamstrung. There was no longer any popular mileage to be made out of anti-semitism, and they were left with the empty shell of prejudice. If they were to salvage anything – in a climate where, in the last election of the century, they had only polled a feeble twelve per cent – the monarchists had to concentrate on the Islamic pact rather than the Jewish issue.

Islam and the Muslims therefore became a doubly sensitive issue to the Third Republic. They already had to deal with the 'rebellious' tribes they had taken over; now, by the end of the century, they had inflammatory monarchists prepared to fuel the fire of an Islamic revival for their own interests. For the writer of the anonymous letter to say that Isabelle would 'like nothing better than to excite France's Arab subjects against her' was carefully judged to induce near-hysteria in an army general.

The army's own position, weak since the Franco-Prussian war, had been further demoralized by their unedifying part in the Dreyfus affair, particularly since it had come hard on the heels of another débâcle, the 'central African Mission'. This army expedition, given an absent-minded go-ahead by the government, had tried to reach Lake Chad, and had come to shameful grief the summer before Isabelle arrived in El Oued. The officers in charge, Voulet and Chanoine, had become increasingly crazed with both the symbolism of their mission and the heat of the desert, and had ended up in a frenzy of butchery, even felling their own men. Reports of this humilating affair reached Paris in August 1899, in the midst of the Dreyfus trial, and left the army looking sheepish. *Le Temps* admitted the events 'make us blush', and France's 'civilizing mission' in Africa was beginning to look distinctly questionable even to its participants.

The army and the Republic needed to 'assimilate' Algeria effectively, but without any hint of swashbuckling. Their tactic, developed by Galliéni and his lieutenant Lyautey in the Far East and Madagascar, was called 'pacification'. The army would win over one by one the cooperation of the local sheikhs, by trade-offs, until, like trumped tricks, all the southern tribes would fall and the French would reach the Sudan. The monarchists found this approach mealy-mouthed and unworthy, and thought the government was corrupting the dignity and traditions of the natives by involving them in commerce on their terms. Where was the respect for the grandeur of Islamic beliefs, for their social hierarchies (dear to the monarchists' hearts), for their family traditions? French conquest should be *justified* by benevolent but firm protection, and by moral progress. Their ideas were by no means all wrong. But to the Republic and the army they were naive and grandiose: they had no idea of the 'realities' of the desert.

This broad picture of political intrigue and insecurity filtered right down to El Oued in a quite specific way. The army there had made one strong alliance, with the Tidjanya tribe, and its sheikh, Si El Aroussi. They cited his 'integrity' on the grounds that he was a proven ally of theirs. However, the traditional rivals of the Tidjanya in the area, the Qadrya, were treated with suspicion as 'untrustworthy'. Now to the monarchists *this* was the naive view. To them the Tidjanya had sold out to the French, had betrayed the Muslim cause, and were mere puppets. This was predictable, they felt, since one of the tenets of their sect was to cooperate fully with whoever was the ruling power. The Tidjanya was a recent, non-Sufi sect limited to Algeria. The Qadrya was the oldest and most revered brotherhood within Islam. The Qadryas accepted the French rule, since Allah had decreed that they should temporarily have power over them, and they cooperated to a limited extent, but without ever losing sight of their religious or social autonomy.

Isabelle was a Qadrya. The anonymous letter had been written a few weeks before her initiation, but Dechizelle would soon find out about it. It instantly reinforced the suspicions the letter-writer had been seeking to sow, putting her on a line of force which ran through El Hachemi, the late de Morès, the monarchists, anti-semitism, and a would-be Franco-Islamic alliance, and ranging her implicitly against the Tidjanya, the army and the Third Republic. She was a dangerous commodity for the army to have in El Oued; her 'domestic happiness' was indeed, as she had sensed, threatened by politics.

*

Dechizelle at once sent off a copy of the letter to General Larrivet in Batna, who sent it down the line to General Pujat in Touggourt, who sent it to Captain Cauvet, asking for his opinion of the newcomer and asking for her to be kept under 'strict but discreet surveillance'.

Cauvet, as we know, had already been doing this on his own

initiative since Isabelle's arrival. However, much as he personally disapproved of Isabelle's sexual conduct, seeing her as a European who had used disguise chiefly to gain Arab lovers, he did not dispute her right to indulge in it, and took an objective view of her general behaviour. He wrote laconically on 25 November 1900 that 'up until now nothing has surfaced that could justify the fears entertained on the army's behalf by the author of the letter', and he denied that she had any prejudice against the army. He cited her liaison with Slimène, but said it was 'discreet', and 'indeed only someone very much *au fait* with what is happening in the El Oued garrison would know of it.' As for the problems she was supposed to have had with the Russian and Swiss police, he felt they must be 'at the very least exaggerated', since she had come to El Oued perfectly openly, and since he had not been contacted by any foreign police. His own view, which 'is only a supposition', was that she had come partly on behalf of the de Morès family or its agents to try to gather information about the marquis's murder: 'her alacrity in going to Touggourt when the *naïb* of the Ouargla Qadrya passed through, her relations with Si El Hachemi and above all with his close associate, the schoolmaster Adbelkader ben Saïd seem to confirm this hypothesis.' If he were right, he felt it a good reason for letting her be, and letting her find out for herself the 'error' of El Hachemi's accusations that both the head of the Tidjanyas (Si El Aroussi) and the French residency in Tunis had been party to de Morès's murder.

As for her connections with *L'Aurore*, Cauvet astutely deduced that the writer was piqued by some recent articles it had run attacking Captain de Susbielle for his brutality and sadism. Cauvet felt they could not have been written by Isabelle, because 'such a well-informed person would never risk attacking officers of the Arab Bureaux when she is living within military territory'. Cauvet concluded that the letter smacked of some personal grudge against Isabelle. Although not in de Susbielle's handwriting, the letter (which was kept in the military files from now on) might well have originated with him, as Cauvet was delicately implying. Cauvet wrote that he personally would not even recommend vetting Isabelle's correspondence through the local post office, although the general might think otherwise.

General Pujat transmitted Cauvet's letter to Dechizelle, together with a covering letter of his own, drawing similar conclusions to Cauvet's. 'Officers who know [Mlle Eberhardt] consider her as a crank rather than as anyone dangerous,' he wrote, and he thought she was an 'unconscious accomplice' in El Hachemi's attempts to implicate the Tidjanya and the Tunisian residency in de Morès's murder. At this stage, neither Cauvet nor Pujat saw any need for a punitive approach, and took the letter with a pinch of salt, feeling it had all the hallmarks of a disappointed lover. General Dechizelle, however, was another matter. He was nearer to the Paris military paranoia, not the dyed-in-the-wool Saharians that Cauvet and Pujat were. He wrote a secret and confidential note on the bottom of Pujat's letter on 6 December, just as Isabelle was forecasting to Augustin clear, un-clouded skies ahead: 'In my estimation, Mlle Eberhardt should be expelled from El Oued and Touggourt. I also consider that Sergeant Slimane should be dismissed from El Oued and replaced.' The Acting Governor-General of Algeria, M. Célestin Jonnart, endorsed his rec-ommendation, on the condition that a formal 'personal report' was compiled on Mlle Eberhardt for the record. Cauvet undertook to supply the report.

4

WINTER

'This beginning of December is curiously reminiscent of the same time in that deadly year 1897,' Isabelle wrote in her diary, 'same weather, same violent wind, whipping the face furiously . . .' Her house had no glass in the windows, and she could not afford a fire, so the shutters were kept closed all the time, adding to the December gloom. She was beginning to find herself as poor as she had foreseen, and dreaded, for some time. She still hoped that the legacy might yield something, and was running up debts she thought it might cover. But the weather, her anxiety over money, and the lack of food were beginning to take their toll. The mere climate and diseases of the southern oases – there had been a virulent outbreak of typhus in Amiche only that autumn – swiftly eroded the health of newcomers, and by early January Isabelle was feeling too weak to write, and Slimène's health was poor. Financial worries were exacerbated by growing anxiety over their security. Their friend Abdelkader ben Saïd had suddenly been ordered out of El Oued by the authorities, six weeks after Cauvet had mentioned his name to Dechizelle, on the grounds that he 'owed money'. And an ominous message had come through from Captain Cauvet asking Isabelle to submit her papers to him. Slimène was frantic with apprehension, and went straight to Cauvet, asking him to say frankly why he wanted the papers. Cauvet – in good faith, trusting the outcome of his recommendations – promised him they had nothing to fear whilst he was in charge in El Oued. Isabelle herself was sure he liked them both 'very much'. Slimène tried to strengthen their position by writing off to his superiors in Biskra, requesting permission to marry. Isabelle wrote to Augustin, asking him to send her papers urgently.

Cauvet filed his report on Isabelle, without waiting for most of Augustin's papers to arrive. It nevertheless detailed Isabelle's background and movements since her mother's death with well-informed accuracy. On 14 January Pujat capitulated to his superior Dechizelle's opinion that Isabelle's presence in the area was provocative. But he felt that the best way to get her out of the Souf was by posting Slimène back to Batna.

Four days later Isabelle wrote a long, plaintive letter to Augustin. The fasting of the month of Ramadan was leaving her 'so thin that it hurts to lie on my bed', she wrote, she had lost all taste for food, and she had a recurrence of an 'old problem', cystitis. Slimène, too, was still weak. She was beginning to despair about her predicament. Surely, she begged Augustin, *something* was owed her from the legacy, and could he not send her an advance on it? For the moment, they had managed to pay off their debts, so that at least they had fended off the 'nightmare of people complaining to the Arab Bureau, which would be the most disastrous thing of all for us two'. In any case, she wrote, 'there can be no question of moving for me now, no possible change of existence,' particularly since she was so attached to the area 'although it's one of the most desolate and dismal that exists.' She adds, 'Do you remember the passage from [Loti's] *Roman d'un Spahi* which begins "He loved his Senegal, poor fellow"? Yes, I love my Sahara, with an obscure, mysterious, profound, inexplicable, but very real and indestructible love.' But Augustin did not reply at all, irked by his sister's miseries, which he saw as self-inflicted, and preoccupied with his own: Hélène and the baby were both ill, and he had had to take a menial job working for a shipping company to make ends meet.

On 23 January the bombshell fell: Isabelle and Slimène learnt 'by chance' that Slimène had been posted back to Batna. Isabelle saw it as another cruel and arbitrary blow from fate: 'Once again, everything is shattered and destroyed in my sad existence!' They may have suspected that the decision was linked to their liaison, but they had no idea yet that it was part of a concerted effort, from high up the chain of command, to manipulate Isabelle out of the country.

Isabelle decided to follow Slimène, although the prospect of living in the bleak garrison town of Batna was dismal to them both, especially since they would find it difficult to meet. Exile from what she now felt was her only home – El Oued – had a particularly bitter taste for Trophimowsky's daughter, born into exile. They also owed a hundred francs, which they could not repay, and now needed to find the money to set up in a new place. They spent an anguished night smoking *kef* and drinking, then Isabelle rode off the next morning to Amiche to beg

El Hachemi for help. Finding him surrounded by pilgrims preparing to go to Nefta, she could only 'mouth banalities' at him for an hour, before managing to arrange to meet with him on his own after sunset.

Isabelle returned to find Slimène in despair. They met later in the evening on the road to Amiche, and rode out to El Hachemi's lodge by the thin light of the crescent moon, with Slimène 'looking as if he might fall off his horse at any moment from anxiety'. For Slimène, with his family background, to sense that the authorities were against him was as worrying as the looming separation from Isabelle. El Hachemi received them by candlelight in his huge, arched room, and they sat in front of him on the large red rug spread on the sand floor. 'I felt that my poor Rouh' [beloved] was unable to speak at all, and I myself felt as if someone were strangling me. Then I saw tears coming into Rouh's eyes and wanted to weep too.' Isabelle managed to explain the situation to the sheikh, who listened sadly, absently. Slimène's eyes were beginning to cloud over with fever, and Isabelle, gesturing towards him, beseeched El Hachemi with her eyes. At last he rose and came back with 170 francs, saying 'God will pay the rest.' 'Then, without saying anything, without even taking the notes, Rouh' looked at them and laughed, with a crazed laugh which terrified the sheikh and me . . . a silent laugh, which was sadder to see than tears. I wondered if he wasn't going to lose his sanity completely.'

Two days later Isabelle and Slimène went to see Si El Hussein on the same mission. Slimène still looked like a walking ghost, giving Isabelle intimations of his fragile health. The sheikh wept at their story, and at the prospect of their departure. He had fond memories of his association with Isabelle, of their long talks and 'the mystery of common enterprises'. Whether these were Sufi mysteries or de Morès-related affairs hangs tantalizingly in the air.

*

The evening before Abdelkader had been sent back to Ouargla, he and Isabelle had made a journey out to the nearby lodge of Elbeyada, setting off at six in the evening and returning in darkness at nine o'clock. There had been a heavy silence around them as they had approached the first houses on the outskirts of El Oued, until some ferocious dogs in one of the yards heard them coming and set up a raucous yelping. At the same moment, in the west, a shooting star had appeared, then slipped slowly down towards the horizon, where it suddenly burst out into a brilliant blue flame, 'like a silent roman candle', lighting up the whole landscape with a magnesium glow. Abdelkader had said, 'It's the torch of the prophets of Islam. Sometimes it comes down like that towards those who are going to die.'

5

ASSASSINATION

Isabelle wanted to see the blue-eyed blond 'giant', Si Elimam, the third of the brother sheikhs, before she left, to 'try the same approach with him which had worked so well with his two brothers'. The sheikh was setting off on a pilgrimage to Nefta, and on 29 January 1901 Isabelle rode out with El Hachemi and other Qadryas to meet up with him on the road there. They reached the village of Béhima, some twelve miles north-east of El Oued, in the afternoon. As they approached the village across a desolate tomb-studded plain, they saw its grey walls and single enormous palm tree standing silhouetted against the horizon, with the sirocco whipping up the sand like shrouds around it. When they reached the village, they stopped off at the house of a local dignitary, Si Brahim ben Larbi, who was surrounded by a group of Qadryas. El Hachemi retired to a neighbouring room for the afternoon prayer, and Isabelle stayed in the main room, which had an ante-chamber giving on to the square outside. Surrounded by some five or six local Arab notables, Isabelle sat on a trunk between ben Larbi and a young businessman from Guémar, who wanted her to translate three business letters for them. As she pored over a particularly inscrutable letter, the hood of her burnous, pulled over her turban, prevented her from seeing a man approaching her, drawing an iron sabre from beneath his burnous. She felt a violent blow on her head, followed by two others on her arm.

I looked up and saw a badly dressed individual, obviously a stranger to the house, brandishing a weapon above my head which I took for a truncheon. I leapt up and ran to the opposite wall to try to seize El Hachemi's sword, which was hanging there. But the first blow had hit the crown of my head and dazed me, and I fell on to a trunk, aware of an acute pain in my left arm.

Two young Qadryas wrenched the sabre away from the assassin, but he escaped and ran off into the crowd, shouting, 'I'm going to find a gun to finish her off!' As one of the young men brought the bloody sabre over to show Isabelle, crying 'This is what the cur wounded you with!', Sheikh El Hachemi came running in. They told him the culprit's name: Abdallah Mohammed ben Lakhdar, a Tidjanya from Béhima. El Hachemi sent at once for the Tidjanya sheikh of Béhima. When he arrived, he refused at first to do anything, claiming that Abdallah was a descendant of the prophet. El Hachemi retorted that if the assassin was not apprehended, he would denounce the Tidjanya sheikh to the Arab Bureau as an accomplice. The sheikh gave in reluctantly, and Abdallah was found.

Meanwhile Isabelle had been laid on a mattress, bleeding profusely, but still conscious. When Abdallah was brought in, he feigned madness, until local people who knew him called his bluff, knowing him to be a 'reasonable, calm and sober' man. Then he took the line that God had sent him to kill Isabelle. Isabelle searched his face to see if she might have seen him before, but realized that he was unknown to her. She asked him why he had done such a thing, and he replied that although he did not know her, he had come to kill her, and if he were set free, he would try again. Isabelle asked what he had against her, and he answered, 'Nothing, you've never done anything to me, I don't know you, but I have to kill you.' El Hachemi asked if he knew Isabelle was a Muslim and he answered yes. El Hachemi made the sheikh from Béhima report the matter to the Arab Bureau, and demanded an officer to take away the attacker and charge him. Only then, rather late in the day one might feel, did he call for a doctor for Isabelle.

Six hours later an officer and a doctor arrived from El Oued. The doctor found that the wounds to Isabelle's head and wrist were negligible: by luck a washing-line had been strung up just above her head, which had deflected the full force of the blow, which would otherwise have killed her. But the sword had severed the bone and muscle in her left elbow, and she was judged too weak to make the journey back to the El Oued hospital that night. The next morning she was taken there on a stretcher, and laid out on an operating table. She watched her blood mark the black oilskin cloth she lay on, as she waited for the doctor to come and operate.

In the days that followed, she kept trying to lift her left arm with her right one, to find some position that eased the agony. Weakness and fever made her see her situation in the blackest light. Remembering it later in her diary, she lapsed into Russian, as she had with her mother's death, as if it was the language of grief: 'Despair took hold of me, and my chest was gripped with cold fear: "No, I shan't escape the assassin's hands." And everyone, everyone, even the doctor, seemed part of the plot.' There was a piece of paper pinned up on her wall with the hospital rules written on it, and suddenly, incongruously, it became overwhelmingly important to be able to read what it said. She squinted at it urgently, in a kind of referral of pain, but she could not make it out, and it depressed her out of all proportion. Thinking back to the assassination attempt, she remembered her first thoughts, as she seemed to be falling into a dark abyss: 'Death . . . no sorrow, no fear. "There is no other God but God and Mohammed is his prophet."' Her arm throbbed with pain, and 'childish' tears streamed down her face. 'Death itself does not frighten me . . . I am only frightened of suffering, of long and absurd suffering . . . and also of something dark, undefined, obscure, which seems to surround me, invisible, but which I alone can feel . . .'

*

On 30 January, General Dechizelle sent a telegram to General de la Roque in Constantine: 'Attempted assassination yesterday afternoon of Isabelle Eberhardt. Wounds do not endanger her life; assassin arrested; letter follows.' The letter which followed on 2 February described the attack. 'The motive for the crime seems to be religious fanaticism; the assassin was arrested immediately by the natives present; an enquiry follows.' On the same date the Governor-General of Algeria sent a confidential note to Dechizelle saying 'Mlle Eberhardt is affiliated, they say, to the Qadrya. One might even suppose that this affiliation, and her intimacy with the religious head of this sect, are not entirely alien to the act of fanaticism of which she has been a victim.' Two days later Dechizelle, in a note to General de la Roque, had escalated 'intimacy' into the less ambiguous 'intimate relationship': 'According to the commanding officer in Touggourt [Pujat], Mlle Eberhardt is an initiate of the Qadrya. Rumour has it that she has an intimate relationship with the *marabout* [i.e. the sheikh, Si El Hachemi]. The commanding officer considers that this relationship, which is said to have been going on for a year, could have unfortunate consequences.' In fact, Isabelle had only known El Hachemi since July, but such details did not matter: the French military version of events was thereafter pinned firmly to the two notions of 'intimate relationship' and 'religious fanaticism', which seemed to say it all, within their terms of reference. It was difficult for them to imagine that any young woman in frequent tête-à-têtes with a sheikh, whose sexual prowess had been so vaunted in the Western 'orientalist' vogue, could be engaged on any other than physical business. As a French colonel was to tell Isabelle later in the year, she had been the subject of 'd'innombrables convoitises' whilst she was in El Oued, amongst the female-starved military. Similarly, to an unlettered Arab, and particularly one belonging to a rival sect, El Hachemi's relationship with a free-acting foreigner could only have one implication. And so Isabelle was condemned on hearsay of something it is difficult to believe actually happened, knowing her frame of mind during this period, her reverential attitude towards the brother sheikhs, her love for Slimène, and his jealousy of their domestic life together. Similarly, 'religious fanaticism' was a convenient cloak under which many political manoeuvrings could be hidden, then as now.

The generals and the Governor-General continued to exchange memoranda on the affair during February. They also sent letters to the Russian consul, requesting permission to expel Isabelle, as a Russian subject, from Algeria.

6

CONVALESCENCE

During the four weeks Isabelle spent in the El Oued hospital, recovering from the shock, the wound to her arm, and the haemorrhage, her moods swung back and forth between feeling that the assassination had given her life its long-awaited meaning, and feeling that it had drained all meaning away. Signs from nature and the outside world, to which she had always been sensitive, now became portents, one way or the other.

Sitting up in her hospital bed on 3 February 1901, Isabelle saw a tiny black-collared coal tit, 'grey as the desert sand', perching outside her door on its spindly claws. As it hopped about and sang, as if for her, she suddenly fancied it was her mother's soul – the 'White Spirit', as she always called her in Russian in her diary – coming back in this 'gracious form' to offer her consolation. The bird and even the assassination attempt itself she felt were good omens, signs that 'destiny' was beckoning her in some inscrutable, but momentous, way. That she had been singled out for such an attack meant that 'holy' martyrdom for Islam might indeed be her lot, the cause 'for which I long to spill my hot blood one day', as she had written in Bône. The fact that the assassin was 'miraculously' prevented from killing her had, she felt, a sacramental significance, the outward sign of an inner grace. More prosaically, from an outsider's point of view, she was in need of an identity, and the attack seemed to confer a role on her – and indeed the role of victim was very much nearer to the truth of Isabelle's life than that of swashbuckling hero, in which she has been cast. Like Joan of Arc and Lawrence of Arabia, she was in search of a cause, waiting for the call, quietistically, curiously pass-ively. (It was a characteristic that made her singularly able to incarnate other people's fantasies, as well as her own.)

What Isabelle secretly believed was that the attack heralded the possibility that she was destined to be a *maraboute*, or mystic, although she was careful to write about it only obliquely, even in her diary. On

9 February, she wrote from the hospital, 'We are living in the thick of mystery and we both feel the powerful wing of the Unknown brushing us in the really miraculous events which favour us at each step.' The attack had been a 'favour' in practical terms alone, deferring their departure from El Oued, and rallying a certain amount of support around them. But on 3 February, when she had seen the bird, she had also seen Abdallah being transferred into a prison cell, and the sight confirmed her intuition of a special significance in the whole event:

Profound impression of pity for this man, the blind instrument of a destiny whose meaning he doesn't understand. Seeing that grey silhouette, standing with his head bowed, flanked by the two blue uniforms, I had perhaps the strangest and deepest impression I've ever had of *mystery*. Much as I search my heart for hatred towards this man, I can find none. Even less contempt. The feeling I have is curious: it seems to me that I'm close to an abyss, a mystery whose last word – or rather whose first word – hasn't yet been spoken, and which would contain the *whole meaning of my life*. As long as I don't know the key to this enigma – and shall I ever know it! God alone knows – I shall not know *who I am*, or what is the reason or point of my destiny, one of the most incredible there has been. Yet it seems to me that I'm not destined to disappear without having some understanding of the whole mystery which has surrounded my life, from its strange beginnings to the present day. 'Madness' sceptics will say, who like easy solutions and have no patience with mystery. They are wrong, because to see the chasms that life conceals and that three-quarters of the population don't even suspect exist cannot be treated as folly, in the same way that an artist's descriptions of sunset or of a stormy night would seem ridiculous to a man born blind . . . If the strangeness of my life were the result of *snobbery*, of a *pose*, yes, then people could say: 'She brought these events on herself', but no! No one has ever lived more from day to day and by chance than I have, and it is very much the events themselves, inexorably linked to one another, which have brought me to where I am and absolutely not me who has created them.

It is interesting to see Isabelle intuitively linking the 'mystery' she saw in her life to its 'strange beginnings'.

Slimène was the only person to whom she felt she could confide her feelings over her possible religious destiny, and it drew her even closer to him. But he was due to leave El Oued for Batna on 9 February, and when he did so she was left bereft again. She wrote him a letter which would reach him at his next stop, saying 'I must soon, soon get better so that I can leave and join you – you without whom I feel myself absolutely incapable of living.' She wrote in her diary, 'I'm alone, poor, ill . . . I cannot expect any favours or help from anyone . . . Mama is dead, and her *White Spirit* has left for good the earthly, depraved life that was so alien to her. The old man-philosopher has also disappeared into the shadows of the grave; the *frère-ami* is too far away.' She looked back with a heavy heart on her idyll with Slimène: 'We shall never sleep in each other's arms again, under the white vault of our small room, tightly entwined together, as if we had an obscure premonition of enemy forces in the shadows, seeking to separate us.'

There was, however, some unexpected consolation in the presence of the military doctor, Dr Léon Taste, to whom Isabelle could talk intimately about Slimène, if not about her religion (about which he was sceptical). Five years older than she was, and a recent arrival in Africa, he was intensely curious about what lay behind Isabelle's wayward persona. They had 'interminable conversations', first when she was in bed, then in his studiedly simply white room. Isabelle described him in some notes:

Sometimes gay, sometimes edgy and acerbic, an observer and thinker, a soul-searcher, amazed by me, brotherly, admiring and often aggressive, particularly over the religious question, Doctor Taste soon became my intimate *friend*. Taste was above all passionate, and often used to open his soul to me, telling me of his mistresses and his ideas, his adventures and his dreams, curious above all about sensual things, looking for rarefied sensations, strange experiences, sounding out my past, particularly my recent past, sensing perfectly well that of everything I could tell him, the only true and sincere things were what I had been taught, unconsciously, by the only person whom I've really loved and who loves me, because the miracle of love, I was going to say the sacrament of love, only works when love is *shared* and not one-sided. Taste tried to find out about the romantic and sensual side of Slimène's personality, in order to get to know mine better, having at first got me completely *wrong* on the first, through caste prejudice, or rather *rank* and most of all *race* prejudice, the Frenchman imagining the Arab as uniquely instinctive, animal, seeing nothing but the brute act in love-making, without any refinement or finer feelings, the officer seeing the subaltern typecast – and even this, he believes, is doing him a big favour – as the sentimental musketeer who goes straight from the dubious rose-water of turgid declarations (like Abdul–Aziz) to the animal act. His interest in the matter and his genuine admiration for me grew from the moment he appreciated things about Slimène that Slimène himself hardly knows: how *unusual* his quite exceptional nature is, unlike anyone else's, either in good things or bad.

Yet Taste's presence did not prevent her ricocheting moods, nor her *cafard*. On 19 February, going for a ride for the first time since the attack, she found even the surrounding landscape had lost its charm:

the Souf is empty, irrevocably empty ... As long as the aspects of nature surrounding us *respond* to our state of mind, we think we see a special beauty there, but from the moment our fleeting feelings change, everything evaporates and disappears ... How could I have believed in the reality of something mysterious which I thought I sensed in this country, and which was nothing else but the reflection of the sad mystery of my own soul. And I'm condemned to carry my whole unformulated sorrow, this whole world of thought along with me like this, through the countries and cities of the earth, without ever finding the Icaria of my dreams!

If it was only her internal world which conferred meaning on things, this, too, might one day be withdrawn. If the 'unfathomable *ennui noir* which sometimes takes hold of me became my *constant* and normal state,' she wrote, 'I should immediately find the strength to avoid that eventuality by a very calm and very coolly premeditated suicide.' 'Life in *itself* genuinely means nothing to me, and death exercises a strange fascination on my imagination.' However, the very next day her spirits revived: 'No! The Souf is not empty and the great Saharan sun is not extinguished ... It was my own heart, the other day, which was empty and sombre.' It amounted to the same thing: the external world was a reflection of her inner state. In the end she concluded, glumly, 'About myself and about the external world I *know nothing*, nothing ... That's perhaps the only truth.'

On the same day, 20 February, she wrote a letter to Slimène's brother Mouloud in Bône in a quite different vein. For the first and only time she made it clear that she thought the attempted assassination was a put-up job, and pointed a finger at the 'enemy forces in the shadows'.

Avoid like the pest the crowd of French politicians who are shamelessly playing with the Muslims and who have all abandoned us in the most cowardly way, after setting us up for the imbecilic role of scapegoat. Before accusing others of all kinds of crimes, they should not have landed innocents like Si Mohammed Taïb, Si Hachemi and others we know all too well in the mire – and Slimène, who has had to pay the price for the rest of us. The future will prove that we've been hideously abused. Understand that there's nothing dishonourable in turning your back on these people, since I'm not advising you to betray them or to seek the favours of other people. No ... stay the good Muslim and faithful Qadrya that you are, but do not continue to help people who, far from wishing well to the brotherhood and our sheikhs, are calculatedly pushing them to their ruin. Before I go, I'm going to tell all this to Sidi Hachemi and leave him the advice as a testament, probably for ever.

She adds: 'The advice I give you here is by the way exactly what I'm planning to do myself. I'm going to Batna and want nothing more to do with these people.'

She left hospital on Monday 25 February to make the journey to Batna and rejoin Slimène – 'too early', in Dechizelle's opinion, who wrote in a confidential army memorandum that she had not yet properly recovered. But Isabelle could not wait to see Slimène, 'this young soul who is mine, whom I love jealously and whom I shall try with all my powers to shape not in my image, which would be a sacrilege, but as I would want him to be, above all as *the White Spirit* would have wanted him to be! Oh, *She* would have loved him, certainly, with all her heart, for naive generosity and purity of mind were everything to her!' Her idealizing of her mother, and her need to please her even after her death, were symptomatic of the way the relationship with her parents had put her slightly out of kilter with reality; and her Pygmalionizing of Slimène suggested she was not going to be able to see him clearly, in realistic terms, either.

Meanwhile she left the Souf nostalgically, knowing she would miss not only the 'prestigious landscape where I should have liked to live and die', but even the hospital, and particularly her talks with Dr Taste, who 'had understood that underneath all the strangeness and incoherence of my life, there is a fundamental honesty and real sensibility and that there is still a gleam of intelligence in my mind'.

*

Three weeks afterwards, the Governor-General of Algeria wrote a confidential memorandum to General de la Roque in Constantine, enclosing the Russian consul's reply to his letter of the previous month. The consul wrote to Isabelle:

Based on the information you have been kind enough to communicate to me, I can see that her presence could only lead to difficult incidents, as you also feel, and in spite of her Russian passport, issued in Moscow, if you think it necessary I authorize you and even require you to rid the Southern regions of this young Russian woman who dresses in Arab costume, and to accompany her to the frontier, demanding her expulsion. That way we shall be safe for the future. In acting in this way towards this young woman, whom I consider as more than eccentric, one would even be doing her a favour, in view of the fanatical act of which she has just been a victim.

7

SLIMÈNE

Dr Taste accompanied Isabelle, who was riding her horse 'Souf', for some half dozen miles, as far as Tarzout. From there Isabelle and Lakhdar travelled on to spend the night at Si El Hussein's *zawiya* in Guémar. The next day the two joined up with a motley caravan of ten Arabs travelling up north. The journey to Batna took them seven days, travelling at first over different kinds of desert: soft sand dunes, with tufts of white broom here and there, hard, stony ground, on which Souf slipped so much that Isabelle had to dismount, and over the vast salt flats 'a horizon-less milky sea, studded with small white islands', with their baked, patchy blue-, white- and plum-coloured ground. By day they drank coffee or salty water from wells, and bought hares to cook and eat. By night, sleeping in simple rented rooms, they could hear the doleful song of toads in the desert silence. In spite of an initial headache and fever, Isabelle found her spirits rising towards the end of the journey. On 1 March she wrote:

Had a feeling of boundless energy and of boldness and daring towards fate all day . . . especially this evening. And yet, another thought haunts me and keeps me from sleeping, although I'm tired: up in Batna, a rapturous sensuality awaits me, and the very idea makes my heart contract in exhilaration. The day after tomorrow or in two days' time, I can give free reign to a desire which is driving me mad this evening, and relive those abandoned nights of El Oued . . . hold my master in my arms, close to my heart, which is heavy at the moment with too much unfulfilled love . . . This evening, I'm aware that I'm still young, that life is not at all black and empty and that hope is not lost.

Slimène rode down to meet her just south of Biskra, and as they were about to enter the city, they turned their horses round for a last look at the Sahara. 'It's our country,' Isabelle said, 'Insh' Allah! We shall soon come back and never leave it again.' After Biskra, Isabelle was sad to feel 'real earth' underfoot again, and see mountains on the horizon.

Although in their own minds they were already married, having had their Muslim marriage vows witnessed at some unspecified point by the brother sheikhs in El Oued, it was still imperative for them to marry under French law, or they would remain at the mercy of the authorities. However, within days of their arrival Slimène's colonel summoned him and told him he would never be allowed to marry Isabelle 'for reasons which he would not disclose'.

Isabelle wrote the news plaintively to Augustin in a letter of 7 March in which she listed their miseries: they still owed money to the sheikhs and were both having to exist on Slimène's pay, now only one franc a day; her arm had healed badly and would no longer bend at the elbow; and as an unmarried and impecunious woman she was finding it difficult to find rooms, in spite of the fact that in deference to Slimène and to her vulnerable position within military territory she was now wearing Arab women's clothes. She urged Augustin to write to the lawyers to ask why the sale of the Villa was still held up, two years after Trophimowsky's death, and threatened to follow in Vladimir's footsteps if Augustin did not help them. Augustin forwarded the documents she had asked for months before, but still without an accompanying letter, which further depressed her. Slimène now wrote to Augustin, entreating him to write to Isabelle as she was 'suffering inordinately from your silence of over a year'. He told Augustin that Isabelle and he were already married according to Muslim law, although not in the eyes of the 'hypocritical Europeans'. Augustin responded, and Isabelle blessed Slimène for having 'brought Augustin back to me'. That night she dreamt that 'Vava' came to her 'lavishing tenderness on Rouh', full of appreciation for him, his voice just as it used to be'. This dream-sanction sealed her love for Slimène, who was now 'my *only consolation*, my only joy in this world where I'm the most dispossessed of people and yet feel richer than anyone because I have a priceless treasure.' On 20 March 1901 she wrote, 'So: the great love of my life has been born, unconsciously and unprompted.'

Their meetings were increasingly difficult. Isabelle had found two small rooms to rent amongst *spahis* and their wives, who seemed to spend their time 'wandering from room to room and quarrelling'. With Slimène virtually confined to barracks, they could only snatch

an occasional meeting, often with a barrack fence between them. By
26 March Isabelle was in 'complete destitution. No food, no money,
no heating, nothing!' Although her poverty increased her vulnerability
to the 'enemy forces', she was protected, ironically, by her previous
extravagance. 'I was right to throw money out of the window two
years ago, here and in Biskra: my reputation for being wealthy is as
useful as a defence as the reality of wealth would be. Oh! if those
blackguards knew that I was in the direst poverty and that they could
ruin us with the least little vexation, they would certainly do so! I was
right to act as if the miserable kind of life I'm leading here was a result
of nonchalance and eccentricity: that way, my poverty doesn't show
up too much.'

She knew now that her every move was being watched, and even
knew the policeman who 'has undoubtedly been detailed by the enemy
to spy on me'. The policeman himself suggested that he thought a
certain person wanted her death, and that the assassin would go
unpunished. In her diaries, the person is only referred to as 'P . . .',
but it was almost certainly Pujat. If this was true, Isabelle wrote, 'it
will be my death sentence wherever I go in the south.' Pujat's words
had been reported back to her: 'This madwoman [*détraquée*] could
cause us a lot of trouble.' (In fact, if there had been secret orders for
her death from the French military, they had initiated from higher up
the chain of command, as we have seen.) Isabelle added in her diary,
'What crimes they must have on their conscience . . . Otherwise, why
don't they arrest me for example for espionage, or expel me?' She
spoke too soon. Less than a week later, the Governor-General of
Algeria was drafting a confidential memorandum:

There would be serious inconvenience to the colony in allowing this person
to continue living in Algeria. M. le Général commanding the Constantine
Division [Pujat] and the head of Police are both of the same opinion.
The Consul-General of Russia in Algiers, whom we consulted, approved
in advance any measure of expulsion which might be taken against Mlle
d'Eberhardt. In these circumstances I believe there can be no hesitation.

On 3 May an order for her expulsion from Algeria was conveyed to
her. It was in a sense the martyrdom which she had almost solicited
in her diary a few days before: 'To me the soul's supreme achievement
would be fanaticism leading *harmoniously*, that is through the path of
absolute sincerity, to martyrdom.' As with the assassination attempt, it

both devastated and strengthened her. 'I am like a beast being pitilessly hunted,' she wrote two days after the expulsion order, 'with the clear aim of killing it, of annihilating it . . . For years I've known with *certainty* that I would reach this degree of misery.' And yet 'I shall not weaken, for two things are intact in me: my religion and my pride, and I'm proud of suffering these uncommon blows, proud of having spilled my blood and having been persecuted for my faith.'

As soon as he heard of the order, Slimène wrote a letter to Augustin asking him to look after Isabelle for him for as long as was necessary:

You know that my wife knows how to live on very little, having unfortunately had the opportunity and the time to get used to it, above all here in Batna. So she will cost you virtually nothing. I am a poor soldier living from the pittance the State gives us in exchange for our health, our time, our work and above all our liberty. We did not get to know each other in good times. We two are already old comrades in misfortune.

Isabelle sold Souf and set off from Batna at four in the morning of 6 May. She stopped in Bône for three days with Koudja ben Abdallah, then, pursued by a 'persistent dark feeling' of the unreality of everything surrounding her, embarked on the *Berry* for Marseilles, travelling fourth-class under the guise of 'Pierre Mouchet, sailor', and reflecting ruefully that the sailor costume she had sported in more affluent days for amusement she now wore out of necessity. The second night on board there was a thunderous storm. Tossed about on enormous waves, and buffeted by a wind howling 'like the voice of death', the small, frail boat seemed to mirror her own predicament, Isabelle felt, as she spent a cold night in semi-delirium.

In Marseilles the next afternoon, she took the tram up the steep Canebière hill behind the port, then trudged the rest of the way up to Augustin's house, carrying her bundle of possessions. She was touched to see the baby, 'poor little Hélène, who, I realize with some tenderness and anxiety, looks so much like me.' Yet Augustin's marriage to his 'good lady' had distanced him further, and Isabelle wondered how much of the previous affinity she had felt with him had existed only in her imagination. Now more than ever she cleaved to Slimène in her mind, 'the only being whom I've ever managed to live with in harmony, and with whom I feel safe'.

❧ 8 ❧

EXILE

On 18 April 1901, whilst she was still in Batna, Isabelle had taken the bold step of writing directly to the Colonial Minister in Paris, thus bypassing the military, and appealing for his support for her marriage. Her tactic paid off. When she arrived in Marseilles, his hand-written reply awaited her:

I read your account with the greatest attention. As far as I am concerned, I am absolutely certain that your private conduct is entirely above suspicion and I am inclined to think that the real motive for the replies which you have received lies in the purely political arena. The long time it has taken to reach the final decision regarding your marriage, and the hesitations which seem to have preceded it, confirm this view. In the circumstances the military authorities, who are the sole judges, are also the only people responsible, and it is not possible for me to intervene officially, but I am convinced that your integrity and probity, and the sincerity of your feelings, will triumph in the end. Have courage in these difficult circumstances.

This was a highly encouraging letter to receive, both personally and politically, and it put new spirit into Isabelle.

Her exile in Marseilles was a good opportunity to collect her thoughts about the events of the past few months and write them down, and the strains and tedium within Augustin's small household were, as so often, an added incentive for Isabelle to write. She wrote private notes, about her conversations with Dr Taste for example, as well as travel notes and essays which she intended for publication. Two of the essays, 'Printemps au désert' and 'Maghreb', were published a few months later in Algeria, and another long essay 'Sahara' was written in Russian, with the intention of getting it published in Russia through her friend Reppmann.

On 15 May Reppmann wrote to her, sympathizing with her over the events of the past months: 'Filonov would have said "Suffering ennobles man: in the economics of good and evil it is a plus for good".

One may take consolation from that.' Isabelle did, echoing the thought in her diary a few days later: 'Suffering is good, because it *ennobles*.' All the same Reppmann added, ruefully, 'Yes, that's all very well, but what about the one who suffers?'

Shortly afterwards, on 23 May, Isabelle wrote to Slimène that destiny seemed to be favouring them after all. She had met up with an old *tirailleur* friend of hers, Abdel Aziz Agréby, who not only owed her a useful amount of money, but was also posted in Tunis and might be able to secure a permutation for Slimène from Batna to Tunis. She drafted a glowing account of Slimène's army career for Slimène to copy out and send off to Agréby. She had been feeling contrite in Batna about her previous 'often harsh and unfair' treatment of Slimène, when she had sometimes got to the point of hitting him, 'ashamed of myself because he didn't defend himself and smiled at my blind anger'. Now, having seen his love and support for her in hard times, she was chastened. She resolved, she told him in her letter, to be 'a submissive and obedient companion to you from now on', and begged him to send a photograph of himself that she could show Augustin and Hélène.

On 25 May a policeman arrived at the door with unexpected news: Isabelle was summonsed to appear in court in Constantine at 6 a.m. on 18 June. Abdallah ben Mohammed was after all to be tried for her attempted murder. In some ways this was excellent news for Isabelle: it seemed that the authorities were not after all colluding in covering up the affair, and that she would have the opportunity to vindicate her conduct and plead her case for being allowed to return to Maghreb. It might have meant that the Colonial Minister himself had had a hand in ordering the trial. In addition, she knew that the publicity, if she handled it well, might strengthen her position – and the prospect of the trial held the promise of a liberating drama. However, she had no interest in taking revenge on Abdallah, and feared that the authorities might be staging a show trial for their own motives, using Abdallah as a scapegoat.

Although to the outside world her approach to the trial was collected and politic, her anxiety came out in a feminine enough way, in a flurry of fretting about what to wear. Of course, that in itself was a political issue for her. She knew that her male Arab dress had provoked much of the antagonism towards her, but complained to Slimène that she could not possibly afford European clothes. He wrote that he would buy her some. She replied, very unsubmissively:

You absolutely *must not buy European clothes, because you've no idea how much it costs and I formally forbid* you to contract a centime of debts. You know me and know very well that I'm prepared to obey you in everything, except when you're talking nonsense. One can tell you know nothing of what it *costs* to dress *not well*, but at least passably as a Frenchwoman: a wig (this costs, for a shaved head like mine, some 15 to 20 francs, because a simple plait won't do), a hat, underwear, corset, petticoats, skirts, stockings, shoes, gloves and so on. All I will concede is to stop *dressing as an Arab*, which is anyway the only thing which would prejudice the authorities against me. I shall therefore dress *as a European* [man], now that I'm properly equipped. I swear to you, [she wrote, protesting just a little too much] *it's not for the pleasure of dressing up as a man*, but because it's *impossible* for me to do otherwise. At court-martial, just like with de Susbielle in Touggourt, they always said to me: 'We quite understand that you wish to wear men's clothes, but why don't you dress as a European?' Anyway, that's all I have to say to you on the subject. It's impossible for me to do otherwise.

Unconvincingly, in view of her opinion of Augustin and his wife, she now gave them the final word: 'European men's dress is what suits me best, so much so that my brother and his wife prefer this on me to any other costume when I'm there. I don't care if I dress as a *workman*, but to wear ill-fitting, cheap and ridiculous women's clothes, no, never . . . I'm too proud for that and I hope you won't insist on such shame for me, in a place where I pass for a millionaire, more or less.' (Her haughtiness when defending a sensitive area was very like her mother's.) Now thoroughly on her high horse, she ended, 'Now what about your photograph, you pig?'

In public, she now took an intelligent initiative. Aware that the French authorities might have ulterior motives in staging the trial, she wanted to pre-empt them playing it their way, as an indictment of Muslim 'fanaticism', which they saw as a dangerous focus for opposition to French rule.

The French had no particular policy on the issue except to assume that any right-minded Muslim would eventually convert to Christianity as the next step in 'civilization'. There had been several recent cases of Muslims rebelling bloodily against the French presence, notably in Marguerritte, where scores of French inhabitants had been massacred. (Isabelle herself had been of course involved in a forerunner of these skirmishes when she first arrived in Bône.) Abdallah's trial could be a convenient occasion to make a scapegoat of someone who had certainly set himself up for the role. Isabelle wanted to make her position clear in advance as someone who was herself a Muslim, and therefore could not be the target of anti-Christian feelings. She also wanted to prevent Abdallah's attack from being presented as an isolated act of fanaticism, and to imply clearly, yet if possible unprovocatively, that she felt he had been hired by others for the purpose. It was a delicate path to tread. The fact that the whole crime had gone unreported in the Algerian newspapers suggested an initial confusion in the authorities' minds over what line to take over the matter, and a desire to brush over its sensitive political implications.

Suspecting that even in court she might still not be able to present her case as she would wish, she now wrote an open letter to the Algiers-based *Dépêche Algérienne*, which they published on 6 June. Having described the incident at Béhima, she wrote:

I was most surprised to note that no Algerian paper breathed a word of this affair, which was nevertheless one of the strangest and most mysterious which an Algerian tribunal has had to judge. I suppose that the press has simply not received any details of it. In the interests purely of truth and justice, I consider it important to tell the public the details of this case before it comes to be judged. I should be most grateful if you would therefore publish the present letter under my signature. I assume full and complete responsibility for it . . . During the investigation of the case against Abdallah ben Mohammed the officers charged with the case frequently expressed their surprise at my declarations of being not only a Muslim but also an initiate of the Qadrya sect, and at seeing me wearing Arab costume, sometimes masculine and sometimes feminine, according to the needs of my essentially wandering life. In order that I should not be thought of as someone affecting Islamism for show, or assuming a religious tag for some ulterior motive, I should like to make it clear that I have never been Christian, that I am not baptised, and although I am a Russian subject, I have been a Muslim for a very long time. My mother, who belonged to the Russian aristocracy, died in Bône in 1897, after becoming a Muslim, and was buried in an Arab cemetery there. I therefore have no reason to convert to Islam, nor to be play-acting in any way – something which my fellow-believers in Algeria have understood perfectly, to the extent that sheikh Si Mohammed El Hussein, brother of Si Mohammed Taïeb, *naïb* of the Ouargla brotherhood, agreed without reservation to initiate me into the sect. I have been anxious to point all this out at the start for the reason I gave above, but also so that Abdallah's attack is not presented as the result of a fanatical hatred against everything Christian, because I am not a Christian and all the *souafas* know it, Abdallah included!

Isabelle then went into an account of the assassination attempt, praising on the way Taste's 'devoted and intelligent care'. She gives credit to Cauvet and other supporters in El Oued: 'In spite of the fact that on my first trip I had some difficulties with the Arab Bureau in Touggourt, which controls the El Oued Bureau – troubles which were provoked purely by the distrust of the Bureau – the Head of the El Oued Annexe and his officers, along with those of the garrison and the military doctor, were eminently kind to me and I should like to express publicly my gratitude to them.'

She then came to the nub of her case: a few days before she left El Oued, she wrote, she had heard rumours amongst the local people that Abdallah, who had previously been crippled by debt, had gone to the main Tidjanya centre of Guémar, and returned not only able to pay off his debts, but also able to buy a palm grove:

At about the same time Abdallah's father went to Sidi Hachemi's *zawiya* and told him in front of witnesses that his son had been paid to attack me, but, since he did not know himself who the instigators were, he wanted permission to see his son in front of someone legally qualified in order to get him to make a full confession. The *marabout* advised him to go to the Arab Bureau. The old man asked to speak to me, through one of my servants, and, telling me 'This crime did not start with us', added that he wanted to see his son in order to persuade him to make a full confession . . . First of all it is clear that Abdallah did not want to kill me out of hatred towards Christians, but because he was pushed into it by others, and then it is clear that his crime was premeditated. I told the investigation that I attributed this criminal attack mainly to the hatred of the Tidjanya for the Qadrya, and that I assumed that it was the Tidjanya *kaba* or *khouans* who had got together to get rid of me, since they saw me welcomed by the enemy . . . I hope that the court martial in Constantine will not be content purely and simply to convict and sentence Abdallah ben Mohammed, but will try to throw light on this nebulous affair. To me Abdallah was only an instrument in other hands and his conviction will not satisfy me, nor, for that matter, anyone who cares for truth and justice. It is not Abdallah whom I would like to see in the dock but rather those who incited him, that is, the real culprits, whoever they may be.

While avoiding actual mention of the French, Isabelle had squarely thrown down the gauntlet.

When the *Dépêche* published the long letter in full, Isabelle wrote a further letter the next day, 7 June, thanking them for their 'well-known impartiality'. However, she was at pains to disclaim the 'honour' they had accorded her by suggesting that she had a certain religious influence amongst the native inhabitants of the Touggourt area: 'I have never played nor sought to play any political or religious role, considering myself entirely unqualified both in terms of rights or necessary aptitude to involve myself with such serious and complicated matters as the religious issues in a country of this sort.' She recounted how, when she arrived in Touggourt in 1899, she had had to defend herself against accusations of being an English Methodist missionary, all of which designations she viewed with alarm. 'I explained that I abhorred all kinds of proselytism and above all hypocrisy, which is the feature of the English character, as unappealing to us Russians as it is to the French.' She got in a dig at de Susbielle, 'a man of an odd turn of mind', and praised Cauvet, 'a man of high intellect and immensely conscientious'. Having had the opportunity to observe her conduct over six months, she wrote with light irony, Cauvet had found there was 'nothing to object to, except eccentricity, and a style of life which was bizarre for a girl, but very inoffensive . . . and he did not consider that my preference for a burnous rather than a skirt and for dunes rather than the domestic hearth could prove a danger to public security in the Annexe.' If she was held in a certain amount of affection in the area, she wrote, it was because she had helped out whenever her meagre medical knowledge allowed her to, in cases of conjunctivitis and other diseases common to the area. 'I have tried to do some good in the area I found myself in . . . it's the only role I've ever played in El Oued.'

At pains to disabuse anyone of the accusation which had plagued her since her arrival in Algeria, that she was a spy bent on anti-French subversion, she wrote:

As for me, all I want is to have a good horse, as a faithful and dumb companion to a solitary and contemplative life, and a few servants barely more complicated than my mount, and to live in peace, as far away as possible from the agitation of civilized life, where I feel myself *de trop*, and which in my humble opinion is sterile. How can it harm anyone, if I prefer the undulating, misty horizon of the grey dunes to that of the boulevard? No, Monsieur le Directeur, I am not a politician, I am not the agent of any particular party, because to me they are all equally wrong to conduct themselves the way they do. I am only an eccentric [*une originale*], a dreamer who wants to live a free and nomadic life far away from the civilized world in order to try to say afterwards what she has seen and perhaps to communicate to some people the charm, the melancholy and the thrill which I have felt in the face of the sad splendours of the Sahara . . . That's all.

She defended herself against the exaggerated fantasies which had attached to her, saying finally: 'It's true that the summer of 1899 was excessively hot in the Sahara and that mirages distort things greatly, explaining all kinds of hallucinations!' The letter, written in patent good faith, is a simple, eloquent statement of her position. It, too, was published in full, and she judged rightly that the publicity would protect her from too capricious action by the authorities. As she wrote to Slimène, 'One must use the weapons one finds in one's path.'

9

TRIAL

She left Marseilles at noon on 13 June 1901 on the *Félix-Touache*, bound for Philippeville. It was a bright, clear day and she was full of the joy she always felt on returning to Africa. Dressed in her Marseilles clothes of rough blue linen trousers, a jacket and a cap, she travelled fourth-class once again, enjoying being amongst the people whose lives interested her. 'It's a great mistake to think that you can study the lives and habits of ordinary people without becoming part of their way of life,' she wrote in a short story, 'Amara le forçat', based on a conversation she struck up during the crossing. Amara was a thin, badly clothed young Arab with a hunted look, who, hearing her speaking Arabic, had cautiously begun to talk to her. He told her he had just come out of prison for killing a man, and later, as they both spent a sleepless night on deck, she asked him his story. His victim, he said, had not only stolen his mare – his pride and joy – but had killed the horse when he risked being found out. Amara could not see that his own subsequent act of revenge was in any way wrong: 'If you don't get revenge, you suffocate, you suffer.' Isabelle, who, unknown to him, was on her way to confront her own would-be murderer, advised him not to be vengeful: '"Live in peace like your ancestors," I told him. "You will have peace of mind. Leave vengeance to God."'

They arrived in Philippeville, on the 'blessed coast of this African homeland', in the evening, the high, black silhouette of the town's hill studded with yellow gaslights. She travelled with Amara as far as Constantine, where she found her way through the tortuous streets to the address of a friend's brother, Mohammed ben Chakar. She changed into her Arab clothes, 'which put me at ease', and the following day Chakar and his wife took her to see the nearby Rhummel gorges. Fleas, and her anxiety at not having heard from Slimène, gave her a bad night, but on 16 June she finally met him at the station. In the evening they had supper with ben Chakar, with Slimène dressed in civilian Arab clothes and Isabelle in Moorish woman's costume. Then followed 'a night of joy, tenderness and peace'. On 17 June meeting three Souafa witnesses at the station, she was overwhelmed by their warm, tearful welcome, and the potent atmosphere of the south they brought with them. Later she met Si El Hachemi on the quayside: 'The dear sheikh smiled to see me,' Isabelle wrote in her diary. They prepared themselves for an early appearance in court next day.

Isabelle had finally decided to appear at the court in female native dress, which proved opportune in view of the fact that Abdallah's defence was to make much play of her cross-dressing. Isabelle arrived early, and sat alone in the witness room. Soon after six p.m. spectators, witnesses and journalists started to arrive, staring at Isabelle as they went past. She saw Abdallah being taken past, handcuffed between two escorting *zouaves*. At seven she was called into court. She did not feel too nervous, she recalled later. Seeing Si Hachemi sitting resplendent in his green and white ceremonial robes in front of the double bench of other witnesses, she went and sat on the chair next to him. Lieutenant-Colonel Janin, presiding, declared the hearing open, and Abdallah ben Mohammed was brought in, looking pale. Amongst those gathered there in the packed court were Mohammed ben Abderrahmane, the Tidjanya sheikh of Béhima – whom Isabelle called 'the traitor' – in his red burnous, General Laborie de Labattut from Constantine and several of his officers and their wives, Dr Taste, and reporters from the *Dépêche Algérienne*. The military tribunal sat 'stiffly and inscrutably' in their uniforms and decorations.

The witnesses, including Isabelle, were then led out, to be brought back one by one in due course. First Abdallah was interrogated in her absence. He claimed that he knew he was striking a Muslim and not a European when he had aimed his blows, but that he done it 'under divine inspiration', urged on by an angel of God to kill 'Mademoiselle Eberhardt, who wore masculine dress, which is contrary to our customs' and who was 'creating disorder in the Muslim religion'. The angel had advised him of her imminent passage through his home village of Béhima, accompanied by sheikh Si Mohammed El Hachemi. For the five days before their arrival, he had fasted and abstained from seeing his wife and children. On the sixth, still urged on by the voice of the angel, he 'took a sabre and committed the crime' – the sabre being the only legitimate weapon for a Muslim bent on sacred vengeance. He claimed that at the time he would have gone ahead with his act even if she had been protected by cannons, but that now he felt differently, and wanted to beg her forgiveness. Cross-questioning him, Abdallah's defence lawyer, Maître Laffont – no doubt eliciting prepared answers from his client – asked what kind of trouble Mademoiselle Eberhardt had provoked, and Abdallah reiterated that she dressed as a man. Then once more he brought out an unexpected weapon, adding, 'I also suspected her of something else: I thought she was sheikh Si El Hachemi's mistress.' There were murmurs in the courtroom. Maître Laffont now took the floor, trying to beam the spotlight of accusation around on Isabelle. He stressed firstly that Abdallah knew he was attacking a Muslim when he struck (he knew that in the current climate, in the aftermath of Marguerritte, the court would be severe on any deliberate attack on a Christian); secondly that Isabelle's cross-dressing was improper and provocative; and thirdly that Isabelle had intimate relations with sheikh El Hachemi. If she was really so charitable and so keen on helping the poor, he suggested, why was she not 'at the bedside of the sick, in their homes' instead of consorting with a '*marabout* in a multi-coloured burnous, a magnificent living tableau but hardly suitable as a close companion'? He aimed his barbs deftly at Isabelle's most vulnerable point in the public eye: her suspicious lack of conventional womanly ways. Isabelle wrote in her diary that 'the defence lawyer exasperated me.'

Isabelle was then called to give her own account of the crime, but the President, Janin, was more interested in taking up Laffont's theme: 'Tell us if the wearing of masculine dress by a woman is considered an insult to the Muslim religion?' Isabelle replied that it was considered merely inappropriate. The lieutenant-colonel asked her why she wore it in this case and she replied that it was more practical for riding.

The Government Commissioner, M. Martin, prosecuting, diverted the enquiry from this tack, which was a red herring as far as the authorities were concerned, and focused instead on the political aspects of the trial. This was where the government stood to make some capital, by trying to deter future 'religious fanaticism', harmful to the stability of the colony, with a heavy sentence. He deplored the numerous recent cases of such 'fanaticism', especially in the Souf, and summed up: 'Criminals must not imagine that our respect for all religions extends to indulging them if they claim that God commanded them to commit a crime.' On these grounds, the Commissioner de-manded the death penalty. The court retired and returned with a verdict of guilty of attempted premeditated murder, recommending that the sentence be commuted to hard labour for life in view of mitigating circumstances. There was a stir in the court at the severity of the sentence. General de Labattut came over to Isabelle and told her, 'You can't say that French justice hasn't thoroughly avenged you!' However, during the adjournment in the middle of the trial Isabelle had been presented with an unexpected ultimatum: she was served with another, formal, expulsion order which banned her from the whole of Algeria, including both military and civil territories. It was, they said, a measure taken for her own safety.

Before she left to return to Marseilles, which she had thought she had left for good, she wrote out a formal declaration, concerned far more with the injustice she felt had been done to Abdallah than with her own. She wrote:

I am firmly convinced, and always will be, that Abdallah was the instrument of people who had an interest – real or imagined – in getting rid of me . . . I think that today's verdict was excessively severe, and I should like to make it plain that I deplore this severity. Abdallah has a wife and children. I am a woman and can only grieve with all my heart for his widow and her orphans. As for Abdallah himself, I feel only the deepest pity for him.

She defended herself again against charges of being anti-French: 'I have never participated in nor been aware of any anti-French action, either in the Sahara or in the Tell . . . I have always spoken well of France to the native people, wherever I have been. It is my adopted country.'

Isabelle then wrote a personal letter to Abdallah, and immediately lodged an appeal on his behalf. As a result his sentence was commuted to ten years' prison, and even Maître Laffont was moved to write appreciatively to her. Indeed, immediately after the verdict was announced, he had volunteered to act for her in appealing against the expulsion order. The trial had created goodwill for her in another way, too, largely as a result of her letters to the *Dépêche Algérienne*. Several journalists, including one called Victor Barrucand, who was a well-known writer both in Paris and Algeria, and who edited the paper *Les Nouvelles* in Algiers, now wrote to the press protesting about Isabelle's expulsion. Barrucand's view in particular was that it would have been far more intelligent of the authorities to use Isabelle's remarkable talents to benefit French policy, rather than alienating her from it. She was beginning to have a constituency amongst people whose opinions mattered in her elected country.

Meanwhile she left believing that, since the order was for her own safety, it would be only a matter of days before it was revoked, since she had undertaken never to return to southern Algeria, which was on the face of it the main bone of contention.

A week after the trial the same Maître Laffont managed to get a complete acquittal for three Arabs who had murdered a Touggourt shopkeeper, and then proceeded to rob him. Abdallah's had been very much of a show trial.

10

MARSEILLES

Isabelle left Constantine early in the morning of 20 June, en route once again for Marseilles. This time, however, she was accompanied by Slimène, who had been given a few days' leave of absence – although they had still not been given permission to marry.

Slimène's first meeting with his prospective in-laws passed unrecorded, but was evidently not promising. Hélène, 'entirely thoughtless and unaware', except over petty material things, as Isabelle recorded bitterly, may have been too threatened socially to accept the dark young Arab sergeant as part of the family, and she and Augustin perhaps also feared being landed with the responsibility for this eccentric and trouble-prone pair when their own affairs were so hand-to-mouth. In dismay, Isabelle saw Slimène off on 4 July from the quayside of La Joliette, as he set off for Philippeville on the *Touareg*: 'Throughout the whole operation my eyes did not leave Zuizou [a pet name for him].'

With his departure, she was left alone with her increasingly ill-disposed relatives, and began to retrench into the private world of her thoughts. Marseilles was like Geneva had been to her, a settled, dreary prison to her essentially nomadic nature: she reflected that 'the *fundamental* need of my nature is *variety* of scenery ... great difficulties and crises of despair recharge my energy and calm my nerves ... *Monotony* and *mediocrity* of settings and atmospheres, these are the enemies.'

Four days after Slimène had left, she noted in her diary how the trial had revived her interest in literature, and in her own writing. 'Before, I had to wait sometimes for months for the right moods to write in. Now, I can write more or less whenever I want. I think I have arrived at the flowering of that gestation which I have sensed for so long.' The trial had also strengthened her morally: 'For me life acquired a meaning from the moment I understood that our passage down here is a gradual process of human development towards another life: it follows naturally that there is an imperative to strive for moral and intellectual perfection – which would be inappropriate, because useless, without an after-life.' Her intellectual development she would pursue by a programme of reading – including Paul Bourget's *Essais de psychologie contemporaine*, and a re-reading of the Goncourt diaries – and writing: that evening (8 July 1901) she sent off her stories 'Printemps au désert' and 'El Maghreb' to Les *Nouvelles*.

But the other question which preoccupies me is of a quite different kind, and one which I could only begin to formulate to Slimène, who is *the only person who would understand* and acknowledge it, and that is the *maraboutic question* – the thought that spontaneously came to my mind the evening when Abdallah was transferred from the civil prison to his cell. And, no doubt with a subconscious intuition springing from our great spiritual affinity, Slimène thought of it too! . . . It seems to me that with will power, it would be easy for me to reach the mysterious goal which would entrance me and open up unpredictable horizons . . . [In Arabic] *Lead us in the straight and narrow path* and I think that, for me, this is the path. God has sown some fertile seeds in my soul: extreme disinterestedness towards all things associated with this world, faith, and an infinite love and concern for everything that suffers. This forgiveness of evil springs from an unlimited devotion to the Islamic cause, the most beautiful of all, because it is the cause of truth . . . Oh, the long hours I used to spend in the shade of the woods, the sleepless nights spent looking at the extraordinary world of the stars . . . wasn't all that meant to be the direct path to religious mysticism?

The mystical experience is notoriously difficult to convey in words, and Isabelle realized that she was laying herself open to ridicule if she mentioned outside of the pages of her diary, or to anyone other than Slimène, her sense that she might have a mystical, even a martyr's, vocation. 'If a scholar or a psychologist or a writer read these words, they would be sure to exclaim "She's one step away from madness!" Well, if ever the flame of intelligence has burned in me, it is now, and I feel that it is only the *dawn* of a *new life*.' She felt grateful to Abdallah for unwittingly having effected this change, and felt sure that, being a devout Muslim, he would have gladly embraced his fate as a chosen instrument of God:

Who knows if his martyrdom will not redeem thousands of other souls, and not just mine, which would be negligible! . . . Abdallah's work, and the seeds he has sown in me, have borne fruit and one day or another will emerge from the place where, for the moment, they remain hidden from all eyes. That is my secret, the one I must not tell, and which I shall never confide to anyone, except to the one who guessed it himself and who never desecrates the sanctuary of my deepest feelings with mockery or laughter . . . for he too is *predestined*.

Isabelle's sense of call, embracing Slimène too, was not purely mystical, but linked in her mind to the wider Muslim cause. The humiliations she and Slimène had suffered in El Oued and Batna, and perhaps also in Marseilles, had made her identify more keenly with the colonized Arabs, and made her determined, simply, to get her own back. Brooding on these matters, she wrote to Slimène:

In order to take a devastating revenge, and one worthy of us both, on all those who have insulted and persecuted us, I want you to become an officer in the very Arab Bureau to which we owe all our misery. The best way – the least expensive and the easiest way – is for you to take the interpreter exams, and we shall work on them so that you will be able to take them when you leave the army. What a triumph! Think of the impotent rage of all the rabble who have something against us! But that's not enough for me: I want you to prove, from your position amongst the officers, that as an Arab and a good Muslim, you are more educated than they are. Nowadays, in order to shine in the world, you don't need to be a scholar: you just need to know about literature. For that reason, whilst you are preparing for your exams you must read a lot of books which we shall get from the library. And in addition I shall try to teach you the basics of my language, Russian. Remember that in working for the goal that I'm setting up here you will be working for all your fellow Arabs, for all our fellow Muslims: you will give those arabophobic and disparaging French *messieurs* the example of an Arab who, starting off as a second-class *spahi*, will have reached an enviable and respected rank through his intelligence and his work. If there were many Arabs like that in Algeria, the French would be obliged to change their opinion in respect of the 'wogs'. This is the way to serve Islam and the Arab cause, not by fomenting useless and bloody revolts which only serve as a weapon against everything Arab, and discourage rightminded Frenchmen who wish our brothers well – for example, in the deplorable case of Marguerritte. 'It's a lot of hard work', you will say . . . but aren't we in this world to work at the perfecting of our souls, with a view to unknown destinies which God is reserving for us elsewhere? You will perhaps object – and I know this is true – that you are free from vanity and have no wish to shine in men's eyes [but] I repeat, each of us has a sacred duty in this world. Yours, mine, that of every Muslim is to work bravely, indefatigably, to *rehabilitate* ourselves in the eyes of the Occident, to assert ourselves by our intelligence and our knowledge. The Muslim who could educate himself and be someone in the public life of his country and does not do so is, for me, a *deserter* and a *traitor*. We are the servants of Djilani and we owe ourselves to him. So let's do everything possible to serve him as he deserves: we have a huge power which no one, except God, can vanquish: *we are two*, with just one soul, just one heart, just one will.

Isabelle wanted Slimène to embark on a programme of reading running parallel with her own, staring with Zola's *Le Travail*, which he was to read 'page by page and attentively to see how unions and disinterested work can one day change the face of the world'. Part of Isabelle's chivvying of Slimène was carried over from her former attitude towards Augustin but part was a lurking apprehension that Slimène's moral fibre needed bracing. He was far less intense than she was by nature, and therefore less pressing about their relationship. He was not keeping to his promise of writing to her three times a week, and by 23 July she was suspecting that he had gone back to his old habit of drinking, since she had received a suspiciously incoherent letter from him. (Just as the French army had brought brothels to the areas they administered, so they brought drink, and the native *spahis* like Slimène took a correspondingly relaxed view of its use, in spite of being Muslim.)

  Isabelle's anxiety was particularly acute since it had become clear soon after her arrival in Marseilles that Augustin, too, was as penniless as she was. The Villa Neuve had still not sold, and the Russian estate was still frozen. By 9 July, Isabelle was smoking leaves from the plane trees in the rue Tivoli, and Augustin had had to pawn his coat, trousers and even baby Hélène's coat. On the 10th, they took in their last pawnable effects. On the 11th, Isabelle told Slimène, her brother and his wife had fallen into despair, and had ceased trying to hide their misery from her. She was acutely concerned about their future: whereas she felt her own troubles would be over when she and Slimène could be together, and knew that the two of them were expert at making do with very little, Augustin and Hélène had 'a façade to keep up', and no bulwark of inner life to sustain their morale for the future. She and Slimène were too poor to help them, and relations were too frayed for them to accept the simple hospitality that they could give. By 23 July, Isabelle had serious fears on Augustin's account: 'I pray he doesn't think of doing what Volodia [Vladimir] did as a last resort! As long as I am here, a collective suicide is impossible. But afterwards?'

  She had been doing her best to earn some money for them all, sometimes managing to get a day's work as a porter in the inspection area of the docks – in spite of her weak arm – which brought in 1.50 or 2 francs a day, or translating the odd Arabic letter for people in cafés. If she could have afforded one outfit of women's clothes, she felt, she would have been in a better position to get work, but that was beyond their means. She wrote off urgently to Lydia Paschkoff, who was now in Paris, asking if she could suggest any paid work in Russian; to Bonneval, the editor of *L'Athénée*, asking if he knew anyone who wanted a book written on their behalf; to her old allies Abou Naddara and Reppmann for loans of money or for any help they could give; to their lawyer in Geneva to try to urge along the sale of the Villa; to Koudja ben Abdallah asking for money he owed her; and to the playwright Eugène Brieux, with whom she had been in correspondence after being introduced by Abou Naddara, and who enjoyed a considerable vogue at the time for his naturalistic, moralistic plays. She also wrote to the mayor of the Vernier district asking for a 'certificate of good conduct', a bureaucratic preliminary to obtaining official permission to marry. She had established good relations with the colonel in charge of the local Marseilles *spahis*, Colonel de Rancougne, who was helping her try to secure a permutation for Slimène and official permission to marry. On the 17 July she finished her ninety-seven-page essay in Russian on the Sahara, and an article on Tunis in French. She wrote to Slimène, 'I shall carry on working towards having the most possible articles ready, in case any of my approaches works out.'

On 19 July 1901, Isabelle heard that *Les Nouvelles* had accepted the two stories of El Oued and its surrounds that she had sent them. 'This success is consoling and opens up a path for me,' she wrote on 25 July, 'so I must persevere and have patience.' She wrote to Slimène asking him to get copies of the magazine sent to Maître Laffont, Eugène Letord and Abou Naddara, and mentioned to him that the magazine's editor was one Victor Barrucand, a well-known Parisian author who also contributed to the *Revue Blanche*. Isabelle wrote she was keen now to maintain her place at the *Nouvelles* by writing at least two articles a month.

However, this success had done nothing to improve relations with Augustin, for she resolved in the next sentence to 'keep herself fiercely to herself' and not to speak of her writing or ideas to

these people who do not *understand* them, and who do not *want* to understand
. . . There's no doubt that in spite of all appearances, it was written that *only*
I should be *saved morally* of all those who lived the abnormal life of the Villa
Neuve, which Augustin used to complain about so much at the time and
which now he seems to be intent on copying down to the smallest detail. I
must at all costs adopt a system of silence, of impenetrability, to finish off
this lamentable, horrible stay here.

11

MARRIAGE

Concerned that Slimène should not misunderstand the ground rules of their marriage as she saw them, Isabelle wrote to him on 23 July 1901, 'Yes, certainly, I am your wife before God and Islam. But I am not just a vulgar Fatma. I am also your brother Mahmoud, the servant of God and Djilani, before I am the servant that being an Arab wife entails. And I do *not want*, you understand, you to prove unworthy of the beautiful dreams I have for us both, and of which I have barely told you a fraction.'

Others were entertaining more serious doubts on her behalf about her marriage. Bonneval wrote to her from Paris on 1 August:

I don't think you have reflected sufficiently on this act, the most important one of your life. It will be difficult for you with your intellectual tastes to find a soul-sister in a man; and if you do not get on in this area, you might live to regret it. Think hard about it, think above all about the moral and intellectual side, the range and capacities of your fiancé and only decide when you are certain you know what you are doing. Forgive me this advice. It is only friendship which dictates it.

On the same date Lydia Paschkoff, now back in Odessa, wrote a note to Isabelle in similar vein: 'I knew – I felt – that your life would end up with love and marriage. I was afraid of it, and wrote as much to Abou. At least you are under the aegis of an honest man, even if he's poor. You have opted for happiness. And I for *liberty*. Because I've never really loved. I have never had this happiness. Can one love Russians?' On 21 October Abou Naddara wrote sadly: 'We have the greatest respect for you, in spite of your one great fault, that of sacrificing yourself for people who are not worthy of it.' He did not write his promised ode in sixty-one languages.

Their doubts were pre-empted for Isabelle by the news that Slimène had been taken ill at the end of July and was in hospital. Since she knew he suffered from an 'heredity illness' – which proved to be tuberculosis – she feared for his life, and the possibility of losing him for ever temporarily drove all other thoughts away. If he was taken from her, she would, she wrote, accept it as the will of God, but would at once go down to the south-west of Algeria, 'where they are fighting' – on the Moroccan border – and willingly 'seek out death'. She felt acute remorse at having chided him for not writing to her, and wrote to him that he was 'my only attachment to life'. In her diary she wrote, 'Perhaps I have *never ever* loved him so *purely* and so deeply as I love him now.'

In the event, news soon came through from the military doctor that Slimène was in no danger, and was improving. On Saturday 3 August, Isabelle heard from the playwright Eugène Brieux, who, like a *deus ex machina*, sent her an indefinite loan of 100 francs. Hugely relieved by this timely benevolence, she repaid Augustin money he had finally lent them in El Oued, and, confident through Colonel de Rancougne that their marriage would soon take place, she bought herself a wedding outfit, which, she wrote to Slimène, was in 'very dark blue, pretty, fine wool', with a lilac waistcoat. She would find it impossible, she said, to marry in white, since 'all Marseilles' knew that they had lived together and 'in front of the Colonel and your friends it would be an enormous scandal'. Slimène wrote on the 4th confirming that he was better and had put on over a kilo in weight in hospital, and with the news that he had been given a convalescent leave of three months, and would be joining her in ten or twelve days at the latest. He wrote equably that he was sure she showed all his letters to 'our brother Augustin, because there are no more secrets between us, now that we all constitute a little family.' On his way to Marseilles, he would stop off in Constantine for a day to do some shopping for a 'pair of shoes and so on'.

Her anxiety about his health now calmed, Isabelle wrote back in combative form once more, distressed that, as she felt, he had misunderstood the situation at the boulevard Mérentié, and was being too eager and appeasing to Augustin. He seemed to be looking forward to the relationship with his wife's brother and family just as much as to that with her, and Isabelle wanted to disabuse him on that score before he came. He evidently planned a confidential relationship with Augustin, which Isabelle felt was naive. She referred back to his visit to Marseilles in July:

You made a grave mistake – unwittingly, I know – in speaking to Augustin when I wasn't there and particularly in telling him not to mention it to me. *Don't ever do that again.* Augustin has *profoundly changed* in his attitude towards me. I've *watched him closely* and now I can see it. You got quite the wrong end of the stick with my brother: he doesn't see you in the same way you see him at all. He hasn't any of the feelings you have felt for him, out of love for what I love. Above all don't believe he trusts you: he doesn't at all. Everything he says and does is calculated.

Throughout the hot Marseilles August she sat in her small room in their flat 'suffocating here, between four walls, in a city which has only ever left me with the darkest malaise'. She wrote angrily in her diary of this 'house of unseeing *bourgeois* . . . bourgeois right to their fingertips, clogged up with the vulgar preoccupations of their greedy and animal lives.' Hélène, she sensed, hated her, 'for no reason', and not knowing herself why she did so. It was not this in itself which distressed Isabelle – 'because such an enemy and her ridiculous hatred can only *make me smile*' – but the necessity of having to play a role in order to keep some equilibrium, mainly for the sake of Augustin. She realized he was deeply unhappy, having made a mistake in his marriage which would be difficult to redeem. Isabelle buried herself in reading Dostoevsky, the poet of 'enfants malheureux', whose books best suited her 'vague, shapeless and sad' present mood, and in thoughts of escape: 'Oh, to leave for distant parts, and start a new life again in the free, magnificent open air! . . . To set off, vagabond and free, as I used to, however much it might cost me in new suffering!' She longed for the sensual presence of Slimène, writing on 17 August:

Certainly, all questions to do with sensuality will always continue to interest me, *intellectually*, and I wouldn't want to give up my studies in this area for anything in the world. But in reality, for me the sexual domain is limited clearly at the moment and, banal as it seems to say so, 'I'm not mine any more'. In the sensual domain, Slimène reigns uniquely, incontestably. He alone attracts me, he alone inspires in me the necessary state of mind to leave the realm of the intellect to descend – is it descent? I doubt it – into the realm of amazing sensual realizations.

In the modern world, 'falsified and off course', she writes, the husband is never a woman's sensual initiator, or a friend, but only the custodian of her 'material virginity', and finally a ridiculous figure. It is usually left to some other to introduce her to the world of sensations, amidst lies and deviousness. This, she felt, is what made people indignant about Slimène: that he was both her lover and her friend.

On 24 August Colonel de Rancougne – a 'compelling and attractive personality', who had done a great deal for them both behind the scenes – came personally to tell Isabelle that instead of the much-delayed convalescent leave, Slimène had been granted a permutation to Marseilles, where he could serve out the rest of his term in the army, now only a matter of six months away.

On the 27th, Isabelle left Augustin's house for good. 'In the end, I pardon everything, and it is up to God to judge. I have done and will continue to do my human duty to the end.' She rented a room for herself and Slimène down in the town centre, at 67 rue Grignan. At four in the morning of the 28th, a sunny day with a strong mistral, Isabelle went down to the quayside and waited for Slimène's arrival at 8.30 a.m. on the *Ville d'Oran*.

In her delight at being with him again – 'We are alone and *chez nous* – a delicious sensation!' – she wrote nothing in her diary for the next month, by which time their marriage was only a question of days away. On 27 September Isabelle had heard the news that the Villa Neuve had finally been sold, for 30,000 francs. But hard on its heels came a letter to say that all the proceeds had gone into legal and other fees which had accumulated over the past two years and, as a final irony, Isabelle was left with an outstanding lawyer's bill of sixty francs. Poverty was, after all, still to be their lot.

Isabelle was philosophical: 'God had pity on me and heard my prayers: He gave me the ideal companion, so ardently desired, and without whom my life would always have been incoherent and mournful.' She wrote in Russian, 'Only he who has suffered to the end will be saved,' then 'God alone knows what He is destining us for. So one must be resigned and confront adversity courageously.'

Isabelle's resignation was tested again in September, as Brieux sent back her short story 'Amira le forçat' and the articles on Tunisia she had sent him. All of them had been rejected by the French magazine *L'Illustration*. As a socialist-realist in his own plays, he reproached her for not tackling the subject of the iniquities of colonialism, and suggested that her writing was too simple for the tastes of the time. Lydia Paschkoff put it more bluntly in a letter to Isabelle of 12 September: '[Brieux] told me that you simply haven't got what it takes to write.' Isabelle noted flatly in her diary that she had a lot of work to do on her writing. (Years later Randau wrote that 'there's a grace to her style which, because it's not heavily made-up, used to dismay or exasperate certain men of letters.')

But now her personal life provided a bulwark against such disappointments. On 17 October she was married to 'Selimen Ehnni' in a civil ceremony, wearing her black wig and her lilac and dark blue outfit. Isabelle was twenty-four, and Slimène twenty-nine. Their relationship, and her political security, were now safe, for having married a naturalized Frenchman, Isabelle acquired his nationality and thus the right to live in any French territory.

On 21 October, Lydia Paschkoff arrived in Marseilles, flanked by her two dogs, and invited Isabelle and her husband over to the Grand Hotel to meet her. This was the first time the two women had met, and it turned out to be the last, the disenchantment evidently being mutual. Isabelle wrote in her diary, 'Mme Paschkoff is not a captivating or charming personality. A strange mixture, but there's a lot of unconscious egoism, immense pride and intellectual superficiality. A Russian restlessness, above all *worldly*.'

The rest of the year was eked out impecuniously, the only warmth in a particularly cold November coming from some firewood neighbours gave them out of charity, one of whom had his eye on Isabelle. Slimène cursed such Western deviousness: 'May God damn the unbelievers and their mentality!'

12

POLITICS AND THE HIGH PLATEAUX

Although Slimène could not leave the army until 20 February 1902, by November 1901 it began to look as if he might be able to transfer back to North Africa for the end of his term, through the good offices of the colonel. Isabelle wrote confidently on 26 November: 'It seems more and more likely that we are living through our *last days* of exile at the moment ... God grant that this is so, since the Marseilles nightmare has lasted long enough!' In the last week of December 1901 she made a fleeting visit back to Geneva and the lawyers – 'a sad return, quick and almost furtive'.

By early January 1902 the permutation back to North Africa was settled, the military having been mollified into an attitude of wary acceptance of the couple by Colonel de Rancougne's recommendations. On the 14th the two sailed on the *Duc de Bragance* for Bône, where they stayed with Slimène's family until his enlistment expired. Their plans after that were to go and live in Algiers while Slimène took his interpreting examinations, and Isabelle continued with her writing. The rest depended on the outcome of her mother's legacy, which Isabelle still expected to yield some revenue – perhaps enough for them to buy some property.

Living with Slimène's relatives, 'where hospitality manifests itself by endless quarrels and snubs', was not much different from living with hers, and it undermined their confidence in each other. Isabelle was critical of her husband in her diary:

Here as elsewhere, I notice Slimène's instability of character and the damaging influence that his surroundings seem to have on him. Will this change one day? I don't know. Anyway, with such a character, the life of poverty we are reduced to is more than difficult ... In Algiers I shall have to find someone capable of teaching Slimène what he doesn't know, which is a major task.

Once Slimène was discharged from the army, they moved to Algiers, initially taking a 'horrible hovel' in the rue de la Marine. But at least Isabelle could go off on her trips into the surrounding countryside again, if not on horseback, then by coach, sleeping on benches in railway stations and stopping off at Moorish cafés for food and conversation. These forays were her life-blood, and she now began to make them on her own again, without Slimène.

On 30 March she was invited to meet Victor Barrucand, the editor from *Les Nouvelles* who had taken a keen interest in her story from the moment he had read her letter in the *Dépêche Algérienne*, and who had been responsible for the sympathetic tone the newspaper had taken towards her since then. He invited her up to his house, the Villa Bellevue, in the chemin du Télemly, in the Mustapha region of Algiers.

It was an auspicious meeting. Barrucand was to have a far-reaching influence on her life and an even more far-reaching effect on her reputation after her death. She knew that he had had a 'brilliant career' in Paris, and counted him as 'one of the masters of journalism in Algeria'. She recorded the meeting briefly in her diary: 'An agreeable impression. A modern, fine and subtle mind, although influenced by the ideas of the century.' From Barrucand's house, Isabelle went on to meet Mme Suce ben Aben, an intelligent, 'dear and good' woman who ran an embroidery workshop for the local women. She wrote, 'Felt some pleasure in this conversation with intellectuals, a feeling long since forgotten.'

Barrucand, who had only arrived in Algeria in 1900, had just been devastated by the loss of his wife, and was throwing himself into work in an effort to forget. He was about to try to extricate himself from his position at the *Nouvelles*, with whose owner, Senator Gérente, he disagreed on several matters of principle. Barrucand wanted to set up his own, more liberal, bi-lingual French and Arabic newspaper. A forty-eight-year-old Frenchman, born in Poitiers, he had published well-received novels 'of ideas', as well as articles in the *Revue Blanche* in Paris, of which he was a corresponding editor. He had written about Herzen and Bakunin, for whose ideals he had some sympathy, although he sought a liberal evolution of ideas rather than revolution. Isabelle's background and character were bound to appeal strongly to him. He saw at once that she would be the ideal collaborator for his new magazine, and began to find ways to help her which were mutually beneficial. Isabelle noted in her diary some two months later, on 8 June:

I am beginning to understand the character of the two people who have helped us here, Barrucand and Mme ben Aben, both of them good people and very tactful: Barrucand, a dilettante in matters of thoughts and above all of sensations, and a moral nihilist, is, however, a man who in his practical life is very positive, and *knows how to live*. Mme ben Aben is the second woman I have known after my mother who is good to the core, and enamoured of ideals. Yet in real life, how ignorant the two women are! *Even I*, as someone intimately convinced that *I do not know how to live*, even I know more than they do.

Thanks partly to Barrucand's support, living in Algiers was beginning to be an enjoyable experience for Isabelle, in spite of the fact that she felt she had to have the moral strength for two at the moment, since Slimène, like Augustin, would not shape up to her dreams. In early May 1902 they moved to 17 rue du Soudan, which led into the Casbah. She liked the new lodgings, the area they were in, and beyond that Algiers itself: 'Algiers bay is, together with that of Bône, the most beautiful, the most deliciously intoxicating corner of sea that I have ever seen . . . In spite of the dross introduced here by prostituted and prostituting "civilization", Algiers is still a graceful and a good place to live in.' The more she read about the history of Africa, she found, 'the more I see that my idea was right: the land of Africa devours and absorbs everything which is hostile to it. Perhaps it is the *predestined country* from which the spark will come one day to regenerate the world!' She experienced, too, a more specific kind of African magic, writing on 4 May that she had just been to a 'magician's' – 'I've found the certain proof of the *reality* of this incomprehensible and mysterious science of Magic.' She wrote a haunting short story, 'Le Magicien', based on her visit, which was published in the 2 November issue of the Paris magazine *Le Petit Journal Illustré*. The sense of magic, in its various manifestations, was indelibly linked to what attracted her about Africa: she wrote on 8 June, 'In the really Arab towns like the *ksours* of the south, the poignant and bewitching atmosphere of the land of Africa is quite tangible.'

In a mood to recapture something of the *ksours*' flavour, and still haunted by the possibility of a mystical vocation, she left on 29 June for Bou Saada, in the middle of the high plateaux behind the coastal Atlas mountains. She particularly wanted to visit the nearby *zawiya* at El Hamel of the woman *maraboute*, Lella Zeyneb. The June weather was oppressively sultry, with the heat and the sirocco turning the countryside into a 'Turkish bath'. Isabelle travelled alone, taking what transport came to hand, coach, mule or horse, and sleeping wherever she could find a corner, on a trunk, on a mat under an arcade, or 'bitten by fleas' in a courtyard. For food she relied mainly on the ready hospitality of the local people, or made do with the bitter coffee of the region, often laced with flies and muddy water. To wash, she used the Turkish baths.

On 2 July she made the journey on horseback out to the village of El Hamel and up to the fortress-like, green-shuttered *zawiya*. Lella Zeyneb had inherited her position from her father, Si Mohammed Belkassem, who had no male offspring. A tanned and wrinkled figure approaching fifty, she suffered from a malady of the throat which made talking difficult. Isabelle never wrote of the content of her conversations with her spiritual mentors; she merely mentioned briefly in a travel note that Lella Zeyneb, sensing a fellow spirit, had confided in her about the loneliness and difficulties of her position.

Politically the Bu Saada journey had been something of a test case for her, but afterwards she noted, 'I can see now that I can easily return to any military post without any particular trouble.' However, the military were still keeping a close watch on her – much of the time, one feels, because they had nothing better to do in the garrison towns – and no doubt she knew it. Six months later, when she returned to El Hamel to visit Lella Zeyneb, the Governor-General himself wrote a confidential note to the police, saying, 'This woman can no longer be affected by the expulsion order which was served on her because she has acquired French nationality following her marriage, but she should still be kept under surveillance because of her eccentricities and her relationships in the Muslim world.' On this second visit, in early 1903, the police were still doggedly tracking every detail of her moves, down to the minute she was taking a Turkish bath. The one thing they were unable to find out was the subject of her conversations with Lella Zeyneb. They were sufficiently interested to try: the Governor-General himself wrote a private memorandum on 28 February 1903 to General Bailloud, commanding the Algiers division of the army, saying he would like them to try discreetly to find out the subjects of the two women's conversations.

Isabelle returned from her first visit – 'as rapid as a dream' –

refreshed and strengthened, confirmed in her feeling that the nomadic life had always been the only one for her, ever since she had yearned for the 'white road' from the Villa Neuve. 'I shall stay a nomad all my life, in love with changing horizons, unexplored, far-away places, for any voyage, even to the most crowded and well-travelled countries, is an *exploration*.'

The day that she returned from this trip, on 4 July, Isabelle was greeted by the news that, through the good offices of Victor Barrucand, Slimène (who had passed his exams) had been offered a post as *khodja* – interpreter – in the *commune mixte* of the town of Ténès, on the Algerian coastline some hundred miles to the west of Algiers. The particular nature of the *commune mixte*, and of Ténès, fraught with cabalistic intrigues, were sorely to test Isabelle's own moral fibre, in the way in all the world she would least have liked it to be tested. Much as she sought out the mystical route, and awaited the call, it was politics which kept insistently, mischievously, snapping at her heels.

13

MISCHIEF

The only link which the small town of Ténès had to the outside world at this time was the five-horse coach which jolted its way once a day to and from Orléansville, with jangling horse-bells and a cargo, as Robert Randau put it, of 'sullen travellers and a reasonable number of starving fleas'. Otherwise the inhabitants still travelled on horse-back, and in winter the whole town could easily be cut off by rain, left to fester even more than usual in its rife intrigues and small-town scandal. On 7 July 1902 Isabelle and Slimène arrived there on the mal-odorous coach, and booked into the Hôtel des Arts. Unknown to them, two men sitting at a table in the hotel were watching the immaculately dressed young Arab couple crossing the hallway. One was Fernand Carayol, general rubber-stamper of all property matters in the town, and the other was M. Vayssié, the local magistrate and author, who, under the pen name of Raymond Marival, had written two novels, and wrote for the *Mercure de France*. Marival, seeing the newcomers in their ample white burnouses, and noticing that one of them had excep-tionally delicate hands and an unmannishly smooth complexion, ex-claimed, 'Goodness, that looks like a woman!' The maid serving them said under her breath, 'Yes, it is a woman, but she signed herself in under the name of Si Mahmoud.' The two men, recognizing her name from the newspaper reports of the trial, went over and introduced them-selves. They were to become much-needed allies of Isabelle's in Ténès.

A few weeks before their arrival, at the beginning of the summer, another writer had arrived in town. Like Marival, he had taken a pen-name, Robert Randau – with only the advantage of alliteration over his real one, Robert Arnaud. Born in Algeria of French colonial parents, he wrote books evoking Africa and the French presence there in the roundly colonial fashion of Kipling, rather than with the outsider's romantic exoticism of Loti or Flaubert. Like Marival, he wore two hats, but with his balding head, rimless glasses and clipped moustache he looked more the administrator than the writer. Yet his writing style was both robust and richly ironic, and its full-bloodedness earned him in his lifetime the title of the 'African Rabelais'. Roland Lebel described him as having a 'double personality, erudite and condottiere, philosophical and conquering, in touch wih action and thought, a hearty fellow infused by the rich blood of Africa. He was a typical colonial, in love both with strength and with ideas.' He himself said his aim was not to make a name for himself in the literary world of Paris, but to 'liberate myself from certain obsessions', and to see 'an original intellectuality and strong and succulent works' born out of North Africa. The mannered irony of the title – *A l'ombre de mon baobab* – and chapter headings of one of his later books suggest something of his outlook on life: 'Curiosity is the enemy of good living; It is vital to love twilights; It is vital not to be sentimental; It is vital not to take life, or women, too seriously; Eating people is the beginning of altruism' (because 'Cannibalism is, for the superstitious person, without any doubt the most practical way of assimilating the best intellectual qualities of a friend or enemy').

Randau had come to Ténès to take up a post as third assistant to the administrator, taking over from a friend of his who had fled the local intrigues in horror. The administrators were uniformed French officials running the *communes mixtes*, the poor relations of the *communes de plein exercice*, which governed the richer, larger towns. The *communes mixtes* incorporated local Muslims into the administration. It was an uneasy compromise on all sides, especially since the administrator was specially recruited by the Governor-General, not elected like a mayor, and enjoyed full judicial, administrative and police powers. However, to add to the confusion there was also a mayor of Ténès, M. Martin, who was not only at daggers drawn with the administrator, but had also been suspended from his duties for a month in 1898 for corruption. A virulent anti-semite, he was a self-made man whose wholesale misap-propriation of funds had made him a millionaire. His corruption was the only thing which lent his enemy, the administrator M. Bouchet, any qualities, on the grounds that he was not quite as bad as Martin. A small, sharp, monocled and authoritarian ex-*spahi*, Bouchet was paranoid about any newcomers defecting to the mayor's camp, and was curt, suspicious and condescending to Randau on his arrival.

Early in the morning after Isabelle and Slimène arrived in this divided town, they rented rooms in the upper storey of a plain but convenient house in the rue d'Orléansville, parallel to the northern rampart of the town which ran down to the quayside. They set out their few effects in the one room and a kitchen: a table, inkstand, mats to sleep on, and a passage from the Koran, copied out in Isabelle's elegant Maghrebian Arabic calligraphy, and pinned up on the bare white walls. At ten they called in at the *commune mixte*, where they encountered Randau for the first time, in his bureaucratic role. Randau wrote that

two strangers in native costume were announced to me in my narrow office (more like a passage) where . . . I was about to embark on a promisingly boisterous confrontation between a cattle thief and some shepherds. One of the strangers was very dark-skinned and sickly-looking, but with regular and appealing features. He was called Si Slimane Ehnni, the new *khodja* of the *commune mixte*. His companion, elegant and slim, was a cavalier in a *haïk* and a fine, immaculately white burnous, the tight, soft *mestr* [leather boots] of the *spahi*, and with extraordinarily shining black eyes, a pale face, prominent cheekbones and reddish-brown colouring. Underneath his turban, near the ears, and around his discoloured lips, his skin had the tone of parchment. 'May I introduce Si Mahmoud Saadi,' the dark visitor said, 'that is his *nom de guerre*; in fact it is Mme Ehnni, my wife.' [Isabelle's 'extraordinarily shining black eyes' were partly due to the effect of *kef*, which by now had become a habit with her.]

Shortly afterwards Slimène left for his duties, while Isabelle stayed on and talked with an increasingly intrigued Randau:

Isabelle spoke slowly, as if she were searching for the words, with the most disagreeable and the most monotonous nasal accent in the world; she smoked cigarette on cigarette, and . . . spiced every sentence with mild swear words. She laughed easily, showing all her teeth but no exuberance; her most typical gesture with her right hand was to lift her cigarette to her mouth; her other hand stayed resting on her knee. Her bearing was always dignified, even grave; I should add that she completely lacked sex-appeal.

Once they had discussed their mutual passion for literature, Randau turned to a topic which had fascinated him ever since he had read the newspaper reports of her trial the previous summer. Indeed, he even had a copy of the text of the trial to hand, and asked her to explain why she had claimed that Abdallah had been pushed into his act by persons unknown. Who was she referring to, he asked; what was the real story?

I tried to press her to answer, but she turned away evasively and avoided the issue. I tried to take a different tack; but each time she dodged any precise question. I pinned her down: was there any correlation between certain of the grey areas which she claimed formed the basis for the mysterious affair, and the police measure which was taken against her? She stared hard at me, and looked troubled, implicitly reproving my impertinence. I took it as said; after that I never again brought up the subject which seemed to be so painful to her.

It is a mark both of Isabelle's prudence and of her defensiveness that she could not air her suspicions to Randau, even when she knew him far better. (Thirty years later Randau was still on the same track, asking one of the then Governor-General's officials, and the Police Department in Algiers, to search through the records to see if there was any trace of what had been going on behind the scenes before the assassination attempt. He was told that the Governor's archives had 'disappeared' and that the police records had probably been eaten by rats after they had been transferred to the local vaults. The memoranda between the military and the politicians before the trial – which had not all been 'eaten by rats', and which Randau never saw – now strongly suggest that his and Isabelle's suspicions of a conspiracy to get rid of her were accurate.)

However, Isabelle was more expansive with Randau on the subject of a visit she had made earlier that morning to Bouchet, who had received her – as opposed to Randau – with unctuous charm, knowing that she was a friend of Victor Barrucand's and seeing the propaganda that might be made through the literary pair. He launched into a litany of the grievances he had against the mayor and others in Ténès, explaining how the native people were being exploited and how he wanted to help them, and asking Isabelle to join his cause. Would she travel around the local countryside interviewing the people, and report back to him on their views? Although she agreed with his broad aim, she was disconcerted by his proselytizing and politicking. She told Randau: 'It was awkward; I don't want to get involved in all this – I am just looking for a quiet corner to get on with my work as best I can.' She told him, laughing, that Bouchet had warned her about Randau's cavalier attitude, the way he seemed 'not to give a damn and to consider us cretins'. Isabelle had at once reckoned that Randau would be the person best qualified to tell her what was going on in Ténès.

With ironic relish, Randau now filled her in on the bitternesses and hatreds in this 'aquarium', which, he said, ensured a 'slow and cruel poisoning' for anyone getting officially involved. There were elections coming up for mayor – though Martin had been acquitted of the charges of corruption on appeal – and the various factions were lining up for a fight to the death. When he had finished, Isabelle exclaimed 'My, my, my! What kind of a hornet's nest have we got into, my husband and I? We've got nothing to fear and nothing to hope for, but we shall no doubt get taken aside by one of the factions; well, in order to avoid getting covered in mud I shall plan to leave Ténès as often as possible during this period. For as far as I'm concerned I don't accept any race hatred and, like Barrucand and Zola, want nothing to do with anti-semitism.'

That evening Randau invited her over to his house, where she drank her favourite drink of strong anisette, and established a swift rapport with his wife. Even better for Isabelle, they went on to visit his stables, where a new grey mare had arrived that day. She was white, with a black star on her forehead. Without a single glance at Randau's own solid, workmanlike beast (he wrote ruefully), Isabelle at once fell in love with the mare, saddled her, took her out of her box and through the streets of Ténès at a gallop. She praised the mare wildly to Randau; he told her she could give her a name. Isabelle called her Ziza, Slimène's pet name for her, and from then on she took her out almost daily into the surrounding *bled*, which consisted mostly of mountains ending abruptly in deep, wooded ravines, scrub, and slopes of fallen rocks.

The local *fellahs*, some of whom already knew of her by reputation since Béhima, quickly got to know and like her. 'She was very approachable,' Randau wrote, 'and wanted them to think of her simply as a young *taleb*, a student from a *zawiya*. All of them knew that this svelte cavalier in her immaculate white burnous and soft red leather boots was a woman. The innate courtesy of the Arabs is such that in her presence none of them ever made any allusion, even by so much as a wink, to a quality she did not want to acknowledge.'

When she was not out riding, or writing at home, Isabelle liked to browse in Randau or Marival's extensive libraries. Marival's was well stocked with symbolists, many of whom had personally given him copies of their works. Randau claimed that she had no knowledge of or interest in the lyrical or symbolist poets – which was not entirely true because she had several books of Baudelaire's, and had copied verses from *Les Fleurs du Mal* into her diary in El Oued. But her main interest, true to Trophimowsky's grounding, certainly lay with the realists: Zola (she subscribed now to a complete edition of his works), Daudet, Descaves, Paul Adam, Rémy de Gourmont, Anatole France. On the other hand, grand ideas still attracted her: she read Schopenhauer, something of a fellow-spirit in his contradictory temperament and orient-inspired philosophy of the relinquishing of individuality. At Randau's mischievous insistence, she also read Nietzsche's *Also Sprach Zarathustra*, which he knew she would dislike. Revealing a touch of superman fantasy herself, she told him, 'I am sorry that the superman did not come and reduce humanity to slavery and impose his law of the two moralities. I would have had the supreme happiness, I think, of ridding our planet of this monster.' Randau wrote off to his literary friends Marius and Ary Leblond in Paris and Sadia Lévy in Sidi-bel-Abbès, alerting them to the presence of this remarkable creature in Ténès, and the word began to get around.

Meanwhile Barrucand had resigned from his editorial post at the *Nouvelles*, to the enduring chagrin of its owner Senator Gérente, for Barrucand's new paper would be a rival to his own. It was to be called *L'Akhbar/El Akhbar*, taking over the name of a defunct paper, and was to serve equally the interests of the French and of the indigenous population, with the articles printed in both Arabic and French. Barrucand rejected any notion that it would be francophobically arabophile: 'I have no other aim than to serve France in her natural inclination towards justice and racial equality, avoiding the excesses of the arabophiles as much as of the arabophobes.' Others did not see it this way, and Senator Gérente particularly had an interest in making the magazine suspect to the French authorities.

One day when Barrucand was in Ténès visiting Isabelle, the administrator Bouchet invited them on a tour of the neighbouring villages to meet the local *caïds* and notables. The tour lasted a day and a half, and was to provide much fuel for gossip for the rest of Isabelle's stay in Ténès. The village people had no idea of what a journalist might be, and Bouchet introduced Barrucand to them, according to Randau, as 'a wise man whose pen, inspired by God, would denounce the abuses of the moneylenders, and regain for them their own rights over Algerian land'. However honest the intentions of the trio were, and they were probably in better faith than the laconic Randau gave credit for, their opponents swiftly made a meal of their visit. Rumour had it that this was a propaganda trip, trying to get the rich local people to fund their newspaper, and promising in return that it would take an anti-French stand. By associating herself with Bouchet, however loosely in her own mind, Isabelle had unwittingly set half the town, including the mayor and Senator Gérente, against her. By associating himself with Isabelle, Bouchet had given his enemies an easy target.

Another incident gave Isabelle a more personal enemy for the future, this time from within the offices of the *commune mixte*. Isabelle told Randau how the deputy there had

made a pass at me, without any provocation on my part, and as if he were dealing with a banal administrative matter. He even made it clear that I had to take that route if I wanted him to be good friends with me, to our mutual benefit. I don't know who this person took me for, and I have no interest in his friendship at all. So that he should be quite clear on the matter, I was very explicit, and told him that rather than sleep with him, I would prefer to kiss the open mouth of a stiff who had died of Asiatic cholera.

When she told Randau of the episode, he said, 'Congratulations, you handle metaphor very prettily.' The deputy, who liked easy conquests, and did not like rejection, was now, like de Susbielle before him, bent on revenge.

Isabelle wrote in her diary on 18 September 1902: 'In itself, all this *boue* means nothing to me, yet it does annoy me when it starts to get too close. There is, though, the precious resort of flight, of solitude on the open roads to the tribal villages.' She took refuge in the peasant life of the *fellahs* in what Randau felt was an unhealthy way, 'in the same pathological way she loved twilights': 'she was not repulsed by the dirt, the vermin, or the lack of hygiene of these people.' She liked nothing better than to crouch down in their smoke-filled, airless *gourbis* on the hillside, which reeked of the smell of the animals who lived with them, and hear stories of the details of their lives, their feuds, and their legends, while scratching the back of the household sheep, or cuddling the children. Randau wrote that 'she felt this destitution represented a bit of herself.' She used to help them with advice on vaccination, encourage them to go to doctors, sit by the bedside of the sick, and 'avoid like the pest those who wanted to engage her in political or religious matters to do with Arab nationalism; she was well aware that her most anodyne comments would be reported back to the administration.' These Europeans, even those not politically against Isabelle, were disconcerted by her ideals, feeling that she was indulging in ridiculous fantasies which had no practical aim in view. Interestingly, even the 'intellectual natives', Randau said, treated her with condescension and a shrug of the shoulders, since they had broken since childhood with the notion of resigning oneself to the will of an all-powerful God, and considered themselves *évolués*.

As for Ténès itself, Isabelle wrote, 'there is only my friend Arnaud whom I enjoy talking to. He, too, is despised by the band of pretentious philistines who think they amount to something because they wear tight trousers, a ridiculous hat or even a striped kepi.' Her frequent exasperation induced a pipe-dream of escape, and she thought briefly of leaving with Slimène for Palestine, and 'escaping from Europe, even transplanted Europe, into an Arab country, no doubt like the one I love, and living another life'.

Her wariness at what use would be made by her enemies of any pro-Arab activity prevented her from a project which she initially envisaged taking on in October 1902: reporting the trial of the Arab nationalist insurgents at Marguerritte. If she had gone through with her plans to cover the trial, which was to take place in France in February 1903, she would no doubt have become a public figure in France, but she shied away from it, ostensibly for lack of funds. Her reluctance was not only a capitulation to possible hounding: at root her espousal of the cause of Arab nationalism was not the dominant force of her life, but a romantic, human bonding born as much of the complexities of her background as of political realities. In the end she saw politics as too narrow and corrupt a way of making the changes that needed to be made if the future of Algeria was to be rescued from bloodshed and disaster: she wrote, in a letter to Randau of 12 October 1902, 'The more I look at the Algerian political hotch-potch, the more profoundly it disgusts me . . . As for the future, it promises nothing good.'

The following day she was in wistful mood, thinking back on the Villa Neuve, and writing 'Ah, Mother! Ah, Vava! Look at your child, the *only one*, the only child to have followed you and to honour you, at least after your death.'

*

There, were, however, many light-hearted moments in Ténès, which we know of only because Randau was there to recount them: Isabelle

tended to confide mainly melancholic or self-searching moods to her
diary, and rarely wrote of her gay and ebullient side. Randau described
a party she gave on the beach one evening, to which he and his wife,
and Marival and Carayol, were invited. They arrived to find Isabelle
already tending a fire she had made to prepare a large couscous for
them all. She was busily peeling vegetables, cutting up a chicken and
some lamb, seasoning the sauces, crushing almonds and peppers, and
blowing on the embers of the fire. They settled around her on the
sand, barefoot, bombarding her with contradictory advice about the
best way to cook this and that. Isabelle was in high spirits, suggesting
they all pretend to be a tribe which had just pillaged another and was
sharing out the booty. Marival teased her, saying she was too puny
to pillage anything, and she leapt up and tussled with the small judge,
bringing him down to the ground and putting her foot on his chest in
mock victory. Later, knowing that he had a phobia about cheese, she
put a piece in his jacket pocket. As his fingers eased in to the pocket
to get a cigarette, they made startled contact with the cheese, driving
him to near hysteria. She herself was rolling on the ground in 'trans-
ports of hilarity', then realized she had gone too far. She ran and put
her arms solicitously around him, begging forgiveness.

They told stories, Isabelle even danced on the sand, and she sighed,
'Yes, I am happy, because you're all happy and because the wine is
good! Damn it, if I were always happy I would never write a line, you
know, because I would be completely satisfied!' They washed the
borrowed plates in the sea, then sang loud café songs as the sun went
down. Isabelle's voice rose loudest of all, and most out of tune. As
they walked back, Isabelle, in maudlin mood, confided to Randau:

I've smoked too much today. I've got the wretched habit of *kef*. Oh, my dear
Arnaud, I loathe this countryside, how it stinks; I hate cultivated fields, and
countryside full of greenery and corn. Why have I got this unhealthy taste
for dead landscapes and salty sand? Why do I prefer the nomad to the
harratine, the beggar to the rich man? Aye aye aye! Suffering is a spice for
me, enriching the flavour of existence. Ah! I'm very Russian, underneath! I
love the knout! Above all I would love people to feel sorry for me for suffering
the lashes of existence, and I rejoice when people pity me. I don't even hate
the bastard of an assistant at the *commune mixte* for trying to get me out of
Ténès . . . any more than I hate the madman in the south who wounded me
with his sabre, or than I will hate the executioner who greases the cord that
will hang me. I feel no anger against them, because thanks to them perhaps
I'll kindle some compassion in men's hearts. And yet my friends in Algiers,

and Marival, and you, and everyone here, you are hard people, who do not understand me and will never understand me, because I'm not of your blood.

Slimène – not present at this party – was still the only person Isabelle felt did understand her, although she often severely tested his long-suffering nature with her long absences and independent ways. Randau's opinion was that although Slimène occasionally wanted her to tone down her eccentricities socially, he was excited by her cross-dressing and 'independent allures'. Erotic Arab literature had a long tradition of addressing the loved one as a young man, out of discretion towards the woman, although it was understood that it was not a boy being courted, but an idealized girl. Randau wrote that 'in my opinion, Isabelle's cross-dressing stimulated the handsome young cavalryman's passion; he experienced romantic love and intellectual love at the same time; he was living out literally one of the great poems of his race' – a heady experience.

Once, however, Isabelle presumed too much on the camaraderie within their relationship. A young Arab philanderer within the *commune mixte* had fallen ill, swearing that it was for love of Isabelle, and was refusing to eat or drink. Isabelle teased him, scolded him and told him she would not listen to such nonsense. However, once back home, she reflected on his state, and 'wondered if I had the right to reduce a fellow human being to despair'. Randau, to whom she was telling this, was aghast at her naivety, but she persevered: 'Should I be a cause of suffering for him?' The person to ask, she felt, was Slimène, her soul-brother and the man to whom she had given her love: 'Ah, my friend, what an uproar. I had forgotten that Arab blood flowed through his veins. As soon as I'd started to speak, he drew himself to his full height, looked at me with hatred and cried, "I have never heard of anything so horrible! You feel desire for this fellow (it's not true, you say?), well, just the fact of this desire is insulting to me; it's as if you had been unfaithful to me!"' Isabelle protested, but Slimène was imperiously outraged and insisted that the only possible resolution of the matter was for him to kill Isabelle and the young *mokhrazeni*. 'When you've killed me, do you think you'll be happier than you are now?' Isabelle asked. 'No, because I wouldn't be rid of you, because I'd kill myself after I'd killed him and you, so that I wouldn't abandon you.' Isabelle did not demur, suggesting that the best thing would be for them both to commit suicide together – but not in the room because 'it would get everything dirty'. They should go out in the moonlight to the fortifications looking out to sea, breathe in the fresh air and then 'snuff ourselves out'. Slimène agreed, and they took some cigarettes, a nearly full bottle of anisette and a revolver and walked off to the agreed spot nearby.

As they sat on a patch of grass under an olive tree, Isabelle was moved to recite an old Arab poem. Slimène followed suit. And so it went on. They agreed to dispatch themselves once they had got to the end of the bottle, but they fell into a drunken stupor well before the end, and awoke the next morning at dawn, heavily hung over, with Slimène coughing badly from his tuberculosis. They crept back sheepishly to their rooms and put on some coffee. It had, after all, been just a lovers' row. And Isabelle, when it came to it, was not so terminally enamoured of death: her subconscious had thrown up some astute wiles to protect her survival.

*

By April 1903 the political protagonists in Ténès were in exalted mood. There were elections coming up; candidates were polishing up their heroic images and their rhetoric of golden ages to come. Bouchet's first assistant, whom Isabelle had so rudely rejected, began to act strangely. Ever vigilant, Bouchet suspected betrayal. When he returned to his office one day to find that his papers had been systematically rifled, his suspicions were confirmed: his deputy was after his job, and was defecting to the opposite camp – the Senator Gérente—Mayor Martin axis – in order to do so. He had tried to find compromising papers amongst Bouchet's files; but Bouchet's paranoia had protected him well in advance, and such material as there was had been heavily edited. Gérente and the mayor had decided that Bouchet's Achilles' heel was to be Isabelle, a sitting target. Why did she dress as a man and write what they deemed ridiculous stories? Why was she always travelling? There were only two possible reasons, both immoral: either she was running after men, or she was trying to profit from her husband's situation to make corrupt deals of some kind. Bouchet's papers had yielded no incriminating material, but circumstantial evidence was enough to get going on: a pseudonymous letter, signed heavy-handedly 'Otto Mobyl', was published in Senator Gérente's *Union Républicaine* on 2 April 1903, entitled 'Grave revelations', suggesting that there should be an enquiry into Bouchet's affairs: 'It is intolerable that an official should become the accomplice of M.

Barrucand's and Mme Eberhardt's noxious propaganda, for which the latter has previously been expelled in similar circumstances.' The letter made knowing but vague insinuations, speaking of her 'militant and dominant role in the task that *L'Akhbar* is pursuing . . . Mme Eberhardt, dressed as a male Muslim, lords it at the entrance to her husband's office and holds mysterious conversations with all the natives. In addition, mounted on the administrator's assistant's horse, and escorted by native policemen, she makes no less mysterious visits to the local villages.' They insinuated that she had some nefarious religious influence over the local Muslims.

Isabelle, who had wanted to stay aloof from all the electioneering hubbub, found herself thrust into the middle of it all. Her letters having always proved effective agents, she wrote a long letter to the neutral *Dépêche Algérienne*, protesting that 'I have never made *any propaganda* with the native people, and it is really ridiculous to say that I set myself up as some kind of *prophetess*! Everywhere, whenever I have the chance, I have been at pains to give my native friends just and reasonable views, and to explain to them that, for them, French domination is far preferable to Turkish or any other.' She also defended herself against the charge of anti-semitism which had been imputed to her.

The deputy at the *commune mixte* was not satisfied with this bout, which Isabelle came out of too well. He broke into Slimène's office and searched through his desk to try to find incriminating material. All he could find was a rough draft of a letter from Slimène to a local *caïd* called Goumiri, asking him to honour a debt to a third party. It was in the line of the *khodja*'s usual duties, but the deputy attempted to blow it up into a scandal: Ehnni had been soliciting funds for *L'Akhbar*, trying to extort money from local people. Barrucand vigorously took up Slimène's defence in *L'Akhbar*, insisting that the letter be published to show how little they had to fear from its contents, and the *caïd* Goumiri himself, baffled by all the commotion, protested in a letter of 14 June to *L'Akhbar* that, in spite of several attempts by the deputy to bribe him, he had never given, or proposed giving, any money to the *khodja*. Isabelle now wrote to the magazine *Turco* on 10 May, protesting the straightforwardness and innocence of her role at *L'Akhbar*. The *Union Républicaine* countered with a letter heavy with sarcasm and innuendo: 'What relationship is there between madame Mahmoud, of the *Turco*, madame Ehnni, of *L'Akhbar*, and mademoiselle Eberhardt, of the *Dépêche*? Is this a reincarnation of the mysteries of the Blessed Trinity? . . . Is this young man a woman? Is it a miss or a madame, what is her real name, does she live in Ténès or Mustapha? Oh, cruel, cruel enigma!' Since Isabelle's friends were urging her to hit back harder, she now went ahead and sued the *Union Républicaine* for defamation of character, and was rewarded with gratifying speed with a police endorsement of her complaint and a formal condemnation of the paper.

Yet all the antagonism and character assassination was debilitating to both Isabelle and Slimène. Isabelle had realized since Slimène's illness in Batna that his presence was not something she could take for granted. She herself was undermined by frequent attacks of malaria, which her chain-smoking and growing addiction to *kef* did nothing to help.

At the end of 1902, at midnight on 31 December, she had been in her usual nostalgic end-of-year mood, writing, 'Another year has gone . . . One year less to live . . . And I love life, out of sheer curiosity for its nature and mysteries . . . What does this year hold in store for us? What new hopes and what new disillusions?' On 29 January 1903, in the last entry in her extant diaries, she wrote, 'For a year now I have been on the blessed soil of Africa which I never want to leave again. In spite of my poverty, I have still been able to travel and see unknown regions of my adoptive country. My Ouïha [Slimène] is alive and we are relatively happy materially.'

What the first part of the new year had held was the increasing escalation of the campaign against them, and in spite of the police vindication neither of them had the will to carry on living in such a hostile community. Isabelle and Barrucand judged that it would be better for her to be out of the way during the run-up to the elections, and Barrucand offered her board and lodging at his house in Algiers in exchange for her help in running *L'Akhbar*. (Later he described to Randau what a mixed blessing this collaboration was, since Isabelle spent her time lying on a mat in his office, chain-smoking and, in fits of adolescent hilarity, bombarding him with pencils and raucous laughter.)

With Isabelle now in Algiers for most of the time, Slimène became increasingly reluctant to stay in Ténès as a whipping-boy. In early April he gave in his resignation, which was immediately interpreted as an admission of guilt by his enemies. He drafted an indignant letter of attack to the *Union Républicaine*, which they did not print, protesting that he had freely resigned in order to join his wife and to help her throw light on the 'hateful campaign of which we have been victims'.

*

Not all Isabelle's troubles in Ténès had been with people. The supernatural had played a brief, but temporarily disquieting, role too. Early one morning she had arrived at Randau's house in a trembling and exhausted state. He and his wife thought that perhaps she had been overdoing the anisette, but she assured them indignantly that she had not. She had been out riding late into the previous night with a local guide around the moonlit hills and *maquis* near Orléansville. She stopped at a stream for a drink for herself and her horse, in spite of warnings from her guide that this stream was 'enchanted' and that it was well known that if anyone drank from it they had visions. Isabelle scoffed at him and carried on drinking. But as they rode on she became overcome by a kind of 'lucid somnolence', as if hypnotized—perhaps, she admitted, suggestibly so – 'I rode like an automaton, as if I were surrounded by my own self.' Then she began to see dark clouds swarming on the hills either side of her, which gradually transformed into a silent mass of warriors fighting each other fiercely on foot and horseback. Amongst them she saw with detailed clarity an unusually tall man in chain-mail, with a 'Polish wide-brimmed hat', a scarlet beard and hair falling thinly over his shoulders. His eyes were glassy, and fixed on her insistently, and he beckoned her with his hand. Her horse quaked underneath her, and she remembered that he had also drunk from the stream. The horse bolted, quite out of her control, and threw her to the ground, where a bang on the head brought her to her senses. The visions had disappeared, and all the time the guide had seen nothing. (The horse, of course, need not have 'seen' anything: he would have responded to Isabelle's panic.) Whatever the origins of the vision, Isabelle's interpretation of the incident was telling: she swore it was not a hallucination, but that the warrior was 'my ancestor from the Russian steppes, with a horde of the vandals who conquered Africa. I was covered in sweat, and half dead with terror. My ancestor has called me; I know now that I haven't long to live.' The hallucinated ancestor was from the steppes, from Trophimowsky's ancestral lands.

14

WAR

In spite of Isabelle's flying pencils, Barrucand knew that he could not have a more concentrated symbol of what he wanted to achieve in bridging the gap between the French colonial intentions and the local reality than Isabelle. She represented a unique congruence of Muslim and French, with the suggestion that the integrity of both had been maintained. This alone, apart from her extensive knowledge of the local tribes and of the vernacular refinements and customs, was enough to make her a unique and attractive acquisition for French policy. There was a sense in which she was a figurehead facing two ways, a perfect symbol of equivocation, down even to her sex. When she had first arrived in Algeria, she had been instinctively on the side of the Muslims against the French presence, in taking part in the Muslim demonstrations in Bône. But by a slow process of attrition, as she began to suffer personally and politically from a policy which saw Muslim allegiance as only subversive, only suspect, as she began, through Slimène, to take on progressively the psychological and practical perspective of the colonized races in striving for the next rung up the Western ladder rather than for freedom in their own terms, she had gradually reached a compromised position where she no longer questioned the overall justification for France's presence, but only judged the means by which this was to be achieved. For the rest, the exigencies of her daily life ensured that she no longer had the luxury of taking the broad ideological view.

Although France's 'horizontal' dream of her territories stretching across North Africa from the Atlantic to the Red Sea had been thwarted five years before at Fashoda, there was still the possibility of securing Morocco for France. Indeed, part of the deal in relinquishing Egypt to England had been England's reciprocal promise to France of a free hand in Morocco. With contemporary colonial arrogance, the fact that there was a Moroccan Sultan in charge of the country was

counted a minor impediment – particularly since he happened to be
ineffectual and spendthrift. Yet the way had to be prepared delicately.
The rationale, as it had been in Tunisia, was that it was 'consolidating
the Algerian borders', and it was there that the gentle push should
start. Jonnart, Algeria's Governor-General in 1903, reported to the
Ministry of the Interior that there might be a gradual, uncontroversial
and inexpensive way through to the 'absorption' rather than the
'conquering' of Morocco, by subduing the rebellious tribes of the
Algerian-Moroccan border, thus ridding the Sultan of a traditional
thorn in his side and establishing a strong position from which
to bargain. Jonnart proposed Colonel Lyautey, recently of French
Indo-China and Madagascar, for the task.

Lyautey was unlike most of the military men in charge of the Arab
Bureaux across Algeria: on the whole they were tough, solid career
soldiers, like Pujat or Dechizelle, who did what they were told and
expected everyone else to do the same. The situation was too fluid
and precarious to admit of much imagination or latitude: merely
holding on to advantages already gained was the priority, and there
was no overall view of what to do next filtering down from the Third
Republic. For most of them, it was a holding operation until the next
orders came through. Lyautey was a different type, with a broader,
more sensitive vision, both idealistic and pragmatic. In fact, he was
not entirely suited to military life, and many years later, after bitter
disappointments, took up an activity which suited the boyish, springy
side to his personality better: the Scouts. By the time he met Isabelle,
in October 1903, he was forty-nine years old, and had just been
promoted to general. Two days after his promotion, on 11 October,
he wrote, in a letter to his sister, 'At the moment I'm feeling regret at
having to give up my blue dolman, and I have the impression of ageing
which this venerable designation confers on me; there is no way now
I can be taken for a young man. Since yesterday, every time that my
officers call me *mon général* I look around me to see if it's serious.'
Until well into middle age he continued to write ebullient letters back
to his family peppered with expressions such as 'Africa! Africa!'
'Magic! Magic!', 'Hurrah! Here's the sun, the sun-king, the sun-god',
and 'What a healthy, independent, really virile life!' He felt the same
surges of aesthetic and sensuous response that Isabelle felt towards
the desert – and towards Arab clothes.

In the year of Isabelle's birth, 1877, two years after leaving

Saint-Cyr, he had first come to Algeria on a six-week study trip, sent by the army staff college in Paris. He had chosen to go 'out of a taste for adventure and exoticism, because Africa, then very much in fashion, stimulated people's imaginations'. The young man of aristocratic background, who, like Loti, had been a sickly child and had spent two years of his childhood confined to bed after an accident, was dazzled by the permission given in this new country for enjoyment of the body. He describes a formative visit to an Arab house where he was led through dark passages, hung with soft drapes which brushed his skin, by two 'nearly naked young men'. They then undressed him and took him to a marble steam bath, in preparation for a massage by a waiting Moor, after which he was dressed up as an Arab and allowed to stretch out on a divan. He had already been 'avid for mysticism' at the age of nineteen, and now, four years after this trip, he began to study Arabic, the Koran and Muslim ways. All this would ensure that he and Isabelle would establish an instant rapport, especially since he, too, suffered from long periods of *cafard*, of 'despair which seems incurable'.

It was after a protracted, fifteen-month spell of depression that he was posted to head the subdivision at Aïn Sefra, in the south-west of Algeria, next to the Moroccan border. His return to Africa revived his spirits, as it never failed to do: in Africa his temperament 'found its equilibrium and his life its meaning'.

From his second visit onwards, he had become convinced that a protectorate was a better system than direct administration, which he deplored, particularly for the way it imposed institutions which were absolutely foreign to the natives' own traditions. The policy of assimilation seemed to him grotesque. In 1891 he had written a long essay entitled 'The social role of the officer', which was published in the *Revue des deux mondes*, where he set out his alternative ideals: 'to orientate the army towards reform in human relations, to define a new style of officer, to insert the army into a nation through civic missions and frequent contacts with the most varied professional and social milieux'. When, in 1894, he had become General Galliéni's Chief of Staff in Tongking, he responded avidly to his general's own theories, so similar to his own, which were carried through with a charisma and panache which appealed to the aristocrat and artist in Lyautey. From there, he had accompanied Galliéni to Madagascar where he had 'pacified' (a key term for him) the north-west of the island. However, by 1903 he was well aware that even these policies were not foolproof, and that the groundswell of anti-colonial resentment, encouraged by Arabi Pasha's 1882 revolt in Egypt, and by anti-colonial actions in Tunis from 1881, was now beginning to surface. It was also doing so in areas of which he had direct experience: Madagascar from 1898 onwards – *after* his work of 'pacification' had been done – and now Algeria and Morocco, where the revolts were focused around the 'rebel' Bu Amama in the Tafilalet area of Morocco, close to the ill-defined and disputed Algerian border.

Lyautey's plan of operation from Aïn Sefra was not, as it had been previously, endless small bulldog attacks on the local tribes, who could always retreat faster than the army could pursue them, but systematically to win over the cooperation of the wavering tribes, and force the resolutely hostile ones into submission by keeping them out of the oases, on which they were dependent for their survival. It has been called 'the Aïn Sefra method of psychological conquest and "contacts" with a flavour of aestheticism', or Lyautey's 'hearts and minds' policy. Lyautey himself saw it as setting up 'a centre of attraction and not a pole of repulsion', and saw his overall goal as 'pacific penetration' into Morocco. His intentions were relatively benevolent, but by redefining the vocabulary of colonialism he was only adding a gloss, not changing its nature. The effect of being colonized gently was in many ways as pernicious as being colonized brutally.

*

Victor Barrucand, who had been producing his newspaper *L'Akhbar* out of Algiers since January 1903, had similar ideas to Lyautey's on the possibility of achieving a positive fusion between the best of Islam and the best of French culture. He and Lyautey had corresponded, and in autumn 1903 he had the idea of sending Isabelle down to the south-west to report on the army's skirmishes with the 'insurgent' tribes of the Tafilalet, and on its expected push into Morocco – a move which Isabelle had foreseen three years previously. He put the idea to Isabelle: she should make a wide-ranging tour of the Sud-Oranais region, reporting on the progress of Lyautey's campaign, describing the unknown country the French were taking over, and eventually compiling a book of her writings. Isabelle was elated at the prospect. Randau said he watched the transformation: 'We were no longer in the presence of someone crushed by fate. Her eyes shone; she held her head high, and her gaiety was a pleasure to behold.' It was a vindication of a long-held dream: to follow the army. It must, too, have been an irresistible temptation for her to accept the approval of the establishment, in the person of Lyautey, on whatever terms, after the humiliations of Batna and Ténès.

On 18 September 1903 Slimène had obtained another position as *khodja* in Guergour, west of Sétif, and his preoccupation with his job left her leeway – which she might have taken anyway – to move around. In September there had been a siege at Taghit and a confrontation at El Moungar in the south-west, in which Captain de Susbielle had for once distinguished himself, and it was these events, in which both tribesmen and French soldiers had been killed and wounded, which prompted Isabelle's departure. She left in late September, taking the railway down to the Sud-Oranais.

The Paris newspaper *Le Matin* had also decided to send a correspondent to the region, on the heels of the recent skirmishes. His name was Jean Rodes. He had already written a short piece about Isabelle for the *Petit Bleu* in Paris, at the request of Randau's friends the Leblond brothers, and when a 'robust lad, *imberbe*', dressed in native costume, arrived at his hotel asking to see him, he guessed at once who it was. Isabelle thanked him for the article, and they compared notes on their projects. She was living 'in native fashion' in Aïn Sefra, sleeping wherever there was a corner of a café or courtyard. She gave him some advice on travelling in these regions: 'Guns and powder are the most precious of jewels around here. If you travel into the *bled* alone, go with your hands in your pockets or, at least, with your weapon carefully hidden; that way you may be able to travel with impunity. If they catch the least sight of a weapon, you're lost.' (Advice de Morès could have used.)

Later, Rodes and Isabelle visited Figuig together, accompanied by a small escort of *mokhrazenis* and an interpreter. Rodes remarked that 'Isabelle was in these circumstances completely astonishing in her profound knowledge of colloquial Arabic and Arabic customs, and she used endlessly and fluently to reciprocate their long rituals of salutations and pious exclamations.' He said that the most refined and scholarly Muslims took an evident pleasure in the ritual perfection of her language, and used to make a point of trying to get her to speak as much as possible. Rodes was not so complimentary about her looks: 'She was ugly, with an ugliness unredeemed by any pleasing feature of her face, with her very prominent forehead, her high cheekbones, very tiny eyes and an appallingly nasal voice. In contrast her walk, the way she held her shoulders, very squarely, belonged more to a hardened cavalryman, a real *spahi*; unless you had known, you would never ever have taken her for a woman.' The next day they both found themselves in Figuig, and Isabelle bedded down in a corner of Rodes's room. Both of them wrote their articles on tables in the same room. They were joined by the painter Maxime Noiré, another friend of Randau's, whom Isabelle had known in her Ténès days, and who slept in another corner. Rodes said that Isabelle was extremely talkative and expansive, saying without the least inhibition everything that came into her head 'usually about her life and adventures in the Sud-Oranais. She never said a word, in my company, about the troubles she had in Ténès.'

At some time during this period she was introduced to General Lyautey by the head of the Béni-Ounif annexe, Lieutenant Berriau. Lyautey welcomed her warmly. His opinion of her is expressed in a note he wrote to Barrucand after her death. 'We understood each other very well, poor Mahmoud and I, and I shall always cherish exquisite memories of our evening talks. She was what attracts me most in the world: a rebel [*réfractaire*]. To find someone who is really *himself*, who exists outside all prejudice, all enslavement, all cliché, and who passes through life as liberated as a bird in space, what a treat!' His words, of aristocratic grace and airiness, had some semblance of truth, but it was a romantic view, more a yearning for a quality he longed to see embodied than a true perception of Isabelle's character. His phrase 'someone who is really *himself*' subconsciously got the heart of the matter: it was a contradiction in terms. Isabelle never did find the right mode to be really *herself*.

In Aïn Sefra, Isabelle began frequenting the military quarter, getting to know the soldiers of all nationalities who were serving there in the Foreign Legion. She had a soft spot for the thin, weary, fever-ridden Legionnaires, who had been 'sent to rest' here, in between fighting in Tongking and Madagascar. She could be seen playing the piano for them in one of the French cafés in the square – called bluntly (and probably descriptively) *Le Môme qui Pue* (The Stinking Kid) – or talking with the foreigners amongst them in their own languages. Her German, apparently, was better than her Russian. One German legionnaire, Richard Kohn, who met Robert Randau many years later, told him how delighted the German soldiers had been to meet someone who could speak their language so fluently and elegantly:

She was interested in our private lives, told us that her brother had been in the Legion, questioned us as to why we had signed up. And on her part she told us endless fascinating stories, particularly of her wanderings in the *bled*. Between ourselves, too, we were secretly flattered that she should prefer the company of soldiers to that of officers. We knew she was close to our chief, Lyautey; I once saw her sitting face to face with him at his desk. They were leaning towards each other and whispering together. But I must make it clear that none of us ever flirted with her, or took any liberties with her. Although there were sometimes a dozen of us chatting with her, not one of us would have ever allowed himself to use any coarse language in her presence. Besides, she had nothing provocative about her and was far from being pretty. Several people who did not know her have claimed that she behaved badly. Not one of the legionnaire she knew in Aïn Sefra would have corroborated that opinion. There were even people who would swear that Lyautey, either as a colonel or as a general, had her as a mistress. This, Sir, is a pure calumny; and I can say so, because very often, in the evenings, my companions and I would meet our chief coming back up to the barracks in the company of women from the *café-concert*, whom he was taking back to his quarters on delicate business.

Although there are naturally no records of the arrangement, there is no doubt that from now on Lyautey engaged Isabelle to do reconnaissance work on his behalf. She was the ideal agent: she could pass anywhere amongst the Muslims and the local tribes, even into the *zawiya*, where no European could normally go, and which were suspected of being strongholds of Muslim resistance. In her capacity as a journalist, she also had a cover for being in the most sensitive and potentially dangerous areas. From November 1903 onwards she began to send back two kinds of story: the first, lengthy, rather plodding and repetitious accounts of the tactics the French army were adopting in the region, and the other short, quickly-drafted, soft-focused sketches of local people, incidents and tales she had met with on the way.

The clearest sign of her agentship is in the reports she began to send back to the *L'Akhbar*, which were infused with Lyautey's own ideas. In two lengthy articles of November 1903 and February 1904, entitled 'Choses du Sud-Oranais', she set out her opinions. The three tacks which had been used up till then had proved expensive and ineffectual – bellicose expeditions against tribes which could not be reached, and would anyway return, or endless defence against their raids and *razzias*, or systematic extermination of the nomads. None of these, she wrote, had worked, nor could they. She pointed out that there were two distinct populations in these Atlas areas, with on the whole opposed interests: the sedentary *ksouriens*, attached to the soil and so interested in pacification; and the nomads, who by their nature and tradition had always quarrelled and pillaged. These nomads – the Ouled-Djérir, Doui-Ménia, Béni-Ghil, and Amours – were not in any sense waging a holy war; they fought in the same way that they wandered, out of habit and tradition. The region had always been *bled-el-baroud*, powder-country, and they called the French *el khian*, the bandits, just like any other tribal enemy or rival. They were causing the trouble in the area, but to pursue them or to exterminate them was no policy. There was another, economic and humane way, as formulated by 'the fine and calm General Lyautey': to isolate the Saharan market-oases and keep them under close surveillance. The markets were the life-blood of the nomads, so they needed to be controlled, and forbidden to the dissident tribes. In this way a few police measures would succeed where costly military expeditions would not:

In order to justify our presence in the south-west Oranais, France has the most imperative duty to ensure a benevolent peace in the area and to use all kinds of economic measures to improve the country's position . . . Without this, the conquest of this area, which has already been so controversial, would be an absolutely pointless venture, and one which any sensible person would not hesitate to condemn severely.

These are unambiguous words: '*la conquête . . . resterait une équipée sans utilité aucune, et que tout esprit sensé n'hésiterait pas à condamner sévèrement.*' She was, she was saying, against colonial conquest – *except* if it brought improved conditions of life to the local people. Having shared their poverty, she felt keenly the daily hardships of their lives, and it was on this basis that she, a Muslim, an ex-anarchist, and a champion of the underdog, could endorse Lyautey's policy to the point of actively working for it.

However, she was also dazzled by Lyautey's sophisticated views and broad command of a situation which he had so recently come into, and this led her to adopt uncritically his overall plan of manipulating these regions away from Morocco. In Lyautey's mind this was the first step towards a gradual assumption of French 'responsibility' for the whole of Morocco, which he felt could be gently wrested from the frivolous Sultan. Isabelle herself, in aiding and abetting Lyautey's plans for the Tafilalet, was being manipulated for a grander plan: the takeover of Morocco. Isabelle wrote, in what was surely an echo of Lyautey's words to her:

It would not be impossible for us to gain some profit from our conquest and to organize it without disturbing Morocco's *illusion* that it possessed these regions . . . We could not be better inspired than by confiding this important mission to General Lyautey, young, with incomparable energy and capacities, and who has managed, in so few months, to get such a good grasp of the situation and instigate a plan of action.

These politically oriented reports of Isabelle's gradually ceded place during the first half of 1904 to more picturesque and human essays on life in these south-western oases, and particularly in Béni-Ounif and Figuig, in amongst the *mokhrazenis*, the native soldiers who worked on a day-by-day basis for the French army, without the ties and commitments of the *spahis* or *tirailleurs*, slept rolled up in their special blue burnouses 'with the absolute nonchalance of the southern peoples, used for so long to sense danger lurking in the shadows of the night', and laughed and joked as they fought. She wrote in essays under the general title of 'Sud-Oranais' of living amongst the white tents of the *caïds* and officers; of the hubbub of the markets; of the increasing cold and wet of the approaching winter, with the sparse trees left gaunt, and the dunes and mountains surrounding the oases becoming covered in snow, a quite different landscape. She described the rumours rumbling around about the legendary old 'agitator' Bu Amama, the chief thorn in Lyautey's side, 'still venerated, but whose influence is still hostile'. (Her use of the word 'hostile' puts her squarely in Lyautey's camp at the time.) Or she wrote of the long conversations she had in German, with a nostalgic German Foreign legionnaire, or the languid, periodic flicking of the desert lizards, or the degradation of an old woman, half-mad from having lost her son many years ago, or the tears and last spasm of a dying camel, or the specific nomadic sadness: leaving, especially under these cold winter skies, with heavy greenish clouds 'like shreds of putrefied flesh'. 'And so my memory is full of families, of homes, of bivouac fires. At times when I'm alone or daydreaming I conjure all this up in the smoke from a cigarette, and it's more of a tonic than my memories of great enthusiasms, which leave troughs behind them, or of great hopes, based on expectations of others, which always finish, almost always finish, in disillusion and failure.'

By this stage she now knew that on short journeys her guides might take her completely at face value, as Si Mahmoud, the young *lettré* from Constantine, but that on longer contact the Arab and Berber tribes were not deceived:

'Si Mahmoud,' they would say, 'stay amongst us. We have got used to you; we are your brothers now, and we shall miss you if you go, because you are a brave lad, and have eaten bread and salt and ridden alongside us.' They knew perfectly well, from all sorts of European indiscretions, that Si Mahmoud was a woman. But, with beautiful Arab discretion, they argued that it was none of their business, that it would have been inappropriate to allude to it, and they carried on treating me as they had at first, as an educated and slightly superior friend.

Isabelle's words echoed Randau's perception.

It was around this period that Isabelle recorded visits she made, in her guise as Si Mahmoud, to two brothels. They excited the voyeur in her and she enjoyed her equivocal position, being lightly flirted with by the young half-caste or Negro prostitutes, who saw her as a slightly aloof young scholar, merely accompanying the other soldiers' 'more urgent business'. At the door, her companion, a young *mokhra-zeni* called Abdelkader, hiding his blue burnous, since any Arabs in the French army were not viewed kindly in these contingently Moroccan regions, was impatient. 'For him, it's not artistic curiosity which has led him here,' Isabelle wrote. Another visit she made is recorded in her essay 'Joies noires', where she describes the dances of Negro prostitutes from the Sudan, sinuously undulating their firm, highly articulated black bodies 'with artificial shivers' and languorous looks from half-closed, chestnut-coloured eyes, their bracelets jangling against each other. The *kef* was passed around. Isabelle watched two fine Sudanese and a *spahi* watching them, fixed and spellbound, with furrowed brows. 'This black hovel gives off a violent and savage sensuality, which is finally profoundly disturbing.'

*

After three months in these southern regions, Isabelle returned to
Algiers in December 1903 to report back to Barrucand and to spend
her fourth Ramadan with Slimène. She took a long and slow route by
mule across the high plateaux through Géryville and the mountains
of the Ouled Naïl, up to Berrouaghia, which was then the southerly
terminus of the railway to Algiers, accompanied only by a *mokhrazeni*
and by a new acquisition, a long, black-haired dog, Loupiot. The
voyage took a toll on her health, since the nights could be freezing at
that time of year, and she had to rely on nomads' tents for shelter.
The stories, impressions and nomads' songs she gathered from this
journey were published in *L'Akhbar* in June 1904, and later within
Dans l'ombre chaude de l'Islam and *Notes de route*.

Although Isabelle's journalistic reports on the French penetration
into Morocco were guardedly pro-French, her copious stories of local
life cumulatively present a rather different picture, politically well
ahead of her time. In her book *Isabelle Eberhardt*, Simone Rezzoug
points out that 'from the beginning [Isabelle's] texts establish an
underlying assumption: the fundamental alienness of the colonial
system to the Algerians. The social and economic organization denies
their existence; but in their turn, and with a force which one would
not expect from such disinherited people, they are refusing a world
which they despise, and ceasing all significant relations with it.' Isabelle
does this not didactically, but instinctively, by building up a strong,
coherent picture of the life and customs of the native Algerians to set
against that of the conquering civilization, subverting simply by her
powers of observation and understanding the colonial cliché of civilization versus barbarism. What she creates instead is a picture of two
opposing civilizations, with individuals doomed more often than not
to be destroyed when they get caught up in the clash between them.
The conquered civilization is not seen as pitiable or weak. On the
contrary, it is marked, as Simone Rezzoug notes, by 'a tragic grandeur,
which the colonial oppression involuntarily confers upon it'. As a
result Isabelle's writing, by now far removed from any 'orientalist'
exoticism, or from any colonial patronage towards 'suffering' people,
was on its way to becoming a milestone in Algerian literature.

Nothing is recorded of the few weeks Isabelle now spent in Algiers,
but it is clear from subsequent events that it marked a change in her
relations with Slimène. They must have been together, in Algiers or
Sétif; and there must have been some kind of showdown. It seems

that Isabelle's long absences had finally taxed Slimène's patience, and that he may have taken a new lover. Whatever the precise details, Isabelle's mood now became markedly more detached and wistful.

She probably planned to return down to the south anyway in the new year, but the way she did so in the end was abrupt and spontaneous. Barrucand and Isabelle were on their way to Oran by train, some time in February 1904. Barrucand was still prey to grief over the death of his wife two years before. Throwing himself into work on *L'Akhbar* had indeed proved an antidote to morbid thoughts – 'the appeal of the tomb', as he put it. The train stopped at Perrégaux (now Mohammadia), at the intersection of the Algiers-Oran line and the new railway running down to Aïn Sefra. In a scrawled note Barrucand wrote to Isabelle after her death, he recalled: 'I can still remember the moment at Perrégaux when we looked at the railway line that disappeared down to the stony south, and you took me by the hand and led me out on to the carriage platform. Look hard at that time, you said. If we took it we could be in another country tomorrow, and breathing another air, we could forget everything that needs forgetting and live each hour as if it were new.' Isabelle's desire to 'forget everything that needs forgetting' no doubt included the emotional rift with Slimène. Although they carried on to Oran that day, three days later Barrucand had 'given in' to Isabelle's wish. On their way back to Algiers, they stopped off at Perrégaux and took the great rail route to the south together.

Arriving in Aïn Sefra, they found Lyautey's policy bearing fruit. A delegation of five sheikhs and a *caïd* from the Béni-Ghil tribe, long loyal to Bu Amama, was coming to have talks with Lyautey and with representatives from their rival tribe, the Hamyan from the Mécheria region. The talks were to take place in the house of the agha Si Moulay of Tiout, chief of the Amour tribe, with whom Isabelle was on particularly good terms. 'Si Moulay,' she wrote, 'has managed to maintain the dignity of his bearing as much with the French officers as with the nomads and the *ksouriens* who are in effect his subjects . . . [The French] have had the sense to leave the Tiout *marabouts* with all their authority and all their influence, which have often been precious.'

When the talks came, in late February, Isabelle and Barrucand were both present, and Barrucand recalled the evening they first arrived in his note to Isabelle: 'The flickering light from an *arar*-wood fire in the hall played over a large, hanging blue and red carpet, and over the faces of the deputation of Moroccan nomads, who stood waiting like mummies.' In her article on these peace talks, Isabelle described the Béni-Ghil in their long, finely woven blue *djellabas* and white turbans, with their 'handsome bronze faces, very closed and very energetic in the firm delineation of their features and in the fiery looks in their long, wild eyes. The austerity of their dark Maghreb costume adds a particular cachet to them, so different from the Hamyan chiefs, in their long scarlet burnouses hung with French medals.'

The Béni-Ghil had come to accept the French proposals: to reintegrate their abandoned mutual territory with the Hamyan, to do their best to find and hand over those amongst their number who were still 'dissidents', and 'genuinely and sincerely' to abandon Bu Amama and his leadership. Isabelle wrote that 'the Béni-Ghil themselves will not be long in feeling the benefits of peace, and their example could be beneficial to other dissident tribes. This sort of declaration of peace the Béni-Ghil have made is, it seems to me, the direct result of the firm and ingenious policy General Lyautey has been adopting towards the nomads.' She felt it was important to monitor the translation of their promises into acts, and, on their part, 'never to compromise our dignity, either through weakness or by acts of brutality or provocation. We must rigorously respect our promises to them, in order to have the right in return to demand the same respect and even faithfulness.'

As they stood in the firelight amongst the nomads, Barrucand turned to Isabelle and asked her, 'What are you, a stranger, doing amongst all these nomadic warriors?' She replied 'with a wicked look': 'I'm obeying my destiny.'

15

PEACE

The winning-over of the Béni-Ghil was not the only fruit of Lyautey's 'firm and ingenious policy'. Even before his arrival in the area he had obtained a blanket authorization from Paris to occupy the 'Béchar region', even though Béchar itself was at the time probably within Moroccan territory. It was only 'probably' because the borders between south-west Algeria and Morocco were notoriously ill-defined, giving useful leeway for interpretation, which Lyautey and the French amply exploited. The fact that 'Béchar' was the name of a region, a town and a mountain added to the convenient confusion.

On 13 November, just over a month after his arrival, Lyautey took the independent initiative of occupying the town of Béchar itself, which he had designated as an important strategic base. It was occupied 'without incident', Lyautey wrote to his friend and mentor General Galliéni the next day, but not without sleight of hand: he added in brackets, 'It is understood and agreed that in order to make things easier for diplomatic sensibilities, Béchar is no longer called Béchar, but Colomb.' The reports went back to the Quai d'Orsay: a town called Colomb had been taken. Lyautey wrote to Galliéni that if there were objections 'of protocol' to their presence in Béchar, they would insist that it was necessary for the immediate security of their military posts and nationals in the area. If this was not enough they could always 'present it as a military base for our police in order to help *our Moroccan friends* out of a situation which they cannot cope with on their own.' In the event Colomb-Béchar, as it became known, soon became the desired 'centre of attraction' for the south-western regions, which he wanted to take over by 'tact, patience and method' and the swift enabling of 'material prosperity' in the area: in essence to win over by economics and charm.

With Bu Amama in the north Lyautey took a ruthless tack. With the Doui-Ménia and the Ouled-Djérir in the south he adopted a 'soft approach', and within this he felt one particular man had an important role to play: the head of the Ziania confraternity in Kenadsa, Sidi Brahim ould Mohammed. If Si Brahim could be won over to the French cause, most of the region from Figuig over to the Tafilalet, with its defiant, mainly Berber tribes, would follow his lead as the most influential religious leader in the area.

The town of Kenadsa was some eighteen miles south-west of Colomb-Béchar, within Moroccan territory, and subject to the suzerainty of the Moroccan sultan. In his letter of 14 November to Galliéni, Lyautey twice stressed the importance of gaining the chief's favour. Two months later, in a confidential report of 13 January 1904 to the Governor-General, he wrote: 'Our relations are good with the *zawiya* at Kenadsa. Sidi Brahim has introduced himself to the Commander-in-Chief in Tagda, making great protestations of friendship, but he seems very demoralized and discouraged by the prospect of being caught between us and his neighbours' – not surprisingly, one might feel. In the same file is a rare letter in Arabic from the Algerian leader Bu Amama to a fellow-chief, which had been intercepted by the French and which shows his view of the conflict, very different from that of the French: 'The French authorities have betrayed me many, many times and until now they have endlessly stolen from me and killed my men; whilst I have only wanted peace and tranquillity. At the moment all the people from the west [i.e. eastern Morocco] are asking me to march against the French; but I only want peace and tranquillity.' His one brief note stands as a reminder, if it were needed, not to be hoodwinked by the mass of prolix and loaded verbiage by which an occupying power justifies and insinuates its presence.

To ask Isabelle to go and stay in the *zawiya*, as she was able to do as an initiate of the Qadrya, and particularly as a friend of Lella Zeyneb, who was close to the sheikh of Kenadsa, must have seemed a brilliant stroke of diplomacy on Lyautey's part. Not only could Isabelle furnish them with an intimately informed reading of the sheikh's allegiances and intentions, but it would be a sojourn of personal benefit to Isabelle herself, with whose religious views and thirst for an inner peace Lyautey sympathized. How clearly Lyautey spelt out to Isabelle what he wanted from her voyage to Kenadsa, or how much Isabelle herself may have been a pawn, is difficult to say. However, in the isolated position she would be in, her main role could only be to gather long-term information or at most to predispose Si

Brahim to go a little further along the road towards collaboration with the French.

As for Isabelle herself, her copious writings during her stay in Kenadsa suggest the personal side of the challenge it represented was paramount throughout. In one of her first essays – none of which were printed in her lifetime – entitled 'New Life', she described her initial feelings on arrival:

I am the guest of these men. I shall live in the silence of their house. Already they have brought me all the calm of their spirit, and a shadow of peace has entered the recesses of my soul . . . Is this the life that I came to find? Will all my longing finally be appeased, and for how long? . . . I dream of a sleep which would be a death, from which one would emerge armed and strong, with a personality regenerated by forgetting.

Isabelle travelled down to Colomb-Béchar with a guide, Djilali, noting with nostalgia the pervasive scents of cut fruit, saltpetre and humid palm groves, potent reminders of her travels in other oases. As she travelled westwards, even the settled village people became more silent and mistrustful, suspecting anyone from the east of being collaborators. From Béchar it was a day's journey to Kenadsa across the dunes and rocks which ran below the dominating silhouette of the Béchar mountain. The chief of the Ziania *zawiya* in Béchar had provided Isabelle with a Negro guide, Embarek, for the last stage of her journey. Kenadsa was a village centred around its monastery, which had been founded, along with the Ziania order, by an ancestor of Sidi Brahim's, Sidi M'hammed-ben-Bou-Ziane. Its mellow clay houses sprawled agreeably over a small hill, their fertile gardens spilling down 'in graceful disorder'. At the approach to Kenadsa stood a brilliant white tomb to one of Si Brahim's ancestors, the Muslim *maraboute* Lella Aïcha, surrounded by countless other tombs decaying in the invading sand – all there, Isabelle wrote, 'as an expected margin to the dwellings of the living. All these Saharan cities begin with cemeteries.' It was the echo of an old obsession.

When they arrived at the *zawiya*, Embarek introduced her as he knew her: Si Mahmoud ould Ali, a young Tunisian scholar travelling from monastery to monastery for instruction. Si Brahim, advised of her arrival, came in due course to greet her, and they exchanged the usual courtesies. She gave him a letter of introduction from a Ziania *khouan* in Aïn Sefra. When he had left, she took stock of her new surroundings. She was installed in a large, square, four-pillared room dimly lit from above, with a square basin in the centre and a jug of water for the ritual ablutions. There was a pit in the floor with an iron grid and a chimney above, for preparation of tea, and the wooden doors were painted with naive, faded pictures of flowers. 'Rugs are laid out; I am *chez moi*.' All the same, bearing in mind her experience at Béhima, and the political aspect to her visit here, she automatically checked the room in her mind 'for security'. Portly, with a greying collar of beard and a face marked by smallpox, Si Brahim came in once more to welcome her and question her discreetly. His slow, dignified manner and gentle, welcoming smile reassured her, and as he left, in his very white, simple garments and large turban, she was left with an 'impression of security'.

She had been struck by the various doors closing behind her as she had entered the monastery, and after a week she began to be troubled by the austere isolation that was expected of an initiate such as herself. (It would also have impeded any information that Isabelle might have been getting out.) Nothing could be done without the express permission of Sidi Brahim. 'Why was I not allowed to go out? It began to weigh on me and even worry me. My cherished solitude was no longer voluntary; my room, so good for inner visions, was too like a discreet prison.' She went to see Si Brahim, who smiled at her concern: 'You must not worry, my child! If you want to go out, it is up to you. But in that case, you must change your costume. You know that the Algerian dress is badly thought of around here.'

In her grey, Moroccan *djellaba*, Isabelle was free to wander in the small town, and the simple discipline of the monastery gave her time to write down her impressions of that outside life, as well as, increasingly, of her inner state, which she was having to face starkly, stripped of the solaces of alcohol or love or companionship. Apart from the Negro slaves – whose lack of finesse in *greeting*, excepting the Sudanese, she rather magisterially deplored – her only regular company was that of Si Brahim, who came in daily to give her news of the outside world. Yet she felt an increasing distance from it all. 'In the monotony of life in Kenadsa, I'm gradually losing all notion of agitations and passions. I have the impression that everywhere, like here, the course of things is arrested.'

Once, a slave came conspiratorially with an invitation to take tea with a group of students from the nearby mosque, whom she had met at prayer. Isabelle remembered that such groups of young men were rumoured to go in for all kinds of perversions in private to make up for the austerity of their routine and the future rigidity of their lives. She was intrigued to see for herself what went on in such clandestine meetings. In the event, although they swore her to secrecy on what they did, it amounted anticlimactically to some guitar-playing, story-telling and even embroidery – an honourable activity for men, even in public. They seemed to take Isabelle at face value as Si Mahmoud. Others, she felt, probably knew she was a woman: 'If anyone has suspicions, they would be very careful not to let me sense them, because it would represent a grave dereliction of Muslim etiquette.'

Another time Si Brahim, knowing that she had been suffering from a fever, invited her to join him for a picnic – in spite of heavy clouds so low they almost grazed the top of the dunes. A carpet and cushions were laid out in a terrace garden, and close friends and relatives were invited. They talked of their neighbouring tribes, they talked of Morocco and the Tafilalet, they talked disapprovingly of Bu Amama: Isabelle would already have had sufficient information to report back to Lyautey on their real feelings. In the branches of the surrounding date trees, a mass of swallows fluttered and twittered. One of the *talebs* said, 'Today is the general assembly of the birds. They are meeting to regulate the affairs of their tribe and to take grave decisions. These tiny little creatures, hardly bigger than flies, make as much commotion as a hundred Doui-Ménia, all talking at the same time.' The solemn *marabouts* laughed at this dig at their turbulent neighbours.

Isabelle, who had always been subject to bouts of malaria during her time in Algeria, and whose health Randau claimed was 'not robust' – in spite of, and because of, presuming so much on it – was now more and more often in a fevered state. Malaria may not have been the only cause of her fevers: it seems likely that she was also suffering from venereal disease, probably syphilis. Quoting her later biographer, René-Louis Doyon, who never knew her, as saying that she only once slept with a European, and that was Letord, Randau writes that 'it must be acknowledged that Isabelle suffered from a chronic, intimate ailment of the most unpleasant kind.' He says no more, although more evidence, ambiguous to the last, was yet to come.

Since meeting Slimène, Isabelle had probably been at least more or less faithful to him. But their long periods apart strained her sensual nature, and she was often overtaken by moments of pure lust. The painter Maxime Noiré, who was (alas for us!) given to hyperbole for the sake of a good story, recounted how he had been with her in Zousfana in the Sud-Oranais in 1903 and how she had suddenly roared 'I want a *tirailleur*! I want a *tirailleur*!' 'By Jove, my dear,' Noiré had ventured, 'I'm here, I'm here!' But Isabelle did not want 'the *ersatz*' and hollered again, 'I want a *tirailleur*.' Whether she got one or not is not recorded.

Now, in Kenadsa, her fever and her cloistered life inhibited her actions, but not her thoughts. She would lie listening to the shifts in sounds coming from the village as evening approached: the clanging of heavy gates, the sounds of horses and goats, the late-night tambourine of the Aïssaouas, seeking oblivion and ecstasy in chanting. And after all of them, Isabelle heard, or thought she heard, the sounds of desire, of moaning, of grinding teeth: 'Under the quiet stars, the ardent rutting'. It troubled her: 'What agony! I almost want to bite into the warm earth, but the real ecstasy is above, in the light of the stars, in the memory of eyes looked into, of hours lived, of hours so beautifully wasted.'

An emotional factor contributed to her increasing abdication from sensual things. According to some oblique references in her notes from Kenadsa, she had had a letter, apparently from Slimène, in which he told her he had found somebody new. 'Yesterday I received a letter all bathed in another sun than mine. What, because some new eyes have smiled at you, can you have become so egotistical as to ask your old friends to share your joy?' Perhaps Slimène had felt excluded from her relationship with Barrucand; her feelings for Slimène appear to have cooled by the time she was living in Algiers; perhaps it was mutual. 'When I return to Algiers, where my heart was troubled, where my desires were no longer fixed . . . what shall we speak of if it's not of us, and how shall we do it?' The letter had brought

a fresh and cruel breath of *insouciance*. Immediately afterwards, I fell back into my feeling of exile, with the urge to bury myself even deeper into the hostile South . . . I put nothing in my reply which was worth reading . . . Why should I? One day the paths separate, destinies go their different ways . . . We must not regret anything, because our happiness, and theirs, will come from letting ourselves be carried along one day by the mysterious currents taking our souls, adrift, towards inconceivable shores. Then we shall taste the intoxication of decay and shipwreck, we shall be beached and lost on the vast night, and we shall feel our hearts burst with germinating grains of sorrow.

This curious and prophetic note, full of concealed pain, leads her to remember 'absent lips, lips which will drink other breath than mine, because my soul could not give itself, because it did not belong within me, but in eternal things, and because I possess it at last in deep, divine solitude, as all my body is offered up to the southern night.' Later, in an account of fever entitled 'The Music of Words', she writes to her 'far-away friend' of songs she knew:

If you sang them to your little love she would laugh in your face, because your little love has never had fever. She only knows how to look at herself in her pocket mirror, gently blink her eyes and purse her lips. She understands with the edge of her teeth. When her eyes close in ecstasy and a dark ring marks her eyelids, don't think she loves you: it's a brief, superficial shiver of egoism. And why should she love you, for your love, like mine, is only a passionate suffering, whilst hers is a light-hearted thing?

It was a bitter insight, to realize that her love had only ever been a 'passionate suffering'. The roots of this incident are obscure: perhaps Slimène had taken his cue from her, and presumed too much on the camaraderie of their relationship, thinking he could share his feelings of new love with her. More likely, her long absences, 'independent airs', and perhaps even closeness to Barrucand, had finally tested him too much. Whatever the case, this loss combined with her spiritual journey in the monastery to detach her gradually from worldly matters.

Increasingly, this journey was towards the inner peace that eluded her, as it had eluded Trophimowsky. She wrote of the 'force and tranquillity of things which seem to last for ever, because they are gently moving on towards the void, without a fuss, without any revolt, without agitation, without even a shudder at inevitable death'. She was achieving a measure of mystical resignation, able now to get intoxicated by the mere thought of a sunset, no longer dependent on drink or love for exaltation. Pure Islamic peace would always elude her, because of her complicated past, but she recognized its appeal:

To be healthy in body, pure of all stains, after bathing in clear water, to be simple and to believe, never to have doubted, never to have battled against oneself, to wait for the inevitable moment of eternity, without fear and without impatience — that is peace, that is Muslim happiness — and, who knows? — perhaps it is also wisdom . . . Gradually, I've felt regrets and desires fading away. I've let my spirit rise and let my will die down. Dangerous and delicious drowsiness, leading imperceptibly, but surely, to the threshold of the void.

She looked at groups of Jews from the south crouched over their fires in the sand, and envied them: 'They are the reproach to my romanticism and to this incurable malaise that I've brought with me from the North and from the mystical Orient, along with the blood of those who have been vagabonds before me in the steppes.'

Some time later – none of Isabelle's writings from Kenadsa are dated – she succumbed to a particularly bad bout of fever. At one point she was laid out on a terrace near a hanging goatskin which was dripping water slowly into a copper bowl. The monotonous drip caused her 'an acute pain, as if the drop were obstinately falling on my inflamed skull', but her mouth was too dry to be able to frame the request to take it away. The image recalls that of the throbbing nail in her head after she heard of her mother's death, and perhaps it did subconsciously to Isabelle, since it caused her such distress. Afterwards, she began to have more pleasant mirages of water – water trickling in streams, waterfalls, springs; but when they evaporated, she was left with 'a burning thirst, an atrocious thirst that nothing could appease, and which was devouring me':

Suddenly, an infinite sadness flooded through me. I was seized with childish regrets. I was alone, alone in this lost corner of Moroccan country, and alone everywhere I had lived and alone everywhere I would go, always . . . I had no country, no home, no family . . . Perhaps I had no friends any more. I had passed through, a stranger and an intruder, only causing reprobation and estrangement around me. At that moment, I was suffering, far away from all help, amongst men who were watching, impassively, the ruin of everything that surrounded them and who crossed their arms in face of illness and death, saying: 'Mektoub!' Those who might have thought of me in other parts of the earth were no doubt thinking of their own happiness. They were not suffering from my suffering . . . Ah, yes, it was indeed written! When I was more lucid and calm, I despised my weakness and I smiled at my unhappiness. If I was alone, wasn't it because I had wanted it in my conscious hours, when my thoughts rose above the easy sentimentalities of heart and body, both equally infirm? To be alone is to be free, and freedom was the only happiness accessible to my nature.

The 'ruin' that people were tolerating all around them was no doubt the disintegration of old values, which the French would add to. Isabelle's earlier enthusiasm for Lyautey's ideas had waned under the influence of what she saw and thought at Kenadsa. She had noticed early on in her stay that

since the *marabouts* have started to have good, neighbourly relations and even a growing friendship with the French, a dull discontent has come over the ordinary people. No one dares to raise his voice and criticize the actions of the masters. They bow, they repeat Sidi Brahim's opinions, they praise him, but, at heart, if it weren't for his great moral authority, they would be quite ready to consider him and his relations *M'zanat* [collaborators].

Towards the end of her stay, she had become more sceptical about the possibility of any foreign presence taking root in Africa:

I wanted to possess this country, and this country has possessed me. Sometimes I wonder if the South will not reclaim all the new conquerors who come with dreams of strength and liberty, just as it has destroyed all the old ones . . . I have felt some profound truths: that it is useless to fight against deep-running and immutable influences, and that a durable transplantation of civilization is not possible. I breathe in the African emanations in the hot nights, like an incense rising up towards strange and cruel divinities. No one can completely reject these idols; in fevered evenings they will come back, monstrous, to all those who lay their heads on this soil to sleep, and who turn their eyes towards the cold stars.

With ideas like these, and with the fevers she was labouring under, Isabelle cannot have had much heart for propaganda in the French cause.

She had hoped to spend the whole summer in Kenadsa, and only leave to set off for more distant parts, further into Morocco, into the Tafilalet. There was no longer any thought of going back to be with Slimène. She could have travelled with a caravan of Berbers, whom she knew and trusted, but she was physically too weak. The only reasonable solution seemed to be to return to Aïn Sefra and let herself be looked after at the hospital, but she kept shelving the decision, lulled into quietism:

breathing with delight the air which poisons me. I close my eyes on the past and on the future, as if I had just drunk the magic waters of oblivion and wisdom. The fact is that I no longer regret anything. In moments of calm and reflectiveness it seems to me that I've found the very point of my vagabond and tormented existence. A great serenity has settled on me, as if, after a painful climb, I had finally come through the zone of storms and had found the clear sky. And yet, I don't flatter myself that I can easily communicate this state of mind. I don't seek to analyse myself, much less to strike a pose. I have no audience. It seems to me that everything that I say is very simple.

The distance which I recognize between my way of seeing things and all the manifold social expectations found in modern books and magazines comes no doubt from a geographic illusion, from my sinking into the past through countries which have not evolved.

These, the last of Isabelle's reflections from Kenadsa, ended: 'I still bless my solitude, which allows me to believe, and which is remaking me into a simple and exceptional being, resigned to her destiny.'

Isabelle left for Béchar, Béni-Ounif and Aïn Sefra, to recover at the hospital for the autumn. She planned to travel to the oases of Touat after she had recuperated, and write notes which, together with her impressions of the Sud-Oranais and her 'reveries' of Kenadsa, would make up a book. Her life would continue in this pattern, and eventually 'lassitude and disillusion will come after some years'. This, she felt, was her future in a nutshell, the day she set off from Kenadsa.

She was accompanied by a Berber, El Hassani, and a Negro, Mouley Sahel, who were setting off too, but in the other direction, towards Bou-Dnib and the Tafilalet. They pressed her to change her mind and come too. It was not only her physical weakness which deterred her. She was concerned at doing such a journey 'without authorization': 'wouldn't this voyage of study and curiosity be badly interpreted?' Reluctantly, she declined the invitation. The two men accompanied her on horseback until the entrance to the cemeteries, where their ways parted. It was a poignant moment for Isabelle: 'My throat is so choked with emotion that I can scarcely reply to the words they are saying to me. Yet I must, up until the last minute, keep the courage of a man.'

*

Even in a monastic retreat in the depths of the Moroccan mountains, Isabelle was not free from controversy and apparently contradictory evidence. Did she have syphilis – was it the knowledge of this which gave her her new detachment? – and was she still 'making love for the love of love'? A Colonel Pariel, who had known Isabelle well, gave Claude-Maurice Robert the following account:

In the summer of 1904 I was in charge of the military post at Colomb-Béchar. One day I was told that the *marabout* of Kenadsa wanted me on the telephone. It was to ask me to send him a doctor. Not the young one, he specified, but *le kébir*, the chief, who knew him better. I did what he asked. When the doctor came back, I asked him why the *marabout* had specifically asked for him. He told me he was suffering from an 'intimate infection', and that it was Si Mahmoud who gave it to him.

Yet in 1906 Barrucand went to Kenadsa with Dr Mardrus – who, together with his writer wife, Lucie Delarue-Mardrus, was a great admirer of Isabelle's – and also spoke with Si Brahim. They asked him if he had ever suspected her identity, or knew she was a woman. He said, 'I have heard say that this well-educated and well-mannered young man was only a *roumia* living in Arab costume: but I don't believe that. They told us that, but we didn't believe it.'

If Si Brahim did make love to Isabelle, he would not have volunteered to strangers like Barrucand and the Mardruses a fact he wanted to conceal even from one of his doctors; nor would he have committed the indiscretion of revealing to them Isabelle's real identity, which was her own affair, when she publicly presented another.

Whatever the case, Isabelle's self-esteem, or more accurately her investment in her selfhood, could conceivably have been at a sufficiently low ebb in Kenadsa to allow her to couple detachedly with the one person she was seeing every day, haunted as she was by others' 'ardent rutting'. If so, it was perhaps the underside of the more exalted, and more touching, spiritual and emotional detachment which she recorded in her notes.

16

AN EQUIVOCAL DEATH

In September 1904 Lyautey received reports from his subordinates, perhaps based on Isabelle's own information, to say that the *zawiya* at Kenadsa was not pulling its weight: 'As we see more clearly into its workings we have discovered that the *marabout* is scarcely more than a cypher, without any force or authority, thanks to his weakness of character and especially to his physical infirmity . . . Kenadsa seems to want to maintain the traditional reserve of the Order towards us and to keep neutral . . . In a word, Kenadsa is more or less no use to us any more.'

Isabelle's own brief flirtation with active propagandizing for Lyautey died away in Kenadsa, and inasmuch as she planned her next travels, it was to suit her writing rather than for political motives. She was installed in the military hospital at Aïn Sefra on 2 October 1904, and on the 15th wrote to a friend in Paris – one Mme Berthe Clavel, otherwise unmentioned in the correspondence – 'I'm working hard and have finally finished copying out "Sud-Oranais". As soon as I'm better I shall go back down to the Saharan oases in Béni-Abbès, Timmimoun and In Salah, and bring back a second volume. Since I shall probably spend the winter in Timmimoun, I'll work on *Trimardeur*, which could then be published in the spring. Before that, no hope of my returning to Algiers.' She explained that she would be in hospital now 'for a long time', having 'picked up a fever en route, in swampy country'.

The military hospital was within the hillside garrison at Aïn Sefra. It looked down to the forked river bed of the Sefra wadi, now bone dry, but which very occasionally late in the year would see yellow mountain waters coursing with breakneck speed along its bed. The town had housed a temporary redoubt from 1884, and a narrow-gauge railway from 1889, but it was only since 1900 that it had been the headquarters of the army's activities in south-west Algeria, thanks to its location close to the border, and its magnificent views over the whole of the Figuig valley. (From a different era, and in a different narrative, it also housed some appealing cave paintings of unrecognizable beasts.) Hundreds of soldiers were stationed in the garrison, scores of officers, a forge, a shop, canteens and 148 horses – one of which was given to Isabelle in exchange for her services in the army. It was a bleak, jerry-built military town worse even than Batna, except for the splendour of its surrounding landscape. Attempting to give it a feel of home, the French had built a Hôtel de la Gare, a small square surrounded by scraggy, unsuccessfully transplanted plane trees, and two cafés – Madame Julia's and the Le Môme Qui Pue, where Isabelle had played the piano earlier in the year.

Slimène Ehnni was an unknown figure to the soldiers in Aïn Sefra. He had not been there as far as they knew during Isabelle's earlier stay at the beginning of the year, and he was not there as Isabelle lay in hospital. But Isabelle wrote to him on 16 October asking him to come down to be with her when she left hospital. She rented a small, crumbling clay house on the corner of a street in the lower part of Aïn Sefra, below the river bed, in amongst the native houses. It seems that by the 20th Slimène had arrived there. They had been apart for eight months.

The German Legionnaire who had met Isabelle earlier in the year, Richard Kohn – a meticulous, dry, pedantic man, according to Randau, who spoke to him later – was in the barracks in October. One evening he was detailed to go up to the hospital, and noticed Isabelle being treated there. 'We exchanged common courtesies. She was in a bad mood, cursing the longwindedness of the treatment and protesting her dislike of the hospital; she wanted to demand to leave, against the advice of the doctor, who recommended she should stay in bed for another few days.' Kohn told Randau that although others had since said she left the hospital that evening, he knew from having been there that this was not so. According to him, she voluntarily discharged herself next day, between eight and nine in the morning. One of Lyautey's lieutenants, Lieutenant Paris (Lyautey called him 'Parisse'), was walking through the town early that morning, and bumped into Isabelle as she was coming out of hospital. He had been particularly interested in her writings, to the extent of reading each chapter of her 'Sud-Oranais' stories as she finished it. She told him her husband had just arrived and that she was just taking her bag of possessions down from the hospital to their rented house. They talked of her book and its progress, and she mentioned that she had sent the manuscript off to an editor in Paris and was waiting for the payment of 500 francs. Other people remembered her saying the same.

Meanwhile Richard Kohn was on orderly duty in the barracks, and took up the story from his point of view:

The town is separated from the military quarters by a deep, torrential wadi, which was spanned at the time by a bridge. The river bed was usually always dry, and so the soldiers ordinarily used the goat-tracks as a short cut to the village rather than use the bridge. At about nine o'clock, the sergeant-major sent me into town on an errand. I did not hang around, and came back shortly after the soup-bell had rung. I took my can and went to the canteen. I was on my way back to the mess when the quartermaster, who was standing by the open door, called out: 'Kohn, come and see this, good God, it's extraordinary. Hurry, hurry! My word, the whole village down there is covered in water! And listen to that racket!' I ran over to him, astonished. A bubbling, yellow torrent was rushing down the valley of the river bed, between the town and the camp, sweeping along with it a mass of rubbish, trees and bushes. I saw the water swallowing up the place where I had just been. Between the town and the barracks was a river of rapids and whirlpools, swirling along and swelling as it went. All communications to the town were cut off. Suddenly there was a noise like thunder; I saw half of the bridge collapsing into the waters. At this point in the day there were hardly any soldiers in the town; the bugles had sounded for lunch, and the legionnaires were eating. The officers themselves almost all lived in the barracks and were lunching in their mess. Now we were all crowded together in front of the camp, watching agonized as the flood swallowed the town.

It was difficult to think how best they could help: one man from Lorraine saw the postman, his wife and small child clinging to the roof of their house, about to be swept away, and, 'en chic type', dived into the water to try to save them. The current swiftly defeated him, and he was carried away in front of their eyes. The surging swell, carrying tree-trunks and debris along with it, smashed into the roof of the postman's house, and the little family disappeared. By the afternoon, the soldiers had managed to swing a heavy rope across the waters and attempted to pull themselves across on it. But the water was icy, and Lyautey ordered them to stop, the task being 'beyond human endurance'. By nightfall, they had constructed a makeshift bridge from pieces of artillery and carts; and the waters were subsiding.

At dawn the next day Lyautey, who had been concerned at once for Isabelle's safety, organized a team of rescue workers, led by Lieutenant de Loustal and including Kohn, to search for her. Nothing had been seen of her, although Slimène was known to be safe. The account Slimène gave to de Loustal of what had happened made them fear the worst:

We were on the balcony of my room on the first floor. Suddenly there was a roar, like a procession of wagons. It came nearer. People ran by shouting 'the wadi! the wadi!' I didn't understand. The weather was calm. There was no rain, no storm. In a minute, the water came down the river bed, rising up like a wall, running like a galloping horse, at least two metres high, dragging along trees, furniture, bodies of animals and men. I saw the danger and we fled. The torrent caught us up in it. How did I get out? I've no idea. My wife was carried away.

On the basis of this account, de Loustal and his team searched the river bed for signs of Isabelle. Drawing a blank, they then went back to the house. They waded through the smelly debris and mud in the street leading to the two-storey *gourbi*. None of the buildings in this area had collapsed, whereas others had done so further down, including the school and various brothels, drowning their inhabitants. They had great difficulty forcing the door open, as piles of stones and mire had heaped up against it from the inside. Ducking their heads as they finally got into the low-ceilinged ground-floor room, they peered across the debris to the primitive staircase in front of them. From the dark hollow underneath it, two 'human feet' stuck out. Wrenching off the beam and rocks pinning them down they found Isabelle's body, her legs bent beneath her, dressed as an 'Arab cavalryman'.

Kohn gave his opinion 'as a man who saw it' of what must have happened: she would have been in her room on the first storey when she heard and saw the flash flood approaching, and gone downstairs to try to get out of the door and escape up onto higher land; but the waters were already too powerful for her, since she was still so weak from her illness. She would have been flung against the wall, perhaps unconscious, and drowned. De Loustal added that when they found her, her hands were clasped behind her head in an instinctive gesture of defence.

Lyautey took charge of the arrangements at once, organizing a simple Muslim burial for Isabelle in the nearby cemetery of Sidi-bou-Djemâa. Ironically, Isabelle had described just such a Muslim burial, in the same cemetery, in a story entitled 'Muslim Death'. Her body, like that in the story, was draped in a white cloth, carried on a stretcher and lowered into its final resting-place 'face to the sun', while a semi-circle of Muslims chanted the last prayer (the only one made without prostration).

Slimène was not at the funeral, and seems to have left almost immediately after the flood, leaving Lyautey to take charge, which he did with efficiency and care. Not that there was a lot to see to in ordinary terms: Isabelle's possessions were few, and the only relative with whom she preserved any thread of contact was Augustin. The waters closed very swiftly over the small material space she had occupied. But there were her manuscripts, and Lyautey devotedly set about trying to find every last piece of her writing that could be salvaged. He wrote at once to Victor Barrucand, assuming, as Barrucand did himself, that he would be Isabelle's literary executor. He was concerned about the manuscript of the 'Sud-Oranais', which she had said she had sent off. There was no trace of it having been registered at the post office, and no one there remembered her having sent it. Lyautey wrote on 9 November to Barrucand: 'We shall keep looking, but I fear that with her usual *insouciance*, she might have simply talked of what was merely a plan, as if it were already done.' He also wrote, 'You can imagine how saddened I was by the loss of our poor Isabelle Eberhardt – for whom I felt admiration and sympathy – between ourselves I can tell you I don't feel *sorry* for her, since I feared that she was so condemned to a life of instability and increasing disappointment.' Lyautey detailed Lieutenant Paris to make a meticulous search of Isabelle's house for any papers, which he did, together with Kohn and another soldier.

On 19 November, almost a month after the disaster, they found Isabelle's letter of 16 October to Slimène, saying clearly that she had sent off the manuscript. On the 27th this seemed to be contradicted when they finally found the whole manuscript of the 'Sud-Oranais' inside a large urn: wet, damaged, but just salvageable. With it were some newspaper cuttings, and some notes on books she had read. (Her fifth diary, which she must have started in January 1903, has never been found.) Lyautey packed up the papers and charged a young officer, Lieutenant Bernard, with delivering them personally to Barrucand in Algiers. Lyautey's own opinion was that Isabelle had spread the word that the manuscript was with her editor to keep her creditors at bay. Whatever the case, most of Isabelle's papers were now with Barrucand. She had already given him a bundle of other manuscripts for safekeeping – including *Vagabond* and her travel notes 'Choses du Sahara' and 'Heures de Tunis' – when they were last together in Aïn Sefra at the beginning of the year. She had told him, tongue-in-cheek, that they were for her 'funeral oration'.

On 10 November, Lyautey had a letter from Slimène asking that Isabelle's body should be exhumed and taken to Bône to lie alongside her mother. He claimed this was what she would have wanted, and he asked the army to defray the costs. Lyautey was alarmed, feeling strongly that 'this exhumation and transportation is absolutely contrary to Muslim customs and religion, which were Isabelle's, and would leave an extremely bad impression on the local people, who buried her according to their rites and with a profound respect.' He felt she was sleeping peacefully now in the Sud-Oranais, which she had loved, and should be left that way. He asked Barrucand to put this tactfully to Ehnni.

As it happened, Isabelle herself had expressed different wishes about where she wanted to be buried: in El Oued ('the only place I would want to be buried'), Algiers ('it would be good to die in Algiers') or 'in the place where my destiny strikes me'. And in May 1900 she had written: 'Under what sky and in what earth shall I lie on the day my destiny meets me? A mystery . . . and yet, I should like my remains to be placed in the red earth of Annaba, where She sleeps . . . or perhaps anywhere in the burning sand of the desert, far from the desecrating banalities of the invading Occident.' Both Lyautey and Slimène were right.

*

In what way did Isabelle meet her death? In a flash flood, yes; stunned by a falling beam, probably. But what was the manner of it, what was her state of mind in face of the death that had stalked her intimately for years? 'Death does not frighten me, I would only wish not to die obscurely and above all pointlessly.' 'For me the supreme beauty of the spirit would express itself in practice through fanaticism leading harmoniously, that is, on a path of absolute sincerity, to martyrdom.' 'To die *consciously*, calmly, *attesting and in order to attest* one's faith, whatever it was, that is pure splendour. But, I repeat, the act must be *conscious*.' There was no religious martyrdom in her death: the catastrophe was natural, or divine, not man-made. She did not die for a cause. But was it all the same a conscious death, did she in some split second weigh up the ironies and misfortunes in which she was steeped and decide that was enough, and that this was an appropriately fateful, elemental way to go?

Years later, Lyautey and René-Louis Doyon – who published Isabelle's diaries in 1923 – talked the matter over. Doyon thought she and Slimène had probably been smoking *kef* (and, it was understood, making love) and that her senses had been confused. Lyautey thought otherwise, seeing the interesting devastation the flood offered to the eyes of 'a nihilist like Isabelle' and was inclined to think she had 'profited from the event to accomplish a kind of suicide'. To judge from her writings in Kenadsa, she was ripe for death, having sloughed off many of the ties attaching her life, particularly Slimène, her 'last attachment to life', as she had said before. They had not met for several months; it looks as if he had found a new love; perhaps he had not come down for a happy reunion, but, in the bare two hours they had together before the flood, for a painful reckoning. Why did Slimène manage to escape, and Isabelle not? Even allowing for the high degree of shock and confusion the flood caused, Slimène's account of what happened is vague and fudged, undoubtedly because he was trying to gloss over his lapse in not looking to Isabelle's welfare. If he had shown concern, he would at least have been aware of what was happening to her. To say that they fled and that she was swept away was a lie, as he must have known, but at that point he did not think her body would be found so clearly trapped within the house, with the door closed. Once it had been found there, his equivocation looked cowardly and suspicious. This may have been why he did not go to her funeral, and why he disappeared so soon afterwards. Everything points to his feelings about Isabelle being equivocal at this stage, and everything points to Isabelle's inner preparedness for death.

Somewhere along the line, it seems likely that they both colluded with the natural catastrophe, that Isabelle, in a split second, chose to meet her death, and that Slimène left her to do so.

*

Although only twenty-seven when she died, Isabelle had in a sense lived a whole lifetime, and most of her reserves had been spent. The shadow of death was so familiar to her that, whatever its precise form when it came, its advent must have seemed like a homecoming.

A note of hers headed 'Reminiscences', undated, but possibly written in the hospital, is probably the nearest we can get to her final state of mind:

The thought of death is familiar to me from long ago, from my extreme youth . . . There is nothing horrible or frightening for me in it . . . I've often found the longing for death so intense in me that I've sometimes almost solicited it, trying to find in non-being the supreme sensual delight . . . It's with a sort of contemptuous weariness that I contemplate the future, a problematic future which is the unknown, and which is perhaps *nothing*! And so once again it seems to me that I'm suddenly approaching death and that I'm skirting the inviting abyss of the void . . . Who knows? Perhaps I shall let myself slip into it one day in the very near future, voluptuously and without the slightest worry or concern? With time I have learned not to look for anything in life except for the near-ecstasy offered by oblivion . . . And I've tasted ecstasy in all its forms, the most refined as well as the most primitive . . . None of these forms has fooled me, and I've rejected them all . . . I have never believed in the possibility of absolute happiness, and I have never bent my head, free of shackles, to any kind of idol. My life passes by like this, and this is the way it will end. At present I fill the days with memories, and thoughts of past delights. And if tomorrow ever arrives, I'll fill it with sweet regrets and warm memories of the present day, which will have passed, and with other thoughts and other delights . . . And so, without illusions and without hope, I shall carry on until the day I disappear into the shadows I came out of one day, an ephemeral and vain creature.

17

POST MORTEM

On 13 February 1905, a year almost to the day since he had made the journey with Isabelle, Victor Barrucand set off from Perrégaux to take the train down to Aïn Sefra. He arrived late the next day, and the following morning made a pilgrimage to Isabelle's grave, in the poplar-spliced dunes of the Sidi-bou-Djemâa cemetery. It was a highly emotional moment for him, and suggests that there was some romantic feeling in his attachment to Isabelle. He wrote a scrawled, sentimental note to her, as if she were still alive:

Here rests my companion and my friend [*amie*]. In the bitter wind whistling across the sand at this cold time of year, I'm still close to you. People think you're dead, but your thoughts are alive in me and soon they'll spread so far that people won't know if it's the voice of an angel of solitude they hear, or of an Arab shepherd beside the Dermel wadi in the dark, rocky sand, or the sound of water cascading into the green chasm of the sky at nightfall. I shall tell of everything you have loved, I'll mix your soul in with it, and those who have ears for the song of the wind in the sand dunes will understand that you could not die, after having conquered the earth. It will be an exceptional communion between a being and a country. Pale Isabelle, with your unsure eyes, at a time when I was tempted by the pull of the tomb, you wanted to bring me back to the most dangerous kind of life. I followed you half-heartedly, and yet the grace of the African miracle worked such a transformation in me that today I can see there was a renaissance there. In my turn now I restore life and speech to you to express what was in us. It will live for ever through us from now on, for the few who understand. I want to situate our love in the warm shadow of Islam. It's the title that I've given to your Saharan adventure. Rest here, and, through my book, in the hearts of those who are like us.

The book was an idea that Barrucand had conceived as soon as he heard of Isabelle's death: a collection of her writings about the Sud-Oranais and Kenadsa, just as she had been planning. Now he wanted to do it as a memorial to her. He would complete her cherished and unfinished business, vindicate her and, along the way, cement the ties of affection between them. The book, as he had written, was to be called *Dans l'ombre chaude de l'Islam*, 'In the warm shadow of Islam', a flowery title which suited his Parnassian tastes better than Isabelle's memory.

As soon as Lieutenant Bernard had delivered the damaged manuscript, Barrucand got to work. It was an arduous task, as the pages were pell-mell, unnumbered, and often disintegrating from the flood. He decided to solve the editing problems by rewriting the manuscript himself, as if it were a novel. On a scrap of paper, he wrote a plan of how the book would be:

A retreat in the desert, the distancing of the old world, serenity achieved, after too much useless agitation. There will be philosophizing along the way – an idea dear to Mahmoud – on love, the future of Africa, the fatalism of the sun [*sic*]. Mahmoud has only described, we shall make her speak, and her constant confidant in Algiers [himself] will lend her a soul more mature than her own, but full of potential and appealing in a *cavalière*.

Later, when he found himself having to justify his intervention, he wrote: 'Isabelle Eberhardt was in our eyes the most interesting of her characters, but it wasn't appropriate for her to say so herself,' and asserted that the book was 'a novel, the novel of Isabelle Eberhardt's nomadic life. The descriptions of the Sud-Oranais, fragmented as they were, gave us the framework; we put Isabelle Eberhardt inside it.'

Barrucand's initial intentions were sincere, and his task laborious. Where he made a mistake was in assuming that she needed lending a soul 'more mature than her own', an unwarranted intrusion. However much he may have been exasperated by Isabelle's naive or doom-haunted sides, his takeover echoed the colonial trespass on an individual scale: remaking someone in your own image 'for their own good'. He heavily, sometimes almost angrily, scored out about a tenth of Isabelle's own text and added revisions of his own, even where the text was complete and undamaged. Isabelle's style of writing was deliberately plain: her drafts show a constant process of honing down. Barrucand added distorting frills. His own personal style, as Randau later remarked, was to 'split hairs in four', to 'stylize the flower'. Where Isabelle wrote 'freedom was the only happiness accessible to my nature,' he would write 'freedom was the only happiness necessary to my anxious, impatient and yet proud nature.' Where Isabelle wrote 'Everyone laughed,' Barrucand elaborated: 'People laughed at his rusticity: this gesture belonged to a shepherd.' These kind of touches introduced an inappropriate, fussy and knowing tone into the writing. Worse than this was the way he evoked Isabelle herself, the central character of his 'novel', exoticizing her, subtly making her into an image of his fantasy, rather than an agent of her own. Sometimes it was not so subtly. He wrote whole passages in what purported to be Isabelle's voice, but infused with a banally pornographic flavour: 'When I sleep out under the stars, under those Sud-Oranais skies which have a religious profundity, I feel myself penetrated by the earth's energies, a sort of brutality comes over me and I need to get astride my mare – and ride straight off, wildly.' This was the image of Isabelle he wanted to cultivate, a stimulating, exoticized fantasy which he sensed would appeal to the taste of the time. It did. *Dans l'ombre chaude de l'Islam*, published in November 1905, went into three editions, and sold over 13,000 copies. Isabelle had become a legend – or rather Barrucand's Isabelle had become one.

This desert androgyne, amazon of the Sahara and nomad with the heart of gold, appealed to what has been called 'Europe's collective day-dream of the Orient', in the same way that T. E. Lawrence did to the British psyche later, and for similar reasons. Both appeared sexually and politically equivocal, both their conquests of exotic territory seemed to speak of more private, inner conquests intriguing to the industrial mind. Both, perhaps, by 'going native' served to appease rumblings of guilt amongst the colonial powers. Both were perfect symbols of escapism for armchair romantics, or for people who had comprehensively compromised in their lives, and wished they had not.

Barrucand had added his name to Isabelle's as co-author of the book, and since his co-author was dead, he collected the royalties. People both in Algeria and in Paris were not slow to pick up on this fact, and he began to be accused of 'tailoring himself a velvet doublet out of the Good Nomad's threadbare burnous'. When the *Nouveau Larousse Illustré* inadvertently entered the volume under his name only, omitting Isabelle's, the sniping became a barrage, and Ernest Mallebay, editor of *Turco*, launched a bitter attack on Barrucand, claiming that he had got into the *Larousse* on false pretences, something which his own 'meagre literary baggage' would never have enabled him to do. Even Randau, whilst recognizing Barrucand's practical help to Isabelle during her lifetime, wrote: 'You don't collaborate with someone who's dead; they cannot be consulted on the matter.' Barrucand was piqued. His original good intentions began to get muddied by defensiveness. After all his work, he was not only getting pushed aside, but also vilified for his part in it – and he, in his own mind, was infinitely the better writer. He claimed, in a vivid enough phrase, that Isabelle 'wrote like an auctioneer' and that all the best bits of the book were his own work – at the same time trying to defend himself from having interfered too much. By 1912 he was scrawling irritably across the top of Isabelle's manuscripts, 'Everything that has been done by M. Barrucand was done in the interests of Isabelle Eberhardt, his friend and collaborator, who, without him, would have remained unknown and unpublished.' Meanwhile he still had a monopoly on most of Isabelle's material, and would not let the originals be seen.

In 1908 he brought out another collection of her stories and essays, *Notes de route*, this time under her sole name, and in a much lower key. After the previous criticism, he took care not to change Isabelle's text, but, perhaps realizing that it might fall a little flat after the previous hype, could not resist conjuring up the raffish image of Isabelle in the introduction at least, devoting it to a story of how, with her hands tied Carmen-like behind her, she was dragged along behind a regiment of *goumiers* (native cavalrymen) on the orders of a young lieutenant who wanted to test and humiliate her. Barrucand took care to emphasize how she had enjoyed the experience.

Over the next decade, two plays appeared about Isabelle, both of them fanciful and romantic, and one of them claiming to be based on a newly discovered story of hers, *Mektoub*. There was another literary skirmish as the impostor, Paul Vigné d'Octon, was unmasked. Meanwhile controversy over Isabelle's true nature rumbled on intermittently in the columns of newspapers.

In 1920 Barrucand, who had by now remarried, published his penultimate volume under Isabelle's name, *Pages d'Islam*. Here the text is Isabelle's own, unedited, and the book has a more detached and sober introduction, dealing with the political value of her life and writing. Barrucand, like Lyautey, was acutely aware of the responsibilities of the colonizer, and felt that Isabelle's great contribution in this area had been to show the way to the only possible resolution of the colonial presence once it was established. Although she had little time for political organizations, he felt her instinctive affinity with the Algerians had embodied the kind of acceptance which was the prerequisite of political stability and integrity. The 'frank acceptance of the native Muslim' had this additional advantage:

It hastens our return to colonial good health and good faith, liberates us from our original prejudices, and brings some order and calm back into our conscience – if the modern conscience has ever been troubled by the scruples and responsibilities of conquest . . . Inevitably in many ways we wronged the native people, who did not ask us to come . . . we make amends to some extent by more intense cultivation, but we shall only really be at peace with ourselves the day when sympathy replaces antipathy.

Isabelle, he said, had been a pioneer: 'From a point of view not far removed from the notion of civilization, we ourselves have a lot to learn from the Muslims, but we don't yet know that. Isabelle Eberhardt goes further, no doubt too far; she reverses the proposition by suggesting that assimilation can be done in reverse, and against the geographical grain.' Qualified as they were, these were still brave words from a Frenchman at the time, and an impressive insight into both Isabelle's position, and the future clouds looming over Algeria. He added prophetically: 'Algeria is evolving: at the centre of our policy towards the Muslims – which, to be good, should never operate against Islam – the native Algerians, who have been treated for too long as a negligible quantity, are respectfully but insistently requiring a charter worthy of us.'

In this he was a voice in the wilderness at the time, and it did nothing to help his reputation. If anything, criticism of him increased. Verbal cross-fire escalated, as he and other admirers of Isabelle's – Raoul Stéphane, René-Louis Doyon, Ernest Mallebay, Alfred Klepping, and Edmond Gojon – battled in the columns of the *Revue Africaine, L'Afrique du Nord Illustré, Annales Africaines, Mercure de France, Belles-Lettres, Ere nouvelle* and the *Revue de la Semaine,* as if they were fighting for a maiden's honour. Doyon, particularly, tried to show that Isabelle's travels and writings were largely the result of a need to escape a complex and troubling background, and that she was a far more vulnerable creature than Barrucand's legend suggested. In an article in 1921 entitled 'A Russian in the desert: the invention of Isabelle Eberhardt', he accused Barrucand of deliberate mystification. The following year, Barrucand launched another salvo by publishing Isabelle's unfinished novel, *Trimardeur,* but this was the last publishable material of hers that he owned, the last card he held.

It was known that other material of Isabelle's existed, notably her diaries, which Slimène had kept. But Slimène became a shadowy figure after Isabelle's death, and died three years later of his long-standing tuberculosis. According to Barrucand, Slimène called him in his dying days, but Barrucand arrived too late, the morning after he had died. Barrucand claimed that his last wish would have been for him to have Isabelle's papers. However, in the event they were taken and kept by Slimène's brother, Mouloud, who eventually approached Barrucand with a view to selling them to him. Barrucand turned the offer down peremptorily, saying they were his by right. But their existence came to be known about, and Mouloud had several visitors, notably Klepping and Mallebay, asking to see and to buy them. By now he was wary of possible exploitation, and of self-publicizing journalists, and refused all offers. However, he learned that a certain Mme Chloë Bulliod, whose husband was something of a press baron in Bône, was interested in Isabelle, and because she was a woman, and not a journalist, but most of all because her grandfather was the general he had served under – Mouloud like Slimène before him, had an excessive respect for authority – he agreed to sell all Isabelle's diaries and other papers to her. It was ironic: Mme Bulliod was perhaps the very type of pampered woman Isabelle would least have liked to have them. She related coyly years later in the *Dépêche de l'Est* how her husband had pressed her to have a fur or some jewellery for her birthday, and could not understand why she wanted some 'dusty sacks' of manuscripts. She planned to do something with them herself in the way of a book, but the war came, then her husband died, then she was ill herself; and there was no doubt she would not have been up to the task. By 1923 she had given up on it, and sold the bundles to René-Louis Doyon, who was longing to have fuel for his long-standing public battle with Barrucand. He had already done some research on Isabelle's early life, and now published her diaries exactly as they had been written, with a long biographical preface by him, both of which, he claimed, revealed Isabelle as she really was. Certainly the diaries were in a sense a revelation, showing a troubled, self-doubting Isabelle, haunted by death, driven by a relentless quest for moral perfection, and lacking the dash and *braggadocio* of her image. However, the contradictions and narrative obscurities, not to mention the unremitting melancholy of the tone, did not make for a good read, and disconcerted a public which would rather have had confirmation of its fantasies. Doyon conscientiously continued, however, publishing two more authentic texts of Isabelle's, *Contes et paysages* in 1925 and *Au pays des sables* in 1944, collections of some of her appealing and evocative short stories. He concluded in the end that 'the subject is still virtually untouched.'

*

Isabelle's short life was caught up in historical moments of the greatest interest: Russia's emergence from Imperial autocracy, nihilism, the emergence of an alienated modern sensibility, the clashes between primitive wisdom and twentieth-century 'progress', Islam versus Christianity, atheism versus religion, the greedy colonial scramble for Africa. All of these issues are alive nearly a hundred years later, only gaining in potency as they unravel into the late twentieth century. Because of the way she lived through these important matters, Isabelle has something of the quality of a modern shaman, bearing twentieth-century malaises and buffetings. There is even an occasional glimpse of the *imitatio Christi* which she sensed once or twice brushing up against her – and then leaving her.

Her journey was interesting from the picturesque side, and coincides with a fashionable interest in travellers; but her real journey, unlike those of many of her intrepid contemporaries, men and women, was an inner one. It was from the new world to the old, from clutter, mental and material, to space, from inherited guilt to redemption, from seething complications to some measure of peace; and from mystery back to mystery. Man was born, it seems, in the desert in Africa, and for Isabelle, loaded as she was with twentieth-century rootlessness and complexities, it was only in the desert in Africa that she could rediscover herself. It was only there that she had the intimation of rebirth she needed to appease her sense of being unwelcome in the world, and unprepared for it. She was particularly fond of the sentence from Matthew's gospel, with which she ruefully identified: 'Friend, how did you get in here without a wedding garment?' (more poignant and rhythmic in the French: '*Ami, comment, n'étant point vêtu des habits de fête, es-tu entré ici?*'). Life was a feast to which she had not been invited, and for which, in the end, she did not have the right clothes.

18

POSTSCRIPT

When Isabelle's few personal effects were auctioned off in Bône after her death, Randau bought her inkstand and the sabre that nearly killed her, which she had kept as a memento.

Augustin de Moerder committed suicide in 1914. His daughter, Hélène Nathalie, also committed suicide, in 1954.

Eugène Letord was made a Chevalier de la Légion d'Honneur in 1904, and married in 1905. Mentioned in dispatches in 1913 as 'an officer of remarkable sang-froid', he died in battle in 1915, 'killed gloriously whilst leading his company against the German trenches, with the greatest bravery and vigour'.

Dr Léon Taste married in June 1908. In 1916 he was cited for his courage in evacuating and treating the wounded under fire. In 1915 he was made a Chevalier de la Légion d'Honneur, and in 1928, an Officier de la Légion d'Honneur.

Adolphe-Roger de Susbielle had shown a spurt of bravery in the attacks on Taghit and El Moungar, which had earned him Lyautey's approbation. However, in 1907 he was put in charge of a regiment in the French town of Stenay, and came into conflict with the police. He had loudly proclaimed his royalist views, physically ill-treated his men, and had repeatedly been seen indecently exposing himself to very young girls and propositioning them. The Minister of War wanted him dismissed, but his influential relatives prevailed, and he stayed on ingloriously in the army, spurned by all regiments.

Marius and Ary Leblond won the Prix Goncourt in 1905.

Si El Hachemi had his charm. In January 1905 he sent his best wishes for the New Year to the President of the French Republic. In January 1906 he sent a telegram to the general in Constantine: 'Hello. Happy New Year. Sheikh El Hachemi.'

General Lyautey left Algeria in 1910, having 'consolidated' the Algerian-Moroccan border for the French, and prepared the way for an eventual French takeover of Morocco. The Moroccan tribes, unsupported by their vacillating Sultan Abdel Aziz, waged fierce sporadic warfare for their country's independence. From 1912-25 Lyautey (who was made a Marshal in 1921) was Governor-General of Morocco, but left with great bitterness, feeling that his paternalistic attitude to the country had not been appreciated. When asked thereafter about Morocco, he would reply, 'Morocco, never heard of it.'

Lyautey and Barrucand continued to correspond until Lyautey's death in 1934. They both agreed on seeing the future for France in Algeria and Morocco as difficult and misunderstood, and chafed at having to play the 'sterile, worn-out and discredited role of Cassandra'. Lyautey wrote to Barrucand in 1915: 'We have the same ideal in North Africa; there aren't many of us to share it, but events are proving us devilishly right and the future will do so even more.' In 1922 he wrote to Barrucand: 'I know you continue to give me your friendship, as I give you mine – and have for twenty-two years! *C'est chic tout de même.*'

Barrucand got a Russian woman married to an Arab to translate Isabelle's writings for him. She wrote him an illiterate, touching letter accompanying her translation:

There are so many spelling mistakes in this, like jasmine blossoms on the tree, because I had to work at it with my kids around me, and there are sticky marks because of them, they were cross because their mother was concerning herself with intellectual things. You cannot imagine how this Isabelle Eberhardt awakened forgotten feelings in me – my unrealized dreams! I understand very well why she idealizes the Arab and Islam so much because it's very characteristic of the Russian soul to get carried away about anything that's surrounded by mystery. But there is one thing that touched me profoundly and that she passes over as if it were unimportant – that's the life of the Arab woman . . . she, the Russian woman . . . the woman who's free as a bird, who's Bohemian, she doesn't see a whole people, millions of women – prisoners, deprived of the most elementary rights in the world, the right to *live*, to think, to see the sun . . . to have respect for their personality. If you knew, dear Sir, how I study them and how I want to cry.

The street names in Algeria, which the French had mainly changed to honour their own citizens ('avenue Jeanne d'Arc', 'rue Gustave Flaubert', etc.), have been changed back since the Algerian revolution to names which are ideologically appropriate to the independent country. Joan of Arc, Flaubert, Delacroix, Mozart and all the French military names, including that of Lyautey, have been swept away. In Algiers only a handful of European names survive: Shakespeare, Cervantes, Victor Barrucand – and Isabelle Eberhardt. The rue Isabelle Eberhardt is a small road which leads off the main avenue Mohammed, and then curves back into it. For her elected country to have honoured her memory is an endorsement of her life which Isabelle would have keenly valued: for Algeria, like her, suffered, was marginalized and exoticized, and has finally been vindicated.

Bibliography

BOOKS BY ISABELLE EBERHARDT

Dans l'ombre chaude de l'Islam, 367 pp., edited by Victor Barrucand, and including a 50-pp. closing biographical essay by him 'Notes sur la vie et les oeuvres d'Isabelle Eberhardt', Paris, Librairie Charpentier et Fasquelle, 1906

Notes de route, 352 pp., edited by Barrucand, and including a 13-pp. preface by him, Paris, Charpentier et Fasquelle, 1908

Pages d'Islam, 337 pp., edited by Barrucand, and including a 24-pp. preface by him, Paris, Charpentier et Fasquelle, 1920

Trimardeur, 280 pp., edited and completed by Victor Barrucand, and with a 24-pp. preface by him, Paris, Eugène Fasquelle, 1922; translated as *Vagabond* by Annette Kobak, London, The Hogarth Press, 1988

Amara le forçat. L'Anarchiste, Les Amis d'Edouard, Paris, 1923

Mes Journaliers, 300 pp., with an 83-pp. biographical preface, 'Vie tragique d'Isabelle Eberhardt' by René-Louis Doyon, Paris, La Connaissance, 1923 translated as: *The Passionate Nomad: The Diary of Isabelle Eberhardt,* trans. Nina de Voogd, edited and with an introduction by Rana Kabbani, London, Virago, 1987

Contes et Paysages, 151 pp., with 3-pp. preface by René-Louis Doyon, Paris, La Connaissance, 1925, de luxe edition of 138 copies.

Au pays des sables, 219 pp., including a 78-pp. biographical preface by René-Louis Doyon, 'Infortunes et ivresses d'une errante', Paris, Fernand Sorlot, 1944

PUBLISHED ARTICLES AND LETTERS
BY ISABELLE EBERHARDT

Nicolas Podolinsky (pseudo).
'Infernalia', *Nouvelle Revue Moderne,* 15 septembre 1895
'Visions due Maghreb', *ibid.,* 15 octobre, 1 and 15 novembre 1895
'Dholema', *ibid.,* 15 avril 1896
'Per fas et nefas', ibid., 15 mai 1896
'Dholima', ibid.
'Le poète russe Siméon Yakowlevitch Nadson 1862-1887', *L'Athénée,* janvier 1897 (III, no 24), pp.181-3
'Le poète russe SYN "Dans la brume"', ibid., février 1897 (III, no 25), pp. 195-6
'Le poète russe SYN "En avant"', ibid., mai 1897 (III, no 29), pp.230-1

'Silhouettes d'Afrique: les Oulémas', ibid., mars 1898 (IV, no 3), pp.35-7
do., ibid., avril 1898 (IV, no 4), pp.54-6
do., ibid., juin 1898 (IV, no 6), pp. 79-81
do., ibid., juillet 1898)IV, no 7), pp. 92-3
'l'Age du néant', L'Athénée, 3 mars 1900, p. 39

Mahmoud Saadi (pseudo).
'Fantasia', ibid., août/septembre 1901 (VII, no 89), pp.108-11

Letter from Isabelle Eberhardt re assassination attempt, *La Dépêche Algérienne*,
    4 juin 1901
do., ibid., 7 juin 1901
do., *Le Petit Marseillais*, 23 juin 1901
'Maghreb', *Les Nouvelles*, Algiers, 19 juillet 1901
'Printemps au désert', ibid., 20 juillet 1901
'Yasmina', *Progrès de l'Est*, Bône, 4 février 1902
'Heures de Tunis', *Revue Blanche*, juillet 1902
'Le magicien', *Le Petit Journal Illustré*, 2 novembre 1902
Letter from IE with account of her background, *La Petite Gironde*, 23 avril 1903
Letter from IE protesting against the accusations of the *Union Républicaine,
    Turco*, 10 mai 1903
1902-1904 articles in *L'Akhbar, La Dépêche Algérienne, passim* including 'Sud-
    Oranais' and 'Trimardeur', in instalments
IE's last letter to a friend published, *Gil Blas*, 24 octobre 1904

SUMMARY BIBLIOGRAPHY OF WORKS
ON ISABELLE EBERHARDT

Lesley Blanch, *The Wilder Shores of Love*, London, John Murray, 1954 (*Les
    rives sauvages de l'amour*, Paris, Plon, 1956)
Paul Bowles, *The Oblivion Seekers*, San Francisco, City Lights, 1972
Denise Brahimi, *L'Oued et la zaouïa: Lectures d'Isabelle Eberhardt*, Algiers,
    O.P.U., 1983
Françoise d'Eaubonne, *La Couronne de sable: Vie d'Isabelle Eberhardt*, Paris,
    Flammarion, 1968
Lucienne Fabre and Constance Coline, *Isabelle d'Afrique*, play shown at Théâtre
    de Montparnasse, Paris, 1939
Henry Kistemackers, *L'Esclave errante*, play shown at Théâtre de Paris, 1923
    (published in *La Petite Illustration* no.168, 3.11.1923)
Cecily Mackworth, *The Destiny of Isabelle Eberhardt*, London, Routledge &
    Kegan Paul, 1951 (*Le Destin d'Isabelle Eberhardt*, translated and with a preface
    by André Lebois, L. Fouque, Oran, 1956)
Jean Noël, *Isabelle Eberhardt, l'Aventureuse du Sahara*, Algiers, Baconnier, 1961
Elise Nouel, *Carré d'as aux femmes*, Paris, Guy le Prat, 1977
Yvonne Pagniez, *Françaises du désert*, Paris, Plon, 1952

Robert Randau, *Notes et souvenirs*, Algiers, Charlot, 1945

Robert Randau, *Les Algérianistes: Roman de la patrie algérienne*, Paris, E. Sansot et Cie, 1911

Simone Rezzoug, *Isabelle Eberhardt*, Algiers, O.P.U., 1985

Claude-Maurice Robert, *L'Amazone des sables*, Algiers, Soubiran, 1934

Raoul Stéphane, *Isabelle Eberhardt ou la révélation du Sahara*, Paris, Flammarion, 1930

Paul Vigné d'Octon, *Mektoub*, Figuière, Paris, 1913

Index

(The spelling of Arab names follows
Isabelle Eberhardt's writings and
contemporary French documents)

Abdallah, Koudja ben 75, 110, 164, 181
Abdel Aziz IV, Sultan 247
Abdel Kader 52, 53, 216
Abderrahmane, Mohammed ben 173
Abdul Hamid II 69
Abdul-Wahab, Ali 46, 49, 54, 55, 81, 83,
    84, 102, 104
Aben, Mme Suce ben 189, 190
Abou Naddara 45–6, 67, 71, 102, 104,
    110, 111, 112, 181, 183
Adam, Paul 26, 198
Africa 27, 32, 33, 51, 107, 116, 121,
    122, 123, 127, 144, 158, 172, 190,
    193, 194, 205, 206, 208, 209, 228,
    240, 245
Agréby, Abdel Aziz 166
Aïn Sefra 47, 209–213, 218, 222, 228,
    229, 230, 231, 232, 236
al-Afghani, Jamal al-Din 28
Alexander II, Tsar 4, 5, 6, 7, 18
Alexander III, Tsar 19
Algeria 19, 31, 32, 34, 44, 47, 48, 50–4,
    57, 61, 63, 64, 65, 67, 82, 87, 91,
    115, 116, 117, 120, 127, 130, 137,
    138, 143, 144, 145, 155, 163, 165,
    168, 170, 175, 176, 179, 184, 189,
    193, 200, 207, 209, 210, 224, 231,
    239, 241, 243, 247, 248
Algiers 50–2, 124, 128, 163, 175, 188,
    189, 190, 192, 196, 201, 205, 210,
    217, 218, 225, 231, 235, 236, 240,
    248
Alsace/Lorraine 52, 233
America 51, 116
Amiche 148, 149

Armenia 28
Aroussi, Si 145, 146

Baghdad 137
Bailloud, General 191
Bakunin, Mikhail 4, 7, 9, 10, 13, 15, 16,
    29, 73, 189
Barrucand, Victor 175, 181, 189, 190,
    192, 196, 197, 198, 204, 205, 207,
    210, 212, 217, 218, 219, 226, 230,
    235, 236, 239–44, 247, 248
Bashkirtseff, Marie 83
Batna 47, 87, 88, 91, 94, 95, 101, 145,
    149, 157, 160, 161, 164, 165, 166,
    179, 205, 211, 232
Béhima 152, 168, 173, 197, 223
Béja 87
Belgium 115
Bellefia, Ribah 63–4
Bell, Gertrude 89
Béni-Ounif 212, 215, 229
Bernard, Lieutenant 235, 240
Berne 101
Berriau, Lieutenant 212
Berrouaghia 217
Bird, Isabella 89
Biskra 87, 90, 128, 134, 148, 161
Bismarck, Count 6
Blidah 30, 31, 32, 44, 57
Bône (also Annaba) 47, 48, 49, 50, 53,
    54, 56, 58, 62–5, 69, 75, 95, 110,
    127, 133, 159, 164, 167, 168, 207,
    236, 244, 246
Bonneval, J. 42, 102, 110, 181, 183
Bouchet, M. 194, 198, 199, 203
Bou Dnib 229
Bou Saada 91, 190
Brahim, Si Elimam ben 137, 140, 152,
    228
Brahim, Si Hachemi ben 137, 139, 140,

Brahim, Si Hachemi ben – *cont.*
    145, 146, 147, 150, 152, 153, 154,
    155, 159, 169, 173, 174, 247
Brahim, Si Hussein ben 137, 138, 140,
    150, 161, 168
Brahim, Si Mohammed Taïeb ben 120,
    121, 136, 140, 159, 168
Brieux, Eugène 181, 184, 186
Bugeaud, General 52
Bulliod, Mme Chloë 244
Burton, Sir Richard 53, 88, 89, 93
Bu Amama 210, 219, 220, 224
Byron, Lord 2

Cagliari 105–8, 119
Cairo 115
Camus, Albert 52
Cape of Good Hope 115
Carayol, Fernand 193, 201
Carthage 82
Casson, M. et Mme 49, 67, 75, 76, 89
Caucasus 28
Cauvet, Captain Gaston 129, 130, 133,
    136, 137, 145, 146, 147, 148, 169,
    170
Chabel, Si Larbi 96, 97
Chad, Lake 115, 144
Chateaubriand, René de 52
Chegga 91
Christidi, Christos 39
Colomb-Béchar 220–2, 229
Congo 115
Conrad, Joseph 13
Constantine 65, 87, 128, 154, 160, 166,
    169, 172, 173, 177, 216
Corsica 31, 32
Crimea 6, 96, 110
Cyprus 92

Damascus 53
Dans l'ombre chaude de l'Islam 240–1,
    249
Darwin, Charles 6
Daudet, Alphonse 198
David, Louis and Cécile 30, 31, 32, 33,
    49, 50, 54, 57, 108

Dechizelle, General, 142, 146, 147, 148,
    149, 154, 160, 208
Delacroix, Eugène 52, 248
Delahaye, Jules 114, 119, 120
Delarue-Mardrus, Lucie 230
Delastre, Hyacinthe 56, 57
Descaves, Lucien 198
Djilani, Abdel-Qadir ben Abdallah 137,
    140, 180, 183
Dostoevsky, Fyodor 6, 83, 110, 185
Doughty, Charles 89
Doyon, René-Louis 60, 224, 237, 243,
    244, 245
Dreyfus, Alfred 114, 143, 144

Eberhardt, Isabelle: birth 14; childhood
    15–18; and puberty 24; education
    26–28; and father 29; and Islam 29,
    62–4, 92–3, 136–9, 226; and
    Augustin 30–7, 44, 75, 95, 102,
    106, 124, 149, 181–2, 185–6; and
    sexuality 39–41, 83, 97–100, 225;
    and disguise 39–41, 56, 89–90; and
    narcissism 40–1; meets Abou
    Naddara 45–6; meets
    Abdul-Wahab 46; meets Letord 47;
    first visit to Algeria 53–7; and her
    mother's death 58–60; and Rachid
    69–72; and 'Rakhil' 74; and
    Trophimowsky's death 76; in Tunis
    83–6; first journey to El Oued
    87–95; and French colonialism 96,
    159, 179, 200, 213–14, 217, 228,
    242–3, 248; in the Tunisian Sahel
    96–7; in Marseilles 102–3, 105; in
    Paris 104, 119–21; in Sardinia
    106–8; last visit to Geneva 121–4;
    in Algiers 127–8; second journey to
    El Oued 128–9; in El Oued
    129–52; and Slimène 132–6,
    157–8, 162, 178–80, 184–6, 188,
    225–6, 237; and Sufism/mysticism
    137–9, 156–7; and fantasia
    139–41; assassination attempt on
    152–4; and convalescence 156–60;
    and trial 172–6; exile in Marseilles

177–88; marriage 187; in Algiers
188–92; meets Barrucand 189; in
Ténès 193–5; meets Randau 195;
joins *L'Akhbar* 210; in the
Sud-Oranais 211–19; meets
Lyautey 212–13; at Kenadsa
221–9; and syphilis 224, 229–30;
in Aïn Sefra hospital 231–2; death
234; burial 234–5; and
'Sud-Oranais' 235–6; circumstances
of death 236–8; posthumous
literary squabbles over 239–245;
last effects 246; and *rue* Isabelle
Eberhardt 248
Egypt 70, 114, 115, 207, 210
Ehnni, Ali ben Mohammed 133
Ehnni, Mouloud 159, 244
Ehnni, Slimène 132–7, 142, 146, 147,
148, 149, 150, 156, 157, 158, 159,
160, 162, 164, 166, 171, 172, 177,
178, 179, 180, 181, 183–7, 188,
189, 190, 192, 193, 195, 200, 202,
203, 204, 205, 211, 218, 224, 225,
226, 232, 235, 236, 237, 244
El Hamel 191
El Moungar 211, 246
El Ouatia 117
El Oued 47, 92–3, 128, 129, 130, 132,
133, 135–7, 140, 142, 144, 145,
146, 147, 148, 149, 150, 152, 153,
155, 157, 162, 169, 170, 179, 181,
184, 198, 236
Embarek 222
England 51, 115, 116, 207
Euphrates 28

Fashoda 115, 207
Ferry, Jules 53
Figuig 211, 212, 215, 221, 232
Flaubert, Gustave 89
Foucauld, Father Charles de 93
France 51, 82, 114–16, 119, 143, 200,
207
France, Anatole 198
French colonialism 51–4, 82, 130,
132–3, 207–8

French Foreign Legion 19, 34, 37
Fridel, Lieutenant-Colonel 90

Galliéni, General, 144, 209, 220, 221
Gasparian, Archavir 122
Geneva 3, 4, 5, 8, 11, 12, 13, 15, 19, 26,
29, 30, 31, 32, 33, 38, 44, 57, 66,
69, 70, 71, 73, 74, 77, 81, 82, 83,
88, 89, 102, 109, 110, 120, 121,
122, 123, 142, 177, 181, 188
Genghis Khan 28
Genoa 105
Germany 115
Gérente, Senator 189, 198, 199, 203
Géryville 217
Gide, André 89
Gogol, Nikolai 9
Gojon, Edmond 243
Goncourt, Edmond and Jules 106,
178
Gourmont, Rémy de 198
Great Britain, *see* England
Guelma 87
Guémar 137, 161, 169
Guergour 211
Guillermet, Françoise 23, 75

The Hague 69, 70, 71
Hassi Mechiguig 117
Hattab, Brigadier Smaïn ben 88, 91, 92,
133
Heraclitus 26
Herzen, Alexander 4, 13, 189
Holland 69, 70

India 137
In Salah 231
Islam 26, 28–9, 46, 50, 56, 62, 63, 64,
110, 138, 144, 145, 210, 245
Istanbul 10, 35
Italy 96

Janin, Lieutenant-Colonel 173, 174
Joan of Arc 98, 156, 248
Jonnart, Célestin 147, 155, 160, 163,
208

Kabylia 52
Kenadsa 221, 222, 223, 225, 227, 228,
    229, 230, 231, 237, 239
Kerkenna 119
Kherson 8, 77
Kinglake, Alexander 89
Klepping, Alfred 243, 244
Kohn, Richard 213, 232–5
Korff, Baron Nicolas 5
Kropotkin, Prince Peter 3, 4

Labattut, General Laborie de 173, 175
Laffont, Maître 174, 175, 176, 181
Lakhdar, Abdallah Mohammed ben 153,
    157, 166, 167, 168, 169, 173–6,
    178, 195
Lakhdar, Hemmouna bent 133
Lambessa 87
Larbi, Si Brahim ben 152
Larrivet, General 145
Lausanne 44
Lawrence, T. E. 29, 40, 156, 241
Leblond, Marius and Ary 198, 246
Letord, Eugène 47, 54, 71, 72, 94, 127,
    181, 224, 246
Lenin, Vladimir Ilyich 2, 9
Lévy, Sadia 198
Livorno 105
Loti, Pierre 26–8, 35, 149
Loustal, Lieutenant de 234
Lyautey, General Hubert 144, 208–10,
    211, 212, 213, 214, 215, 218, 219,
    220, 221, 227, 231, 233, 234, 235,
    236, 237, 242, 247, 248
Lyons 47, 127

Mackworth, Cecily 99
Madagascar 144, 208, 209, 210, 212
Madrid 69
Maghreb 27, 28, 29, 30, 48, 166
Mallebay, Ernest 241, 243, 244
Mardrus, Dr 230
Marguerritte 167, 174, 179, 200
Marival, Raymond 193, 197, 201, 202
Marseilles 31, 32, 34, 65, 70, 73, 75, 82,
    83, 94, 95, 102, 104, 105, 109, 112,

    120, 121, 122, 123, 124, 131, 164,
    165, 172, 175, 177, 179, 180, 181,
    184, 186, 187
Martin, M. 194, 203
Marx, Karl 4
Maseev, Vassily 47, 97
Mes Journaliers 106–7, 249
Mecca 27, 88, 89
Mexico 96
Meyrin 15, 50
Mezrab, Jane Digby El 93, 112
Mill, John Stuart 6
Millet, René 119, 121
Moerder, Augustin de 10, 25, 30–7, 38,
    44, 56, 57, 70, 71, 73, 75, 76, 77,
    81, 88, 95, 102, 106, 124, 135, 147,
    148, 149, 162, 164, 166, 167, 177,
    180, 181, 182, 184, 185, 190, 235,
    246
Moerder, Hélène de (née Long) 32, 73,
    94, 102, 149, 166, 167, 177, 180,
    185
Moerder, Hélène Nathalie de 122, 135,
    149, 164, 180
Moerder, Mme Nathalie de (née
    Eberhardt; IE's mother) 3, 5–10,
    11–14, 15–18, 49, 56, 57, 67, 85,
    112, 168
Moerder, Nathalie de 5, 12, 14, 15, 16,
    20–3, 67, 122
Moerder, Nadezhda Alekeevna 5
Moerder, Nicolas de 5, 12, 14, 16, 19,
    21, 23, 36, 48, 57, 66, 67, 75, 102,
    122
Moerder, General Pavel de 3, 5, 10, 11,
    23, 75, 77
Moerder, Vladimir de 5, 17, 19, 20, 23,
    66–8, 162, 180
Mohammed, Si Brahim ould 221, 222,
    223, 224, 228, 230
Monastir 96
Montreux 10
Morès, marquis de 114–20, 143, 145,
    146, 147
Morocco 50, 51, 123, 207–8, 210, 215,
    217, 221, 224, 228, 247

Moscow 5, 8, 73, 75, 160

Nadson, Siméon 43
Naples 10
Napoleon III 52
Nechayev, Sergei 9, 13, 18
Nefta 137, 150, 152
Nietzsche, Friedrich 3, 198
Noiré, Maxime 212, 225
Notes de route 242, 249

Odessa 183
Oran 34, 35, 56, 57, 218
Orléansville 193, 206
Orschanow, Dmitri 30, 44, 45, 56, 81, 100
Osman, Abdul-Aziz 105, 109, 114, 119, 120, 121, 122, 136, 158
Pages d'Islam 242–3, 249
Ouargla 87, 88, 91, 92, 120, 122, 123, 128, 150
Ourlana 91, 128
Ouled Naïl 217
Ourmès 92

Palestine 200
Paris 31, 39, 41, 45, 46, 48, 67, 69, 70, 71, 74, 102, 103, 104, 109, 110, 112, 113, 119, 120, 121, 124, 136, 139, 144, 165, 175, 181, 183, 189, 194, 198, 211, 231, 233, 241
Paris Commune 5, 52
Paris, Lieutenant 232, 235
Paschkoff, Lydia 110, 111, 113, 181, 186, 187
Pasha, Arabi 210
Pawlowsk 7
Perez-Moreyra, Alexandre (*also* Jules) 19, 20–3, 77, 122
Perrégaux 218, 239
Persia 137
Philippeville 172, 177
Phoenicia 82
Plato 26
Podolinsky, Nicolas (IE pseudonym) 34, 41, 42, 57

Poitiers 189
Popow, Vera 73, 102–3, 122, 123
Portugal 115
Pujat, General 145, 146, 147, 149, 154, 163, 208

Rachid, Ahmed 69–72
'Rakhil' 74, 101
Rancougne Colonel de, 181, 184, 186, 188
Randau, Robert (*also* Arnaud) 27, 44, 53, 56, 89, 99, 100, 187, 193–202, 205, 206, 210, 211, 212, 216, 224, 232, 240, 241, 246
Reppmann 97, 103, 165, 166, 181
Rezzoug, Simone, 217
Richepin, Jean 41, 43
Rimbaud, Arthur 16
Robert, Claude-Maurice 99, 229
Rodes, Jean 211
Roque, General de la 117, 154, 160
Rousseau, Jean-Jacques 4, 26
Russia 3, 5–7, 11, 15, 19, 21, 36, 48, 66, 67, 73, 77, 97, 102, 245

Saadi, Si Mahmoud (IE pseudonym) 45, 56, 86, 89, 103, 112, 140, 142, 195, 212, 216, 230, 240
Sahara 81, 149, 171, 241
Saïd, Abdel-Kader 139, 146, 148, 150–1
St Mandrier 83
St Petersburg 8, 9, 13, 18, 48, 77, 108
Saint-Simon, comte Claude-Henri de 4
Salah 87, 88, 91, 101
Samuel, M. 67, 77, 101, 122
Sardinia 105, 106
Schoenlaub 32, 36
Schopenhauer 198
Schwarz, Charles 38, 39
Senegal 115, 149
Sétif 211, 217
Séverine 70, 110
Shelley, Mary 4
Sidi Bel Abbès 19, 34, 198, 231
Sousse 96
Spencer, Herbert 6

Staël, Mme de 4
Stéphane, Raoul 243
Sudan 81, 94, 115, 144, 216
Sud-Oranais 47, 210, 211, 225, 229,
    231, 236, 239, 240, 241
Suez Canal 114
Susbielle, Adolphe-Roger de 90, 92, 146,
    167, 170, 211, 246
Switzerland 9, 26, 48, 142

Tafilalet 210, 215, 221, 228, 229
Taghit 211, 246
Tarzout 161
Taste, Dr Léon 158, 160, 161, 165, 169,
    173, 246
Ténès 192, 193, 194, 196, 197, 198,
    200, 203, 205, 206, 211, 212
Tigris 28
Timgad 87
Timmimoun 321
Tolstoy, Count Leo 7, 26
Tongking (Vietnam) 19, 209, 212
Touat 229
Touggourt 88, 90, 91, 92, 128, 135, 139,
    140, 145, 147, 154, 167, 170, 176
Toulon 83
Trimardeur see Vagabond

Trophimowsky, Alexander Nikolaevitch
    8–10, 11–14, 15–23, 25–9, 32, 48,
    49, 57, 60, 66–7, 69, 70, 71, 73–6,
    101, 109, 111, 135, 137, 138, 142,
    149, 162, 198, 206, 226
Trophimowsky, Akilin 8
Tunis 49, 55, 69, 81–2, 83, 84, 85, 86,
    87, 95, 101, 102, 118, 119, 146,
    166, 210
Tunisia 50, 51, 81–2, 96, 97, 115, 117,
    120, 137, 143, 186, 208
Turgenev, Ivan 6, 10, 11, 26
Turkey 27

Vagabond (Trimardeur) 30, 44, 61, 74,
    81, 99, 100, 231, 243, 249
Vernier 67, 77, 84
Vigné d'Octon, Paul 242
Villa Neuve 18, 19
Vivicorsi 34, 41
Voltaire 4, 26

Yalta 11

Zeyneb, Lella 191, 221
Zola, Emile 20, 144, 180, 197, 198
Zürich 9, 13